Publishing Director: Laura Bamford
Creative Director: Keith Martin
Executive Editor: Julian Brown
Editor: Karen O'Grady
Design: Geoff Fennell
Production Controller: Clare Smedley
Picture Research: Charlotte Deane

First published in Great Britain in 1998 by Hamlyn
an imprint of Octopus Publishing Group Ltd
Michelin House, 81 Fulham Road, London SW3 6RB

ISBN 0 600 59595 1

A catalogue record for this book is available from the
British Library

Produced by Toppan
Printed in China

A Chronicle of Folk Customs

Brian Day

HAMLYN

contents

How to use this book

Each chapter in which customs are listed refers to either a calendrical, agricultural or ecclesiastical period.

The chapter starts with general notes on the types of custom peculiar to that period.

Events of variable date are listed seperately from those of fixed date – it is advisable to check when these events will be happening with local tourist offices before travelling.

Each event is accompanied by a symbol denoting the type of custom (see key on opposite page).

February customs

Customs in the dark, cold month of February reflected the knowledge that the worst of winter would soon be over, and thoughts could turn to preparations for spring. Farmers who had not already done so made plans to prepare or acquire the use of land. Livestock, seed and equipment would soon be bought, so workers could be hired ready. Many hiring and livestock fairs were held on and after Candlemas, a date when land tenures expired and farmers did their accounts before the new spring season. Salmon and eel fishermen also prepared for their catching season, but took the precaution of having their nets blessed first.

Games played in February were much the same as those mentioned for January.

For those for whom spring meant an opportunity to find a partner, February was the time to turn one's attention to possible future meetings and relationships. The cue perhaps was taken from nature itself, as the first spring flowers bravely pole their heads above the snow and hardy breeds of sheep give birth to the first lambs of the year.

Variable Dates

Beginning of the Easter Cycle
The following two entries form the beginning of the Easter Cycle:
Septuagesima Sunday Lost Sunday, The third Sunday before the beginning of Lent
This can also fall in January, depending on the date of Easter.
Sexagesima Sunday The second Sunday before the beginning of Lent
This can also fall in January, depending on the date of Easter.

Early February

⬤ Hurling the Silver Ball, St Columb Major and St Columb Minor   Cornwall
    TAKE THE A3059 EAST FROM NEWQUAY.

⬤ Roundabout Riding, King's Lynn   Norfolk
    KING'S LYNN IS AT THE MEETING OF THE A10, A47 AND A149.

30 February customs

For quick and easy reference the following symbols accompany every folk event:

⚙ Mixed Celebration, Feast, Sing-Song, Commemoration, Opening of Season, Mock-Mayor Election

🎭 Pagan Custom, Wassailing , Fertility rite, Sacrificial rite, Harvest custom

♔ State event, Crown event, Civic custom, Curfew, Courts

✠ Religious Custom, Wake, Rushbearing, Clipping, Beating Bounds, Walking Day , Blessing, Pilgrimage

🎵 Music, Dance, Drama, Arts

🚶 Parade, Trade Procession, Trade Ceremony

🎡 Fair, Carnival

🏛 Land Rights, Quit rent, Auction, Civic dole

☃ Charity, Dole

⚽ Game, Contest, Competition, Sport

A Sunday in early February

✠ **Clowns' Service, Holy Trinity Church, Dalston**   London
During the service a wreath is laid on Grimaldi's memorial. This famous clown died on 31st May 1837.
DALSTON IS AT THE JUNCTION OF THE A10 AND A104.

In February or March

♔ **The Trial of the Pyx, Goldsmiths' Hall, Foster Lane**   London
The Trial of the Pyx involves testing the coins of the realm, one from every batch minted in the past year, in the presence of 12 Jurors. This is presided over by the Queen's Remembrancer. The Chancellor of the Exchequer, who is Master of the Mint, announces the result at the Pyx Luncheon in May. These are not public events.
FOSTER LANE IS OFF CHEAPSIDE, ON THE NORTH SIDE OF ST PAUL'S CATHEDRAL.

Fixed Dates

1st February **St Bride's Day**
Bride, or Brigid, was a 6th-century Irish Abbess. Dew gathered on this day will beautify your features and make them youthful. This was the Celtic Quarter Day of Imbolc.

2nd February **Candlemas Day, The Presentation of Christ, Feast of the Purification**
Christians celebrate the day when the infant Christ, who was 40 days old, was taken by Mary and Joseph to the temple in Jerusalem. Candle-lit processions, of mothers who had borne children the previous year, in celebration of the purification of Mary were held; candles were blessed and distributed to the congregation. The Catholic Church chose this day for Candlemas in the 5th century to try and replace the ancient Celtic feast of Imbolc, which heralded the start of the lambing season, and was dedicated to the Celtic Goddess of Youth and Fertility, Bride. This goddess was renamed St Bridget and myths were invented to Christianise her. Snowdrops, a symbol of purity.

Trial of the Pyx, Goldsmiths' Hall, London

The regions where each event takes place are listed.

Directions to the event are provided.

Captions relate to listed events, where more information is given.

Illustrations have been chosen to show scenes characteristic of the custom.

Introduction

What is the A Chronicle of Folk Customs? In its simplest form it is a day-to-day listing of current, traditional customs, events, celebrations, meals, games, crafts, habits, superstitions and many other aspects of folklore which are a part of English folk culture today, and which have an association with specific dates or times of the year. Starting from the day you buy this book you can follow through, day by day, a year of England's surviving folk heritage. It reveals many regional characteristics, and the special local circumstances at the time which moulded them, thereby portraying England in all its richness as a tapestry of local cultures, whose interaction over time has, by borrowing, assimilation and adaptation, created the unique complexity of the English character and folk scene.

But the book does much more than give lists, important though these are. For each event currently held, date, travel directions, and starting and finishing times are given, as well as a description of what happens. Some events are not open to the public and these are so indicated. The origins of these customs are also considered, in terms of the beliefs, attitudes and daily lives of those who originated them, providing windows on the soul of Englishness. It also attempts to find out how and why the original customs changed and became what we know today. In so doing, much of our surviving folk tradition is illuminated, explained and put into social, geographical and temporal context. The centuries-old entwinement of folk and ecclesiastical traditions is unravelled, showing how secular and religious forces have influenced and shaped each other to produce the mosaic of elements that make up the way these traditions are manifest today. Recipes for many of the traditional, seasonal dishes are given with full instructions and with measures and temperatures in both imperial and metric units. Games, crafts and other activities are described sufficiently for people to actually play, make or take part themselves, and it is to be hoped that all the entries in the book will encourage parents to recognise the value of passing on these aspects of our common culture to their children so that we do not risk having what could so easily be the first rootless generation in our nation's history.

A Chronicle of Folk Customs has both fixed and variable dates, the most important of the latter being the dates of events in the Easter Cycle. Some events on fixed dates are specifically for a calendrical day, some are periodic, whilst others are at a fixed interval from a variable date. Some cannot be categorised, but in every case the entry is put as near as possible to the months where they normally fall. There are several events for days which are no longer public holidays which have been moved to weekends or nearby public holidays.

Common themes in folk ceremonies are: celebrating the changes in the seasons; celebrating the landmarks of the human life cycle, such as births, weddings and funerals; paying tribute to ancestors; losing one's own identity behind disguises or communal endeavour; letting off steam; strengthening community ties; making explicit the divisions within the community: relishing the enjoyment of the day; and using the occasion as a licence to behave in ways that would not be acceptable at other times. Common ingredients are spring and summer poles; decoration with flowers and greenery; foliate figures; distinctive art, design and craftwork; animal and other disguises; transvestism; period or exotic costume; blackened faces; bonfires and explosions; begging for money/food/drink; and music, singing and dancing. All are here in abundance, which is extraordinary when one realises how vigorous have been the attempts to stamp out many of the customs, and how much our lives have changed in the 20th century.

People celebrate folk customs for many reasons. Some do so because they have always done so, and do not necessarily remember why they started; some wish to express their belonging to the community and want to preserve its character, distinctiveness and history; some participate for sheer enjoyment; some see such involvement as a release from their stressful, regulated lives; and undoubtedly some have personal, unannounced reasons. The contents herein are for those who are already actively involved just as much as for those who are not, as they seek to give an historical perspective as well as to describe what is actually happening now.

It has been a rocky road to the present parlous state of English folk culture. Many customs have gone for ever, and as many more have changed so much with the times that their originators would not recognise them. Some disappeared and were later revived. But one fact remains: folk customs are valuable anchors in a changing world, and it matters not that their roots are in a rural past that is long gone and far removed in character from urban, and even country life, today. There are many quotable examples of the willingness of ordinary folk to embrace revivals or to accept customs of foreign origin that are similar to those that they remember from their youth or which serve a purpose that they can readily identify with. Some Victorian revivals undoubtedly arose because of a rose-tinted vision of an Arcadian past. The mid-Lent custom of Mother's Day revived after World War II, and one of the influences was the celebration by United States servicemen of their own Mother's Day on the second Sunday in May, which had been instituted in the USA in 1907. Similarly, Trick-or-Treat reappeared in southern England in the 1980s, again with American influence, leading to an accusation of its being an 'American import'. In reality, it is just our own Mischief Night returning home to the south where it had virtually died out. In northern England (and Scotland) the custom has always been kept. In contrast, some institutionalised customs have failed because they have no strong roots. An example is Empire Day, founded in 1892 on Queen Victoria's birthday, 24th May. Even renaming it Commonwealth Day

Shrovetide football

in 1958 did not save it, and it has disappeared like most of Britain's foreign territories. The lack of nationalist fervour in today's secular, multi-faceted society has seen customs like those associated with St George's Day fade in significance. But, however much our folk scene has or has been changed, whether it be by Victorian sanitization, such as of Harvest Festivals, or by religious re-orientation by the church, as with church clipping and well blessings, or by other means such as tourism and commercialisation, we must cling to and cherish what remains. Too often, survival of once widespread customs is only found in remote places where community spirit and interdependence survive also, or in places where a committed local family or group of enthusiasts refuse to let go of something they regard as special and worthy of retention.

There are many circumstances which can conspire, and have conspired, to cause a custom to cease, some deliberate, some not. Among these circumstances we can list: industrialisation, agricultural depression and the drift of rural people to the cities to find work; the improvement of travel and communications, leading to the decision to abandon what has suddenly begun to seem rustic and unsophisticated; the movement of townspeople to the country with consequent changes to country life and customs, not least the conversion of simple rural celebrations into drunken revelries; oppression by the Church of pagan rituals; the combining of Church and civic authorities against the riotous behaviour associated with many celebrations; the deaths of those in two world wars who had maintained the customs; the changes in lifestyle brought about by the hardships and contingencies of war; 17th-century Puritan zeal; 18th-century gentrification in the Age of Reason; Victorian prudery; and post-war modernisation and new-age philosophies. All have played a part in eliminating or changing our folk customs. All customs evolve and adapt to current circumstances, which may obscure their original function, but as a part of our heritage they are no less worth preserving because of it.

This book has not been written with a view to recreating the past, but in support of the belief that our folk culture is a vital part of our Englishness, which we are in danger of losing. We save old books, buildings, cars, trees, and so on, but cast away old customs. It may be that we have never recovered from the devastation of 20th-century conflicts and the accompanying desire for recrimination, self-analysis and the acquisition of new brooms and directions. Now that so many of us are exhausted by conflict and the rat race, perhaps we can learn again to look forward without ignoring the past, lest we lose sight for ever of where our roots lie and how they grew to create our present selves and lives.

Some important, historic customs have ceased in the last half of the 20th-century after hundreds of years of unbroken tradition. If this book encourages former participants and their relatives, as well as friends and neighbours, to revive them, it will have served one of its purposes.

The author invites readers to contact him through the publisher with details of current or recently discontinued customs which have not been included in this edition. Please supply notes on the custom, its origins and precise location, and, if possible, photographs. Village or town names alone are not sufficient as there is often more than one place with a particular name in a county. For example, which of the two Northamptonshire villages called Ashton holds the World Conker Championships? Is the Royal Manor of Portland in Somerset or Dorset, and where does the ancient court meet? Extra information on customs that are featured would also be gratefully received.

Whoever you are this book is for you. If you are English, or of English descent, and were brought up in, or in the ways of, England, this book will explain many of the things you and your ancestors were brought up to do but never really knew why or how they arose. If you are not English, or have not been raised in England or in the English way, the book will go a long way towards explaining why those strange, insular people you know, live amongst, or have heard about, behave the way they do throughout the year.

The Folk Regions of England

Although the shires and metropolitan areas of England have undergone boundary changes since the first half of the 20th century, these changes have not obscured the regional character of ceremonies and customs, despite the fact that they may now occur in places whose address contains one of the new counties or urban areas. The folk regions of England are not definitive regions, but are such that the customs pursued therein have many similarities of origin, type and detail.

Some regions of England have surviving aspects of Celtic culture and folklore, particularly Cornwall. The last recorded fluent speaker of Cornish was John Davey of Boswednack who died in 1890, but it may be that the last to have conversed in Cornish for most of her life was Dorothy Pentreath from Mousehole who died in 1777. There is evidence that Cornish was regularly used in the 19th century by Cornish miners who went to work in South Wales coal mines after the closure of their Cornish tin mines. However, in Cornwall itself anglisisation has led to the loss of much Celtic folk culture and many customs are similar to those of the rest of South West England.

The English Folk Regions are:

Northern *comprising Lancashire, Merseyside, Greater Manchester, Cumbria (including the former counties of Cumberland and Westmorland), Northumberland, Tyne and Wear, Durham, Cleveland, North Yorkshire, West Yorkshire, South Yorkshire, Humberside north of the Humber.*

Midland *comprising Hereford and Worcester (formerly two counties, Herefordshire and Worcestershire), Shropshire, Staffordshire, Cheshire, Derbyshire, Nottinghamshire, Leicestershire (including the former county of Rutland), West Midlands, Warwickshire, Northamptonshire, Bedfordshire.*

Eastern *Cambridgeshire (including the former county of Huntingdonshire), Lincolnshire, Humberside south of the Humber, Norfolk, Suffolk, Essex.*

London *before the creation of the outer London boroughs.*

Southern *Isle of Wight, Hampshire, Wiltshire, north Avon, Gloucestershire, Oxfordshire, Berkshire, Buckinghamshire, Hertfordshire, the former county of Middlesex, Surrey, East Sussex, West Sussex (the latter two were formerly one county of Sussex), Kent.*

Western *Isles of Scilly, Cornwall, Devonshire, Somerset, south Avon, Dorsetshire.*

There are certain local areas within these regions with distinctive traditions, for example, in The Lakes area of Cumbria.

Types of Folk Tradition in England

English folk traditions are predominantly calendrical or seasonal celebrations, having their origins chiefly amongst the rural and urban labouring classes of the past. Today, long after the time when they were an integral part of existence and survival, these traditions are popular as a spectacle or as activities to join in. They have been remarkably tenacious: many have survived wars, changing natural, social and working environments, puritanical condemnation and suppression by both civil and Church authorities. Perhaps the blackened faces which are so commonly seen in these celebrations originally arose as a disguise against authoritarian efforts to stop the festivities. Suppression by the Church was seen as the only alternative to assimilation of the tradition into a sanitised celebration of the religious tradition that was nearest in calendrical terms or which had compatible associations. Inventions of saints and their good works were made to supplant the worship and deeds of gods, mythical heroes and natural objects and phenomena. In many places it is now a matter of pride that distinctive local customs should not be allowed to die out or be forced out of existence, even when the circumstances that gave rise to the custom no longer apply to the local people.

Many celebrations in the past got out of hand, particularly those on the 1st of May and the 5th of November. Licentious and riotous behaviour in the former and the accidental burning of property and general unruliness in the latter were the sort of happenings that led to civic and Church opposition. Maypoles were banned during the Reformation, the 16th-century revolution resulting in the establishment of the Protestant Church, but which also led to moves to ban what were seen as pagan rituals. Christmas was banned by Act of Parliament in 1644 but re-established, along with May festivities, by Charles II, the first monarch after the Restoration of the English monarchy in 1660.

There are today surviving examples of the following types of folk custom: traditional dances; folk dramas; folk song and carol singing; parades and trade processions; fertility and sacrificial rites; seasonal customs; heathen customs fitted into a Christian context, including well-dressing, blessings, Beating the Bounds, walking days, church-clipping, wakes, fairs, rush-bearing/hay-strewing; State and Crown ceremonies; civic and manorial customs, including curfews, ancient rights and candle auctions, and the pageantry associated with the London Livery Companies (or trade guilds); ancient courts; doles and charities; sports and games. This book does not deal with wholly private customs, such as those of schools, colleges, universities, clubs, regiments, and so on, which have no folk elements, nor with wholly commercial events.

Styles of dancing include Morris dancing (Black Face, Cotswold, North West Clog, Border), Mollie dancing, sword dancing, clog dancing, garland dancing and step dancing. The bells worn by Morris dancers drive off evil spirits, and their sticks awaken seeds to germinate. Morris tunes are played at weddings to bring fertility to the couple.

Morris dancing may have been introduced in to England from Spain, possibly via France. Spanish Moresco, or Moorish, dances were performed from the 12th century. There is also a French Mauresque dance which is similar. The blackening of faces by some sides (a Morris team is called a side) has been held to be an imitation of the Moors, but is equally likely to have been a disguise at the time when civil authorities were actively trying to eliminate the boisterous nature of many folk activities. Common Morris Dances are the Handkerchief Dance, Bean Setting, Riggs o' Marlow, Trumbles and Blue-eyed Stranger. Sword dancing may be with the one-handled long sword (Yorkshire) or the two-handled short sword, or rapper (Northumberland and Durham). Cotswold Morris was traditionally danced at Whitsuntide; North West Morris in Wakes Week, late summer and in rushcart processions; West England Morris at Christmas; East Anglian Mollie dancing between Christmas and Plough Monday; and North of England sword dancing during midwinter. The dancers, with attendant characters and people in animal costume, also accompanied civic and guild processions, May festivities and appeared at plays.

Folk plays were commonly performed at Christmas, All Souls, New Year, Plough Monday and Easter. Various names for the players are found, such as Mummers (Mumming means 'disguising' or 'masking'), guisers, pace-eggers, and Plough Jags. The main type of Mummers' Play was the Hero-Combat Play in which a self-proclaimed warrior, e.g. St George, kills an adversary, who is revived by a comic doctor. This story is thought to have its origin in fertility rites. The texts of North of England plays were published in 'chapbooks'. Generally the plays had characters who contributed nothing to the main action, e.g. Tosspot, and who would fool around, improvise lines for comic effect, and collect money from spectators. Mummers' Plays predate the Christian era and were originally stories of the seasons or of myths and legends, in which life, death and resurrection played a key role as in the example above. When the Church started to adapt Mummers' Plays for its own ends they began to act out stories of good triumphing over evil. Miracle or Mystery Plays acted out biblical stories, they started in the 9th century as a teaching aid for the illiterate and those who could not understand Latin. Merchant Guilds took up the idea and performed a play each on their special guild days. In the East Midlands Wooing Plays were performed.

Traditional times for carol singing were Eastertide, May Day, Whitsuntide and Christmas, although there are carols for other times of the year as well such as Corpus Christi. Carols exist for many festive occasions during the year, as they were originally songs with refrains to accompany round dances. Many folk carols were the victims of the attention of the Puritans, although some have survived such as the 15th-century Coventry Carol which was part of a Mumming Play.

Common characters in parades were Hobby Horse (a man dressed in a circular crinoline frame with a wooden horse-head mask), the Teazer (a man in clown's costume with a cardboard club), All Sorts (a man in woman's clothes), the Fool or Whiffler (with a bladder on a stick), folk characters such as Robin Hood, Maid Marian, and so on, and characters from Mummers' Plays. Animal Guisers (people dressed as animals) appear in many dance teams, Mummers' Plays and processions and have their origins in the days of human sacrifice. It was regarded as a great honour to wear the head and skin of a ritually slaughtered animal.

Water-worship is the pagan precursor of well-dressing, an expression of thanks for the water supply introduced by the Church to replace pagan rituals. Pagan gods associated with wells and springs were replaced by saints. The relative freedom of villagers with wells from water-borne diseases helped to perpetuate these changes.

When Christian missionaries sought to replace pagan seasonal fertility rites in fields and fisheries, designed to ensure good yields and catches, they substituted blessings and thanksgivings as the reason for the activity. The beating of the earth to awaken sleeping spirits became Beating of the Bounds, or Perambulation, often done in Ascension week. This is a walk around the parish boundaries by the vicar, churchwardens and parishioners to mark and aid recollection of the parish boundaries in the

absence of mass literacy and maps. Boundary walks or rides became social as well as religious events, and some arose by civic charter rather than out of religious observance. Walking Days were originally processions of witness in Northern England, usually held at Whitsuntide. Similarly, Club Walking was done in the North of England by members of clubs and trading associations.

Church clipping is when parishioners link hands and walk or dance round their church. Clipping means 'embracing', and it may have originally been an attempt by the church to eliminate practices at the Roman festival of Lupercalia when people danced around an altar on which goats and young dogs were sacrificed. There are echoes of this in the ceremony at Painswick, Gloucestershire where puppy-dog pies are sold, albeit with a china puppy inside. After the sacrifice the Luperci, or priests, dashed through the crowds whipping them with goat-skin thongs, again similar to the former habit of shouting children running through the streets after church clipping.

Wakes were annual festivals held to commemorate the completion and dedication of the parish church to a saint. Booths would be set up to provide refreshments, and gradually some of the occasions developed into fairs or markets. The following day became a holiday, indeed, the word 'fair' comes from the Latin *feria*, a holiday. Sometimes whole Wakes Weeks would be given over to the festivities. Gradually some fairs took on a more practical purpose, enjoyment becoming secondary, for many were established purely for trade, both wholesale and retail. The Normans granted royal charters to trading fairs. Fairs, then, came to be either trading or charter fairs, established by royal charter (e.g. Sturbridge Fair, Cambridge) or wakes (or revels) to mark a church's patronal festival (e.g. St Giles' Fair, Walton, Oxford). In the North, during the Industrial Revolution, the wake developed into a week's unpaid holiday. Church-ale was often brewed on a church's holy day and sold to parishioners to raise money for church repairs and charitable causes. Hiring or mop fairs were trading fairs established for the hire of seasonal or permanent workers. At hiring fairs labourers would show a token of their trade, such as a mop for maids, a whip for a carter, a straw for a cowman or a crook for a shepherd. The display of a glove or hand outside a fair is a sign that visiting merchants may enter and trade without fear of arrest as long as the charter is obeyed. Delicacies specially sold at fairs are called fairings, such as Fair Buttons at the Great Yarmouth Fair, Gingerbread at Barnstaple Fair and Brandy Snaps at Nottingham Goose Fair. The common feature of roasting oxen, rams, boar, deer, and so on, to sell the meat to visitors may have its origins in animal sacrifice.

A wake was also a vigil and feast for the just departed on the evening before burial. It was traditional to serve guests burying cakes or biscuits so that they can digest the sins of the deceased. Professional mourners may be paid to attend the funeral and relatives would also hire sin-eaters, often poor women in need of food, who would take on all the sins of the dead person as s/he was brought out of the house. The soul, thus unburdened, would ascend freely to heaven. Bees have a strong connection with death, and if the deceased kept bees the hives would be turned round when the corpse was brought out of the house. People also kept vigil on the eve of the saint day of their parish church.

Rush-bearing (or hay-strewing) is the spreading of freshly cut rushes, sedges or hay over the floor of the parish church in summer and the spreading of straw in winter. This became a ceremony in

Introduction **13**

which girls dressed in white walked in procession to the church with bundles of rushes and garlands of flowers tied up with ribbons. The traditional Cumbrian rush-bearing ceremonies used supports or frames, called bearings, on which various emblems of rushes were made.

Curfews were originally signals to the inhabitants to cover their fires (from the French *couvre feu*) in times when most dwellings were built of wood. Later they were used to clear the streets after disturbance or in response to the threat of it.

Preservation of ancient grazing and gathering rights formed the basis of many customs. Of a similar ilk were auctions which were used to grant rights for a limited period to the highest bidder. In candle auctions a candle is lit as villagers start to bid for the right to use land or other facilities for a year. The bidding stops when the candle burns out, the highest bidder securing the right. Sometimes the candle has a pin stuck in the side. When sufficient wax has melted the last bid before the pin falls secures the right.

Many civic customs are the preserve of trade guilds, particularly well represented in the City of London, as they strive to advertise and maintain their privilege, authority and exclusiveness.

More than 80 manorial courts still sit in England. Manorial courts are for the administration of common land and other property, and are of two types, Courts Leet, that may also enquire into felonies, but cannot administer punishment, and Courts Baron, that are purely manorial. Ashburton in Devon uniquely has both. Other types of ancient court include Hocktide Courts; courts for grants of rights; Verderer's Courts for the administration of forests; Admiralty Courts for regulating fisheries and waterways; industrial courts, for example, to regulate local mining or quarrying; courts maintaining quality and standards in retailing; and Pie Powder Courts at fairgrounds, so called because they dealt instant justice to offenders, who were often itinerants, as shown by the dust on their feet (French *pied-poudre* meaning 'dusty feet'. Although surviving courts still have certain powers to supervise and regulate practices, their powers to prosecute and fine are now severely restricted. Probably the oldest court in the land is the Coroner's Court.

Many courts have preserved the ancient names of officials, such as Bailiff, Reeve, Hayward and Pinder (or Pinner). Courts Leet and Courts Baron are essentially feudal customs, a category which could also include rights of land use, some doles not originating from benefactor's wills, and the payment of quit rents.

Padstow Hobby Horse

Doles and charities tend to be feudal, Christian or philanthropic in origin. These days some are distributed by the Church, some by private benefactors, and some by executors or trustees of wills in which the donations were provided for – sometimes with eccentric conditions attached.

Traditional sports and games were played at wakes (days of dedication of the local church), fairs and public holidays. They include horse racing, foot races (for example, the now discontinued Hebden Bridge races where men would run naked and women in a chemise, for a prize of a hat for a man and a chemise for a woman), Cornish and Cumbrian wrestling, knurr and spell in Yorkshire (still played at Norland), billeting (near Norland, Yorkshire), fives in Durham, quoits in Whitby and East Anglia, Trap, Bat & Ball around Canterbury, Stoolball in Sussex (particularly at Easter), Marbles in Sussex, mass football in many areas, hurling (in Devon and Cornwall), camp-ball (in South East England), and lark singing (in the area between Hebden Bridge and Halifax). For the latter, men took nestlings and trained them, keeping them in darkened cages before a competition. Uncovering them was, to the bird, like dawn, and they sang. Judges considered the length and musical quality of the song. Tilting the Quintain survives only at Offham in Kent. Happily some games have disappeared, such as biting the head off a sparrow and pulling the head off a suspended goose, with a greased neck, by riding past.

Many customs are highly individual to a locality and which do not fit into any category. Many have echoes of more profound pagan rituals, however harmless they may seem now.

Folk and Ecclesiastical Traditions

Many folk and ecclesiastical traditions are similar in that they have a mixture of secular and religious elements. After centuries of effort by the Christian Churches to rid people of their folk culture by assimilation of folk festivals into church events, with imposition of Christian customs on the roots of pagan traditions, the Folk and Ecclesiastical Calendars are now as inextricably linked as are the elements of the celebrations themselves. Most of the variable dates in the Folk Calendar either began as part of the ecclesiastical tradition or were converted to such by the influence of the Church. These are the dates in the periods of Shrovetide, Lent, Easter, Hocktide, Rogationtide, Whitsuntide, Trinity and Corpus Christi, collectively called the Easter Cycle, with Harvest dates being largely determined by the weather.

The lives of many of the saints associated with the calendar are shrouded in mystery. It is difficult for research to distinguish between fact and legend, a situation which is further complicated by evidence of deliberate distortion and even invention by the Church in an effort to eradicate the memory of pagan gods and superstitions and substitute 'Christian' role models, events and explanations. In 1969 when the Roman Calendar was reformed, some saints were removed from it on the grounds that no firm evidence could be found for their existence, among them St Catherine of Alexandria. Even some of those remaining are extremely doubtful, for example, St Anne.

Some saints' days were different in different regions of England, some were national and some were confined to specific trades. For example, lacemakers celebrated their patron St Catherine on 25th November. To rationalise this situation the Victorians removed many saint-day holidays and replaced them with national paid holidays a week at a time. Until 1830 the Bank of England closed on 40 saint days. In 1871 national Bank Holidays were established, the first ones being Good Friday, Easter Monday, Whit Monday, the first Monday in August, Christmas Day and the first weekday after Christmas Day.

One of the features of ecclesiastical ceremonies was the use of symbolic colours, called Liturgical colours. These are still used, and are:

White *symbolises life, innocence, purity, glory and joy and is used on: All Saints on 1st November; Christmas on 25th December, Circumcision on 1st January; Easter; Feast of the Annunciation on 25th March; Feast of the Purification on 2nd February; Feasts of the Saints who were not Martyrs; Nativity of St John the Baptist on 24th June; and Trinity.*

Red *symbolises fire and blood, burning charity and the sacrifice of Martyrs and is used on: Corpus Christi; Elevation of the Cross on 2nd May; Feasts of the Apostles and Martyrs; Finding of the Cross on 14th September; Holy Innocents on 28th December; and Whit Sunday or Pentecost.*

Green *symbolises hope of eternal life, being the colour of nature, and is used on all Sundays which are not specific festivals.*

Black *symbolises mourning and is used on Good Friday.*

The Celtic Year and Quarter Days

The ancient Celtic year began with Samhain (what is now 31st October/1st November) and continued through three other Quarter Days, Imbolc (1st February), Beltane (30th April/1st May) and Lughnasadh (1st August). A festival marked each one. Quarter Days were the days when rents and other dues were paid, and hiring transactions made.

Two other sets of Quarter Days arose, one based on the astronomical cycle and the other based on the agricultural seasons. These are known from at least medieval times. The former had Quarter Days at Christmas (25th December, near the winter solstice), Lady Day (25th March, near the vernal equinox), Midsummer Day (24th June, near the summer solstice) and Michaelmas (29th September, near the Autumnal Equinox). The latter was very close to the old Celtic year and had Quarter Days at Candlemas (2nd February, the start of spring), May Day (1st May, the start of summer), Lammas (1st August, the start of autumn) and All Saints' Day (1st November, the start of winter).

The Julian and Gregorian Calendars

The Julian Calendar was instituted by Julius Caesar in 45 BC and based on a solar year of 365 ¼ days, the extra day being added every four years as a leap-year day. However, owing to astronomical computational errors the solar year was too long by 11 minutes and 14 seconds. After 128 years it was a day out, and by 1582 the spring equinox had retrograded to 11th March. The erratic seasons were causing problems for farmers.

In 1582 Pope Gregory XIII instructed astronomers to harmonise astronomical and civil calendars by adding ten days. 5th October 1582 became 15th October. All Roman Catholic countries adopted the Gregorian calendar, but Protestant Britain and its American colonies continued with the Julian Calendar. This is how William of Orange was able to leave Holland on the 11th November 1688 (Gregorian) and arrive in England after a four-day voyage on 5th November 1688 (Julian)! There was a further complication in that England and Ireland maintained the old tradition of starting the new year on Lady Day (25th March), whilst the European countries on the Gregorian Calendar began the year on 1st January. Scotland began the new year in 1600 with the 1st January but retained the Julian Calendar! In the first three months of the year, therefore, England was apparently twelve months and eleven days behind Europe, so that 11th February 1648 in Europe was 1st February 1647 in England! Eventually George II and Parliament authorised a change to the Gregorian Calendar in 1751, and decreed that the following 1st January should be 1st January 1752 and that the days from 2nd September until 14th September should be left out. There were riots in some places with banners saying 'Give us back our eleven days!' Regrettably, May blossom now rarely appears by May Day, and snow rarely falls for Christmas, in many parts of England.

By this time an 11 day variation had developed between the two calendars, and events held according to the Julian Calendar acquired the prefix 'Old'. Many such events survive today, although miscalculation and other factors has meant that the difference is not always 11 days. We avoid the need for future compensation by making every fourth year a leap year, if it is divisible by 4, and add 29th February, except that a century year is only a leap year if divisible by 400.

Celebrations associated with a particular occasion are not necessarily found on the same date. In times past rural people took rather more notice of changing patterns of weather and temperature, growth and activity amongst plants and animals, the changing positions of stars, planets and the moon, and other natural phenomena, than they did of the calendar. Furthermore, when the calendar changed some communities which did hold their festivities on a specific date remained faithful to it on the Old Calendar, whereas other communities changed to the New Calendar. Solstices and equinoxes may change through the course of astronomical events, whereas dates like Midsummer Day were traditionally fixed. In addition to these factors there were peculiarly local reasons why some villages held celebrations at times different from the norm elsewhere. Thus, for example, we find May festivities on 1st May, May Bank Holiday, the Saturday nearest May Day, 12th May (Old May Day), the last Saturday in May, as late as the 9th June. In more recent times popular occasions have been moved to the nearest weekend or Bank Holiday.

The Easter Cycle

Easter is a movable feast. The Easter Cycle begins with Septuagesima Sunday, nine weeks before Easter, and goes through Trinity Sunday, eight weeks later, ending with Corpus Christi the following Thursday. Easter is always the first Sunday following the paschal full moon of the vernal equinox (21st March). Should the paschal full moon fall on a Sunday, Easter is observed on the Sunday following. It never comes before 22nd March, or after 23rd April. The Synod of Whitby in the 7th century fixed the way Easter's date is calculated.

The full Easter Cycle is:
Septuagesima Sunday, or Lost Sunday, the 3rd Sunday before Lent
Sexagesima Sunday, the 2nd Sunday before Lent
Shrovetide
Shrove Saturday
Quinquagesima Sunday, or Shrove Sunday, the Sunday before Lent
Shrove Monday, or Collop Monday
Shrove Tuesday, or Pancake Tuesday, the last day before Lent
Lent
Ash Wednesday, the 1st day of Lent
Mothering Sunday, or Mid-Lent Sunday, the 4th Sunday in Lent
Carling Sunday, or Passion Sunday, the 5th Sunday in Lent
Palm Sunday, the Sunday before Easter
Maundy Thursday, the last day of Lent
Easter
Good Friday, the Friday before Easter
Holy Saturday, the Saturday before Easter
Easter Sunday
Easter Monday
Easter Tuesday
Hocktide
Hock Sunday, or Low Sunday, the 1st Sunday after Easter
Hock Monday
Hock Tuesday
Rogationtide
Rogation Sunday, the 5th Sunday after Easter
Rogation Monday
Rogation Tuesday
Rogation Wednesday
Ascension Day, the 40th day after Easter, always a Thursday
Whitsuntide
Whit Sunday, or Pentecost, the 7th Sunday (or 50th day) after Easter
Whit Monday
Whit Tuesday to Friday
Trinity
Trinity Sunday, the 8th Sunday (or 57th day) after Easter
Trinity Monday
Corpus Christi
Corpus Christi, the Thursday after Trinity Sunday

Daily and weekly customs

Fixed Dates

Daily/Nightly

Hornblowing (9pm) by the Mayor's Hornblower, Ripon North Yorkshire
Dating from 886 this is the oldest civic custom in England. A charter and horn were granted by King Alfred. Until 1604 it was the signal for the Wakeman and his assistants to patrol the streets, but now the Hornblower sounds the horn from the four quarters of the Obelisk and outside the Mayor's residence. The original horn is still used on special horn days: Wilfrid Sunday, Candlemas, Boxing Day, Easter Monday and Rogation Wednesday.
RIPON IS BETWEEN HARROGATE AND THIRSK ON THE A61.

Ringing the Apprentice bell (8am) and the Curfew Bell (8pm), Richmond North Yorkshire
RICHMOND IS WEST OF THE A1. TAKE THE A6108 FROM SCOTCH CORNER.

Ringing the Curfew Bell (8pm), Winster Derbyshire
TAKE THE A6 NORTH OUT OF MATLOCK, TURN LEFT ON TO THE B5057, PAST WENSLEY.

Ringing the Curfew Bell (9pm), Durham Cathedral Durham
This custom began in the Middle Ages to warn people to come inside the city walls. It is not rung on Saturdays as a mark of respect for the death on a Saturday of a former bellringer.
DURHAM IS WEST OF THE A1(M). TAKE THE A690 WEST FROM CARRVILLE.

Ceremony of the Keys, Tower of London London
This 700-year-old ceremony can only be seen by application to the Governor. The locking up of the Tower begins at 9:53pm when the Chief Warder with his keys meets the Escort of the Keys at the Bloody Tower. They go to the West Gate, then to Middle Tower, on to Byward Tower, then to the Bloody Tower at 10pm for the Last Post, and finally to the Governor to return the keys.
THE TOWER OF LONDON IS ON THE RIVER THAMES BY TOWER BRIDGE.

Ely Place Watch, near Holborn
London

This is the only place left in England where a liveried beagle still calls the watch, e.g. 'Ten o'clock and all's well.' From the 13th until the 19th centuries this cul-de-sac was a Liberty of the Bishops of Ely, that is, an area over which they alone had jurisdiction.

ELY PLACE IS OFF CHARTERHOUSE STREET BETWEEN HOLBORN CIRCUS AND FARRINGDON ROAD.

Providing Bread for the Poor, Cartmel Priory
Cumbria

Bread is kept in a cupboard in the church for the poor, who may request it any day, in accordance with the will of Rowland Briggs of Swallowmire, Cumbria who left money for this purpose. He perished in the great storm of 1703.

CARTMEL IS NORTH WEST OF GRANGE-OVER-SANDS, WHICH IS ON MORECAMBE BAY.

Every weekday

Wayfarer's Dole, Gatehouse of St Cross Hospital, Winchester
Hampshire

Established in 1136 by Henry de Blois, Bishop of Winchester and grandson of William the Conqueror, travellers who request it can claim a piece of bread and one sixth of a pint of ale dispensed from an ancient horn cup bearing a silver cross. Nowadays the dole is given to the first 32 supplicants.

WINCHESTER IS JUST OFF THE M3 FROM JUNCTIONS 9 OR 10.

Every Saturday at 4pm

Ralph Greneway's Charity, Wiveton Church
Norfolk

At 4pm the 'Charity Bell' tolls, and 12 elderly villagers receive money (originally two half-crowns) in a blue bag. Ralph Greneway was a member of the Grocers' Company and he provided for these pensions in his will of 1558.

WIVETON IS BETWEEN WELLS-NEXT-THE-SEA AND CROMER ON THE A149.

Every other Sunday

Bede House Procession, Castle Rising
Norfolk

In 1614, the Earl of Northampton founded a charity home for elderly women 'of honest life and conversation' who were 'not haunters of alehouses'. The women parishoners still go to church in Jacobean dress of tall hat and red cloak embroidered with the arms of the Northampton Howards.

TAKE THE A149 NORTH FROM KING'S LYNN, THEN LEFT TO CASTLE RISING

Ceremony of the Keys, Tower of London

January
customs

January has always been a cold, dark month, the first of the present cycle of 12 months, although different sections of England's ancient multi-ethnic society once held turn-of-the-year celebrations at other times, for example, the Celts at the end of what is now October, the Anglo-Saxons at the end of what is now September, and the Vikings at the winter solstice. Welcoming the New Year today is done amid the Christmas period, yet the traditions associated with each have quite distinct origins. Whilst the Christmas period ends on 5th January (or 6th January according to which tradition you follow,) there is no doubt that today Christmas effectively finishes as people get ready to bring in the New Year and prepare for what lies ahead.

Surviving traditions hark back to a time when the next crop cycle was not too far in the future. The associated gods, goddesses and spirits had to be invoked or appeased, with songs, prayers, offerings and sacrifices, in order that a good crop would be had next season. People received spiritual and moral uplift for the coming year from the family, Church and community, and sometimes, particularly for the illiterate, through the medium of Mummers' Plays. In the North of England these plays are often accompanied by the traditional midwinter sword dances. Letting of agricultural land would be concluded, and the sources of food – land and seas alike – and the implements, vehicles and vessels used blessed.

Outdoor games in January depended on the weather, of course, but snowballing, tobogganing and skating were perennial favourites, the latter particularly in the Fens, and also bat and ball. When people were not huddling round the fire telling stories they would be playing chess, backgammon, billiards, Nine Men's Morris, cards, dice or shovel-board/shuffleboard.

Shuffleboard *Wooden discs are pushed from behind a line with wooden shovel-brooms towards a 20-30 ft (6-9m) target marked on the floor. The target is formed out of numbered rectangles. A score is made only if a disc is wholly in the rectangle. A game is won by the first to score 51 points. It is possible that this game played on ice gave rise to curling.*

People made resolutions to keep in the New Year and the young and unattached would dream of future friends and partners. All could now truly say that the struggles and anxieties of the old year were over. A pervasive feeling of hope countered the insistent chill, just as the lanterns, fires and torches accompanying so many activities let it be known that darkness would not rule.

Until recently, 1st January was not a public holiday in England, and seeing in the New Year was largely a private celebration, in contrast to the communal festivities enjoyed in Scotland

Variable Dates

♛ **Opening of the Central Criminal Court, Old Bailey**　　　　　London

Each year the Lord Mayor, the Sheriffs, the Sword-bearer, the Common Cryer and the City Marshall walk in procession from Mansion House to the Old Bailey for the Opening.

MANSION HOUSE IS AT THE JUNCTION OF VICTORIA STREET AND CANNON STREET.

♛ **Court of Common Council Service,**
Church of St Lawrence Jewry, Gresham Street　　　　　London

The Lord Mayor and officers go in procession from the Guildhall to the church for a service to mark the opening of the first session of the newly elected Court of Common Council.

THE GUILDHALL IS JUST OFF GRESHAM STREET (B128).

Fixed Dates

1st January New Year's Day, Circumcision

1st January, one week after the Nativity, is also known as Circumcision, marking the formal admission of Jesus into the Temple of Israel.

As Old Father Time, resplendent in his long grey hair and beard, carrying his scythe, is replaced by a new-born babe, church bells 'ring in the new year'. The making of New Year resolutions is traditional at New Year, as is present-giving and visiting friends and relatives.

First-footers, the first people through your door on this day, are welcomed with a glass of ale, a piece of Yule spice cake and a piece of cheese; also mince pies and **Plum Puddings** *(see p.182 for recipe)*. Traditionally they bring something green (not dead), a piece of coal (for warmth), salt (for wealth), and a loaf of bread or piece of cake (for sustenance), so that the household may have good luck, warmth, prosperity and plenty of food in the coming year. These gifts are collectively known as 'handsel'. A tall dark man (not a woman) is a lucky first-footer, but if the first-footer has auburn hair, a squint, flat feet or meeting eyebrows the house will have strife in the year ahead. An old custom in Coventry is for children to visit their godparents on New Year's Day and give them **God-Cakes** *(see p.182 for recipe)*. Another custom was apple-gifting. Children would decorate an apple by sticking evergreen twigs in it (usually rosemary and box) and carry it from door to door offering a New Year's blessing in exchange for a small donation. In some areas wassailing started on this day. Girls used to go from door to door singing wassail carols and carrying a holly bush adorned with ribbons, oranges and dolls.

It is unlucky to give credit on this day or cause someone to be in your debt by lending something to them. It is good luck to get the Cream of the Well – the first water to be drawn from the well that year, for example at the three wells in Wark, Northumberland, the water of which is said to have magical powers.

Evil and diseases are prevented from crossing the threshold by twisting hawthorn into a globe, seasoning it with cider, and hanging it in the kitchen. In Worcestershire a crown of blackthorn is used. The old one is placed on burning straw and carried across the fields to be dumped. It is a bad omen for the crops if the flames go out. This ceremony is called Burning the Bush. Mummers' Plays are performed on this day and have as their theme death and rebirth.

Until the 16th century the Feast of Fools was held in the 1st week in January, starting on 1st January, but it was banned during the Reformation. It originated from the Roman winter feasts of Saturnalia. A Lord of Misrule was elected to preside over the revelries.

🖐 **Sword-Dancing and Mummers' Plays, Northumberland, Durham**　　　**North Yorkshire**

These dances symbolise the conflict between the death of the old year and the revitalisation of the new. The Yorkshire dancers employ their traditional long steel or wooden swords and the Northumbrians their short, flexible steel swords which they interlock at the end of the sequence to form a 'knut'. The principal Yorkshire teams are at: North Skelton; Lingdale; Handsworth and Grenoside, near Sheffield; The Plough Stots of Goathland and Sleights; and Flamborough Head. The Royal Earsdon Northumbrian dancers can be seen at Earsdon.

The Mummers' Plays have the usual characters such as Fool, Medicine Man, Woman (a man in women's clothes), Beelzebub with his club, and Hobby Horse. The play represents winter's death and the resurgence of spring, as Fool is beheaded and brought back to life.

Burning the Bush at Putley Water Mill, near Ledbury   Hereford and Worcester

Just as the new year arrives 13 bonfires are lit, a large central one surrounded by 12 smaller ones, with a hawthorn globe on a long pole. The globe is stuffed with burning straw, and when the fires are all alight the globe is thrown on to the central one. As it is consumed a new hawthorn globe is made, doused in cider and singed in the embers of the main fire. A chant of 'Old Cider' is made nine times before the globe is hung in the kitchen of the mill until next year.

Formerly Burning-the-Bush ceremonies were held at Brinsop and Birley Court.

PUTLEY IS JUST OFF THE A4172 NEAR AYLTON.

Symondsbury Mummers' Play, near Bridport   Dorset

SYMONDSBURY IS NORTH OFF THE A35, TO THE WEST OF DORCHESTER AND BRIDPORT.

Andrew's Dole, Bideford   Devon

TAKE THE A39 SOUTH WEST FROM BARNSTAPLE.

The first Monday in January

The Landletting of the Poor's Pasture (candle auction), The George, Hubberholme   North Yorkshire

This candle auction is conducted by the local vicar, but is not a public event. At 8pm bidding commences for this 16 acre (6.5 ha) plot of land after a candle is lit. A pin is stuck in the candle and when it falls the auction finishes and the last bidder claims the use of the land for the year. The money paid is distributed to the poor of the parish.

A similar custom was once held in Broadway and Upwey, Dorset, there was no pin because the candle was only 1in (2.5cm) tall, balanced on a knife blade. Bidding ceased when the flame died.

HUBBERHOLME IS NORTH OF BUCKDEN ON THE B6160.

5th January, evening Twelfth Night, Epiphany Eve, Old Christmas Eve, Wassail Eve

As the twelve days of Christmas traditionally started on Christmas Eve, this is the last of the twelve days of celebration, and the time to take down the tree and decorations. This was a night to invite friends and relatives to play cards, games and have a supper of **Twelfth Cake** *(see p.182 for recipe)*, mince pies and to partake of the wassail bowl, filled with **Lamb's Wool** *(see p.182 for recipe)*. Each takes a spoon and eats a toasted apple from the bowl and then drinks the health of those present. Before the calendar change Twelfth Night was celebrated on a grand scale, with a large Twelfth Cake the centrepiece. Twelfth Cake, baked with a bean and a pea inside, is essentially the same as Christmas Cake. Whoever gets the bean is King of the Revel, and whoever gets the pea is Queen of the Revel. Sometimes a penny was put in the cake, and whoever found it became King or Queen. The cake is decorated with red and green knots, yellow crowns and flowers.

The custom of wassailing comes from the Saxon *Wass Hael* meaning 'to your health'. This salutation would be made to all members of the household and all guests as they were invited to drink a toast from a large communal bowl. Travelling vendors would sell the contents of their wassail cups to passers-by. Poor families would go from house to house with an empty bowl (wassail cup), singing wassail carols, and ask for food and drink. They offered good wishes to the household for the coming year, and hoped to be treated to spiced ale. They carried wassail branches, sticks with evergreens tied to them, decorated with ribbons and tinsel. The bowl was also sometimes decorated with evergreens and tinsel. Children did something similar, but instead of a wassail cup took a Doll-in-the-Box, finely dressed and the box decorated, singing carols and hoping for contributions. The box often had dolls dressed as Mary and Jesus. A carol associated with this tradition is the Holy Well, or Withy Twig. On payment of a penny the dolls were revealed. The Church attempted to replace wassail customs with those of Epiphany, but many customs remain.

The blessing of the apple orchards began, to ensure a good crop in the coming season. At dusk songs would be sung, cider poured over the tree roots, and toast hung in the trees for the robins to pick. To frighten off evil spirits guns were fired and noise made with horns, saucepans and so on. On returning home the wassailers were barred-out until they could guess what was roasting on the spit, or could answer another question put to them.

In some areas 13 bonfires were lit, one for each apostle and a Judas fire – which was extinguished early. At Brough in Cumbria a mobile fire of burning holly and ash was carried through the village. This was called Holly Night.

Wassailing, Curry Rivel, near Taunton Somerset
Starting at 6pm the wassailers bear an ash faggot round the village, wassailing door to door, before finishing at the King William pub where the faggot is thrown on to the fire by the oldest wassailer.
CURRY RIVEL IS WEST OF TAUNTON.

Pilgrimage to the Holy Thorn, Glastonbury Somerset
This non-native species of hawthorn, in St John's churchyard, is said to bloom each Christmas. Legend has it that Joseph of Arimathea visited these shores to found the first English church, and after scaling the heights of Wearyall Hill he sat down to rest and thrust his staff into the ground. It sprouted and became the Holy Thorn.

The original Glastonbury Thorn on Wearyall Hill bloomed every 5th January (then Christmas Eve). In 1752 the calendar was put back 11 days but the Thorn still flowered on 5th January. Puritans condemned it as an idol and destroyed it in the mid-17th century but cuttings thrived, one in the grounds of St John's Church, another in the ruins of Glastonbury Abbey.
GLASTONBURY IS SOUTH OF WELLS ON THE A39 AND WEST OF FROME ON THE A361.

Cutting the Baddeley Cake, Drury Lane Theatre London
The comedian Richard Baddeley made a bequest of 100 pounds in 1794 that the Drury Lane Theatre Company be bought a cake to eat every Twelfth Night. At the end of the play currently being performed on this night the cast, still in costume, eat a slice of cake and drink a toast in wine to this former pastry cook who became one of the most successful actors of his day.
DRURY LANE THEATRE IS AT THE JUNCTION OF RUSSELL STREET AND CATHERINE STREET.

6th January Twelfth Day, Epiphany, Old Christmas Day

Epiphany means appearance. Christians celebrate the showing of God to man – the manifestation of Christ to the gentiles. Epiphany also marks the giving to the infant Jesus of the gifts of gold, frankincense and myrrh by the three Magi. It has been considered the final day of the twelve days of Christmas celebrations.

Fancy dress is traditionally worn for Twelfth Day festivities, and is called guisering. **Epiphany Tart** *(see p.182 for recipe)* is traditionally eaten.

Throwing the Hood, Haxey, Isle of Axholme — Lincolnshire

The Haxey Hood Game is said to commemorate the day in the 13th century when men of the village chased and returned the black silk hood of Lady de Mowbray, which blew off in a gust of wind. However, the earliest record of it is in 1828. The 'hood' is tightly bound sacking or canvas, or, in the case of the Sway hood, leather-bound rope. As in mass football the hood is thrown not kicked. This is a very boisterous game and many unsuccessful attempts have been made to stamp it out.

At a committee meeting presided over by the 'Lord' on St John's Eve (23rd June) 12 Boggins are appointed. At midday on 6th January the Lord and Boggins march to the church gate, dressed in red, where one Boggin, the Fool, makes a welcoming speech and outlines the proceedings for the day. Then all process to Haxey Hill on the boundary of the parishes of Haxey and Westwoodside for the first sacking hood to be thrown. The villagers try to wrestle the hood from the Boggins, in a fairly harmless preliminary to the main game. If a villager is tackled the hood is Boggined and goes back to the Lord and another is thrown, until 12 have been competed for.

Then the real game begins with the leather Sway hood. The objective is to force the hood to either one of two public houses at Haxey or Westwoodside. The hood cannot be kicked, run off with or thrown. The game is over when a landlord touches the hood.

HAXEY AND WESTWOODSIDE LIE BETWEEN GOOLE AND GAINSBOROUGH ON THE B1396.

Cutting the Twelfth Cake, Sadler's Wells Theatre — London

After the regular performance the house is emptied and guests who have purchased the special tickets are re-admitted for a show of comic entertainment and the serving of slices of the cake to the guests by members of the company.

SADLER'S WELLS THEATRE IS IN ROSEBERY AVENUE, EC1.

Villagers prepare to smoke the fool as part of the Haxey Hood Game at Haxey Cross

✠ **Royal Epiphany Offering, Chapel Royal, St James' Palace**   **London**

This service commemorates the gifts of gold, frankincense and myrrh given by the Magi at the birth of Christ. The Lord Chamberlain, on behalf of the monarch, presents three symbolic purses during the singing of the Offertory in this 700-year-old ceremony. The gifts are blessed by the Bishop of London. Afterwards the frankincense is given to the Anglican Church, the myrrh to Nashdom Abbey and the gold is returned to the Bank of England, the cash equivalent being given to charities. Attendance is by invitation only.

ST JAMES'S PALACE IS IN MARLBOROUGH ROAD, OFF THE MALL.

The Sunday nearest Epiphany

✠ **Blessing the Sea (Greek Orthodox ceremony) at Hastings**   **East Sussex**

During this service a large cross, decorated with flowers, is dipped three times into the sea to ensure good catches in the year ahead.

HASTINGS IS ON THE SOUTH COAST OF ENGLAND AT THE END OF THE A21.

✠ **Blessing the Sea (Greek Orthodox ceremony) at Margate**   **Kent**

A similar service, but the cross is thrown into the sea, to be retrieved by a chosen swimmer.

MARGATE IS ON THE NORTH KENT COAST, EAST OF CANTERBURY ON THE A28.

7th January St Distaff's Day, Rock Day, St Brannoc's Day

Rock day comes from the word 'rocking', an old word for spinning. This day marked the resumption of work by women after Christmas. 'St Distaff' is not a real saint. A distaff is a long piece of wood, with a cleft, used in the spinning of flax – a job done entirely by women. It thus became symbolic of women's work in general. The men, who were still on holiday, used to burn the women's flax and tow for sport, the women's response was to try and drench the men and the burning flax.

St Brannoc was a 6th-century saint who sailed from Wales to Devon in a stone coffin and achieved a reputation for being able to tame or cure any animal.

The Sunday nearest 7th January

☻ **William Underhill's Charity (money), Eldersfield**   **Hereford and Worcester**

In his will of 1647 William Underhill left money to the 'honest poor, not Bastards nor any known dishonest poor'. The vicar calls the names of the chosen, who receive the money from the church-warden whilst the latter is sitting on a chair at the head of William Underhill's tomb.

ELDERSFIELD IS BETWEEN GLOUCESTER AND GREAT MALVERN ON THE B4208.

A life-size straw bear, Whittlesey

Blessing the Plough, Goatland

The Saturday before Plough Monday

Straw Bear Day, Whittlesey   Cambridgeshire

This is a revival of an ancient festival, now part of a larger festival of folk music and dance. Straw Men were either real men dressed completely in straw or life-sized straw effigies. The effigies were ritually sacrificed, but whether the same fate ever befell the real men in straw is not documented.

WHITTLESEY IS EAST OF PETERBOROUGH ON THE A605.

Plough Sunday Sunday after Epiphany

Traditional Blessings of the Plough on this day have been revived in many places. These are examples of many similar local ceremonies in which local farmers take a plough, as a symbol of all the agricultural work to be done in the coming season, up the chancel steps to be blessed.

Blessing the Plough, Chichester Cathedral   West Sussex

CHICHESTER IS BETWEEN WORTHING AND PORTSMOUTH ON THE A27.

Blessing the Plough, Blunham, Dunton and Wrestlingworth   Bedfordshire

BLUNHAM IS NORTH OF SANDY OFF THE A1. DUNTON IS NORTH OF LETCHWORTH OFF THE A1. WRESTLINGWORTH IS JUST TO THE NORTH OF DUNTON.

Blessing the Plough, Exeter Cathedral   Devon

EXETER IS OFF THE M5, JUNCTIONS 29 AND 30.

Blessing the Plough, Goathland   North Yorkshire

GOATHLAND IS SOUTH OF WHITBY OFF THE A169.

Blessing the Plough, St Agnes Church, Cawston, near Norwich   Norfolk

TAKE THE B1149 NORTH FROM NORWICH, THEN THE B1145 WEST TO CAWSTON.

Plough Sunday Play, St Leonard's Church, Flamstead   Hertfordshire

This is a short play performed by local farmers as part of the Plough Sunday service.

FLAMSTEAD IS ON THE A5, NORTHBOUND OFF THE M1 AT JUNCTION 9.

First Monday after Twelfth Day Plough Monday

On this day ploughmen, with blackened faces and white shirts, decorated their ploughs and went around collecting money, accompanied by characters such as Fool, dressed in skins and a tail, with a stick and inflated pig's bladder on the end, Old Woman and Bessy the man-woman resembling those characters in the medieval Festival of Fools. Sometimes faces were blackened and clothes worn inside out. They were called Jags, Plough Jags, Plough Stots, Plough Jacks, Bullocks or Boggins depending on the area. Anyone refusing to give money or drink was likely to have their front garden ploughed up.

Also the ploughmen featured in village festivities with leaping dances, the height leaped was thought to represent the height of next season's corn. Shepherds and farm labourers would turn out in embroidered smocks, heavy linen shifts with patterns indicating their trades, e.g. tree symbols for foresters, wheels for carters and rams' horns for shepherds.

Blessing the Plough was particularly common in Sussex and Hampshire. Plough Monday Plays were once common in Nottinghamshire, Lincolnshire and other parts of the East Midlands, for example in Revesby and Hibaldstow in Lincolnshire, Hinckley in Leicestershire, and Holton-le-Clay in Humberside (which had a Straw Man). Men then returned to work after the Christmas break, and in the first new furrow they would plant the corn dolly so that the corn spirit would return to the field and ensure another harvest.

The Dancing Plough Stots (Sword-Dancers), Goathland and Sleights — North Yorkshire

This is the most important day for this eight-man team of six sword dancers. They are accompanied by two Mummers, dressed as Fools, who perform antics and collect money from spectators. The swords of the dancers are held in the right hand and after a series of intricate movements become interlocked in a hexagon called a 'knut', which is held aloft by one of the dancers. This hexagon is then undone by a further series of movements.

SLEIGHTS IS ON THE A169, SOUTH OF WHITBY, AND GOATHLAND IS JUST OFF ON THE RIGHT.

The Mumming Play, Revesby — Lincolnshire

TAKE THE A153 SOUTH FROM HORNCASTLE, THEN LEFT ON THE B1183.

The Tuesday after Plough Monday

Straw Bear Tuesday, several places in the area — Fens

A man dressed in straw, with a straw tail and conical sheaf over his head, does comic antics and collects money. This is a similar tradition to that at Whittlesey.

The Thursday after Plough Monday

The Giving of Cakes and Ale, Bury St Edmunds — Suffolk

Carried on unbroken for 450 years this may be the country's oldest charity. Nowadays, after a religious service, money is given to local almshouse residents instead of the original cakes and ale.

BURY ST EDMUNDS IS AT THE JUNCTION OF THE A45 AND THE A134.

9th January St Fillan's Day

St Fillan was an 8th-century Scottish pioneer of a cold-water immersion therapy for lunatics.

13th January St Mungo's Day, St Hilary's Day

St Mungo was a 7th-century Celt who founded a church on what is now Glasgow Cathedral. The 4th-century St Hilary, Bishop of Poitier, gave his name to the Law Courts' winter term. This is the first day after Christmas when it is considered religiously decent to get married, and is traditionally regarded as the coldest day of the year.

15th January St Ceolwulf's Day

St Ceolwulf was an 8th-century King of Northumbria, to whom Bede dedicated his *Ecclesiastical History*, who abdicated and became a monk at Lindisfarne.

16th January St Sigebert's Day, St Fursey's Day, St Henry's Day

St Sigebert was a 7th-century King of East Anglia. St Fursey was an Irish mystic, a contemporary of St Sigebert. St Henry was a 12th-century hermit.

17th January Old Twelfth Night, St Anthony's Day

St Anthony was a 4th-century founder of a hospital for pigs suffering from the disease ergotism. The disease is caused by eating food prepared from rye and other cereals infected with the fungus ergot.

🎧 **Wassailing the Apple Trees, Carhampton, near Minehead**   **Somerset**

After mulling some cider the villagers take it out to the apple orchards and toast the trees whilst singing a wassail song. Cider with toast floating in it is taken to the trees, and the toast placed in a fork 'for the robins' – so they won't eat the buds. Cider is then poured abundantly about the roots of the tree and guns fired in the branches to scare away any evil spirits that may be lurking with intent. Safe in the knowledge that a good apple crop will be had this year, the people retire to the village pub.

CARHAMPTON IS ON THE A39, EAST OF MINEHEAD AND JUST PAST DUNSTER CASTLE.

18th January Old Twelfth Day, St Ulfrid's Day

St Ulfrid was an 11th-century Christian Viking martyred for destroying a statue of Thor.

19th January St Wulstan's Day

Wulstan was one of the few Saxon bishops to retain his see after the Norman Conquest. The crypt of his Norman cathedral survives as part of Worcester Cathedral, where a memorial service is held on this day to commemorate his death in 1095.

20th January St Agnes' Eve St Vigean's Day

Traditionally young girls in the North of England fasted all day and ate a salt-filled hard-boiled egg (with shell) before going to bed looking as beautiful as they could. The reason for this was that they hoped the decidedly unpleasant bed-time snack would enable them to dream of their future husbands, who would appear and offer them water! Swallowing a raw red herring (bones and all) before going to bed allegedly produced a similar result. Another way to dream of a future husband was for a girl to prepare before going to bed a row of pins, pull out each in turn, say a prayer or Paternoster and then proceed to stick each pin in the sleeve. St Vigean was a 7th-century Irish abbot.

21st January St Agnes' Day,

St Agnes, patroness of maidens, was a 4th-century Roman virgin who suffered persecution under Emperor Diocletian because she refused to marry and deny her faith. She was stripped and sent to a brothel.

22nd January St Vincent's Day

St Vincent was a 4th-century martyr, seemingly known for having had a reputation for excessive drinking.

25th January St Paul's Day, Conversion of St Paul, St Dwynwen's Day

On this day the Church commemorates the conversion of St Paul on the road to Damascus in the 1st Century, after he had previously been involved in persecuting Christians in Jerusalem. He was born at Tarsus in Cilicia, Turkey, and beheaded in about AD 65, during the Persecutions by Nero.

Venison with Port Wine Sauce *(see p.182 for recipe)* is traditionally eaten, in memory of the gift in 1224 by the Dean and Chapter of St Paul's Cathedral to Sir William Baud of the manor of Westley, Essex, of 22 acres (9ha) of land, in return for which he promised to donate a buck and doe every St Paul's Day.

26th January St Tortgith's Day

St Tortgith was a 7th-century nun who was admired for the way she kept her faith while coping with extreme ill-health and disability.

30th January Anniversary of Execution of Charles I

Memorial services are held on this day in several London churches to commemorate the day in 1649 when Charles was beheaded after the English Civil War. Among them are St Martin-in-the-Fields, Charing Cross; the Church of St Andrew by the Wardrobe, Queen Victoria Street; St Mary-le-Strand, Strand; St Alban the Martyr, Holborn; St Saviour's, Hampstead and Whitechapel Parish Church.

✪ Charles I Memorial Service and Wreathlaying, Trafalgar Square and the Banqueting House, Whitehall

London

After a service at his statue in Trafalgar Square a wreath is laid at Banqueting House.
TRAFALGAR SQUARE IS OPPOSITE CHARING CROSS (A4).

The last Thursday in January

● Dicing for Maid's Money, Council Chamber, Guildford

Surrey

Many charities were set up in the past to encourage and reward faithful service and good character in maid servants, particularly in Reading and other towns in the Thames Balley and at Guildford. The annual interest on John How's bequest of £400 on 27th January, 1674 is annually given to the one of two chosen good, humble maidservants who throws the highest dice score. To qualify they must be unmarried and have served their employer faithfully for at least two years. The hide dice box, with silver band and bottom, and two dice, are over a century old, and the dice are tossed on the council table. This is not a public event.

About 20 years after John How's bequest a similar charity was set up by John Parsons, but he left £600. The interest was to go to a poor young man who has served as an apprentice for seven years and has less than £20 to his name. If no suitable candidate came forward, then the money would go to a maid who had given at least three years good service to her household. As a suitable apprentice could rarely be found, the Town Fathers eventually decreed that the money should go to the loser of the dice contest, who thus gets more than the winner!
GUILDFORD IS ON THE A3 SOUTH EAST OF JUNCTION 10 OF THE M25.

Dicing for Maid's Money, Council Chamber, Guildford

February customs

Customs in the dark, cold month of February reflected the knowledge that the worst of winter would soon be over, and thoughts could turn to preparations for spring. Farmers who had not already done so made plans to prepare or acquire the use of land. Livestock, seed and equipment would soon be bought, so workers could be hired ready. Many hiring and livestock fairs were held on and after Candlemas, a date when land tenures expired and farmers did their accounts before the new spring season. Salmon and eel fishermen also prepared for their catching season, but took the precaution of having their nets blessed first.

Games played in February were much the same as those mentioned for January.

For those for whom spring meant an opportunity to find a partner, February was the time to turn one's attention to possible future meetings and relationships. The cue perhaps was taken from nature itself, as the first spring flowers bravely pole their heads above the snow and hardy breeds of sheep give birth to the first lambs of the year.

Variable Dates

Beginning of the Easter Cycle
The following two entries form the beginning of the Easter Cycle:

Septuagesima Sunday Lost Sunday, **The third Sunday before the beginning of Lent**
This can also fall in January, depending on the date of Easter.

Sexagesima Sunday **The second Sunday before the beginning of Lent**
This can also fall in January, depending on the date of Easter.

Early February

Hurling the Silver Ball, St Columb Major and St Columb Minor   Cornwall
TAKE THE A3059 EAST FROM NEWQUAY.

Roundabout Riding, King's Lynn   Norfolk
KING'S LYNN IS AT THE MEETING OF THE A10, A47 AND A149.

A Sunday in early February

✠ Clowns' Service, Holy Trinity Church, Dalston   London

During the service a wreath is laid on Grimaldi's memorial. This famous clown died on 31st May 1837.

DALSTON IS AT THE JUNCTION OF THE A10 AND A104.

In February or March

♔ The Trial of the Pyx, Goldsmiths' Hall, Foster Lane   London

The Trial of the Pyx involves testing the coins of the realm, one from every batch minted in the past year, in the presence of 12 Jurors. This is presided over by the Queen's Remembrancer. The Chancellor of the Exchequer, who is Master of the Mint, announces the result at the Pyx Luncheon in May. These are not public events.

FOSTER LANE IS OFF CHEAPSIDE, ON THE NORTH SIDE OF ST PAUL'S CATHEDRAL.

Fixed Dates

1st February St Bride's Day

Bride, or Brigid, was a 6th-century Irish Abbess. Dew gathered on this day will beautify your features and make them youthful. This was the Celtic Quarter Day of Imbolc.

2nd February Candlemas Day, The Presentation of Christ, Feast of the Purification

Christians celebrate the day when the infant Christ, who was 40 days old, was taken by Mary and Joseph to the temple in Jerusalem. Candle-lit processions, of mothers who had borne children the previous year, in celebration of the purification of Mary were held; candles were blessed and distributed to the congregation. The Catholic Church chose this day for Candlemas in the 5th century to try and replace the ancient Celtic feast of Imbolc, which heralded the start of the lambing season, and was dedicated to the Celtic Goddess of Youth and Fertility, Bride. This goddess was renamed St Bridget and myths were invented to Christianise her. Snowdrops, a symbol of purity,

Trial of the Pyx, Goldsmiths' Hall, London

were called Candlemas Bells, and were used in dedications to her. The day was also the day of the Roman festival of *Februa*, at which candles were carried through the streets and women observed purification rites.

It was customary on this day to light a brand from the burning Yule log and keep it alight until sunset. Finish eating the Yule log today.

Old land-tenure agreements traditionally ended on this day, which was a Quarter Day and the end of the farmers' fiscal year. Cattle, horse and general merchandise fairs were held on this day, and the annual fair at Reading, Berkshire is still so held.

✠ Rocking Ceremony, St Mary of the Purification, Blidworth — Nottinghamshire

This may take place on the Sunday nearest 2nd February. It is a version of an old Candlemas play about the presentation of Christ. The Blidworth baby born nearest to Christmas Day is baptised and lain in a decorated wooden cradle. During the service the vicar blesses the baby as he rocks the cradle.

BLIDWORTH CAN BE REACHED BY TAKING THE B6020 EAST OUT OF KIRKBY-IN-ASHFIELD.

☻ Forty Shilling Day, Wotton, near Dorking — Surrey

Five poor boys compete for 40 shillings, under the terms of the will of William Glanville, who died in 1717. They must stand with their right hands on the tomb of the former Treasury Clerk in Wotton churchyard and recite the Lord's Prayer, the Apostle's Creed and the Ten Commandments. They must then read aloud the fifteenth chapter of the First Epistle of St Paul to the Corinthians and write two verses of the Epistle in neat handwriting.

TAKE THE A25 WEST FROM DORKING, THROUGH WESTCOTT TO WOTTON.

☻ Bread Dole, Woodbridge — Suffolk

Endowed in 1638 by John Sayer, this was once a weekly dole providing 'two penny loaves' every Saturday from the bread shelves in the porch of St Mary's Church. Today the bread is provided to local pensioners.

TAKE THE A12 NORTH EAST FROM IPSWICH.

Bread Dole, Woodbridge

3rd February St Blaise's Day, St Werburga's Day, St Ia's (Ives's) Day

St Blaise was a 4th-century doctor who became the patron saint of sufferers from a sore throat and of wool-combers. Wool centres such as Bury St Edmunds, York and Guildford held feasts on this day. St Werburga was the daughter of the 7th-century Christian King of Mercia. St Ia was an Irish virgin who fled to Cornwall.

✙ **Ceremony of Blessing the Throat, St Ethelreda's Church (RC), Ely Place**   London

At this ceremony to commemorate St Blaise two candles, tied together, are touched on either side of sufferers' throats.

ELY PLACE IS NEAR HOLBORN CIRCUS, OFF CHARTERHOUSE STREET.

✙ **Blessing the Water, St Mary's Abbey, East Bergholt**   Suffolk

After the blessing the blessed water is sent wherever there are sufferers of throat complaints.

EAST BERGHOLT IS BETWEEN IPSWICH AND COLCHESTER ON THE B1070.

The day after the Sunday nearest 3rd February Feast Monday, Feasten Day

At wakes and other celebratory occasions in Cornwall **Feasten Cakes** *(see p.183 for recipe)* were eaten.

⊚ **Hurling the Silver Ball, St Ives and Lelant**   Cornwall

This is a local type of handball game. A silver-coated cork ball is thrown by the Mayor at 10:30am to a gathering of children, who proceed to pass it amongst themselves. The child holding the ball at noon is awarded a crown piece.

LELANT AND ST IVES ARE ON THE A3074.

4th February St Gilbert's Day

St Gilbert, from Sempringham, Lincolnshire, formed a monastic order in the 12th century, the only one ever to have been founded in this country.

6th February St Dorothea's (Dorothy's) Day

St Dorothy lived in the 4th century. This is reputedly the snowiest day of the year.

8th February St Cuthman's Day

St Cuthman was a 7th-century Sussex preacher, who lived in Steyning, known for his devotion to his invalid mother.

9th February St Teilo's Day

St Teilo was a former Bishop of Llandaff Cathedral, Cardiff.

11th February St Caedmon's Day

St Caedmon was a 7th-century Christian poet from Whitby, Yorkshire.

13th February

On St Valentine's Eve unmarried people would put the names of their acquaintances of the opposite sex into a vessel and draw them in lots to determine whom they might marry. Boys would sometimes wear their Valentine slips on their sleeves and treat the girls whose names they bore. This practice has given way to the sending of Valentine cards.

✙ **Blessing of the opening of the salmon net-fishing season, Pedwell Beach, near Norham on the River Tweed, then at Berwick-on-Tweed**   Northumberland

Fishermen from both the English and Scottish sides of the river assemble just before midnight with their nets for the blessing and offerings of prayers for safe-keeping. After the service the fishermen go out into the river to get their first catch from which the vicar receives a presentation.

NORHAM IS BETWEEN COLDSTREAM AND BERWICK-ON-TWEED, OFF THE B6470.

14th February St Valentine's Day, Feast of St Cyril and St Methodius

This day combines the commemoration of the martyrdom of St Valentine on 14th February AD 273 at the hands of the Romans with the pagan festival of Lupercalia (held on 15th February) in which young people of marriageable age took part. Boys drew the names of girls from an urn and the couples paired off.

St Valentine, who was renowned for his chastity, has, curiously, become the patron saint of lovers, and it is customary on this day anonymous cards and gifts are sent to those admired from afar. Valentine cards, made of parchment, are known to have dated from as long ago as the 15th century.

Valentine symbolism is commonly heart-shaped. In the past on the eve of this day boys would write girls names on slips of paper and then proceed to draw lots for their sweetheart for the year. A traditional love token is for a boy to buy a girl a pair of gloves – but the glove is also a symbol of authority. By placing a bay leaf under the pillow at night a girl would dream of her future lover.

Valentine Cakes, also known as plum shuttles, and **Valentine biscuits** *(see p.183 for recipes)* are traditionally eaten.

This day was the opening of the eel catching season.

Valentine Fair, King's Lynn   Norfolk

The King's Lynn fair, known as Lynn Mart, is one of England's oldest charter fairs, dating from at least the 8th century. It opens with the ringing of a hand bell and the reading of the old proclamation by the Mayor.

KING'S LYNN IS AT THE MEETING OF THE A10, A47 AND A149.

Valentine Fair, Biggleswade   Bedfordshire

BIGGLESWADE IS BETWEEN ST NEOTS AND LETCHWORTH ON THE A1.

Valentine Fair, Bath   Avon

BATH IS ON THE A4 BETWEEN BRISTOL AND CHIPPENHAM.

Valentine Fair, Wymondham   Norfolk

TAKE THE A11 SOUTH WEST FROM NORWICH TO WYMONDHAM.

Old Candlemas Fair, Devizes   Wiltshire

DEVIZES IS JUST NORTH OF THE SALISBURY PLAIN AT THE JUNCTION OF THE A360 AND A342.

Candlemas Fair, Dorchester   Dorset

This was originally a hiring fair for servants.

DORCHESTER IS BETWEEN POOLE AND BRIDPORT ON THE A35.

17th February St Finan's Day

St Finan was a 7th-century Bishop of Lindisfarne who challenged Catholic dominance over what he saw as an exclusively Celtic Christian Church.

The Saturday nearest 22nd February

Baden-Powell Memorial Service, Westminster Abbey   London

Boy Scouts and Girl Guides attend this service on the Saturday that falls nearest the shared birthday of Lord and Lady Baden-Powell and it is the tradition lay wreaths on the Baden-Powell Memorial.

WESTMINSTER ABBEY IS OFF VICTORIA STREET (A302).

23rd February St Milburga's Day

St Milburga was an 8th-century Abbess of Wenlock Priory, Shropshire.

24th February St Matthias's Day

St Matthias was chosen in the 1st Century, as the twelfth apostle. He spread the faith in Cappadocia and the Caspian Sea, later to be martyred in Colchis (Ethiopia).

25th February St Ethelbert's Day, St Walburga's Day

Though a pagan, St Ethelbert, a 6th-century King of Kent, allowed Augustine to preach and convert his subjects. In 595 he became the first Christian English king.

St Walburga was an 8th-century English missionary who appears to have been confused with the Germanic goddess Walborg, worshiped by witches.

27th February

 **Robert Rede's Twopenny Gift, Eton College, Eton**   **Berkshire**

Robert Rede of Burnham, who died in 1514, bequeathed two-pence in his will to every Colleger in Hall at Eton College who would recall his memory and that of his wife at the altar. When the then Provost Roger Lupton died in 1535 he left money to increase the sum to threepence.

ETON COLLEGE IS ON THE B3022 NORTH FROM WINDSOR.

28th February St David's Eve, St Oswald's Day

As the 29th February does not appear in the calendar of saint days today is St David's Eve. St Oswald is associated with the building of Worcester Cathedral.

29th February Leap Day

This day appears in the calendar every four years and was instituted to compensate for the fact that the year was calculated to be 365¼ days. As it is actually slightly less than this, a further compensation was made by modifying the Leap Year rule to exclude the last year of the century as it is not divisible by 400. So, 1600 and 2000 are leap years, whereas 1700, 1800 and 1900 are not. This is the only day of the year when it is seemly for a lady to propose to a gentleman, provided she is wearing a red petticoat. If the gentleman refuses he is duty bound to buy the lady a pair of gloves or a silk dress.

St. Valentine's Fair, King's Lynn, Norfolk

Shrovetide customs

Shrovetide comprises four days: Shrove Saturday, Shrove Sunday or Quinquagesima, Collop Monday and Shrove Tuesday. At Shrovetide the worst of winter is over and people look forward to warmer days. The merrymaking arises partly from the festivities held at the Roman feast of Bacchus.

This is the period when Christians seek absolution and forgiveness by confessing sins before Lent begins on Ash Wednesday. 'To be shriven' is to be cleansed of all sins. A bell summoned villagers to confession and shriving on Shrove Tuesday, which later became known as the pancake bell. The tradition survives in: Olney, Buckinghamshire; Pontefract, West Yorkshire; Shrewsbury, Shropshire; Claybrook and Belgrave, Leicestershire; Ilmington, Warwickshire; and other places.

The Monday and Tuesday before Lent were times of Carnival (which means 'goodbye to meat') and feasting, as all meat, butter, fat, eggs and cream had to be eaten up before the 40 days of Lent began on Ash Wednesday. Meat that couldn't be eaten was preserved. The pre-Lent period marked the retreat of winter, and the celebrations reached a climax in the three days before Ash Wednesday. Giants featured in the Carnival parade, and also in some civic and Guild processions.

The Monday of Shrovetide was often used for mischief, and the Tuesday for playing sports. Shrovetide football (not to be confused with soccer) is a traditional Shrovetide game (originally called 'camping'), dating from the 12th century, for which each village had a local variant. Whole communities would take part, using natural or village features as goals and streams as obstacles. Brute force was as important as skill in forcing the ball through the goal. There are records of games between bachelors and married men, and a few of games between spinsters and married women. Other popular sports included battledore and shuttlecock (or battledore and shuttlefeathers) – the precursor of badminton, pitch and toss, quoits, skipping (for example, at Scarborough), rope-pulling (for example, at Ludlow, Shropshire), knurr and spell and billeting (Yorkshire and Lancashire), shinney and whipping (last played at Newarke, Leicester), hurling in Celtic areas like Cornwall and Devon, marbles, top whipping, prison bars and, in southern England, Holly Boy and Ivy Girl.

Pitch and toss *The object of the game is to pitch a lead 'pitcher' (which is like an ice-hockey puck, but has head-and-tail sides) as near as possible to a marker such as a stick planted in the ground. The player whose pitcher lands nearest throws the opponents' pitchers in the air and keeps the heads. The second-placed player throws the remainder in the air and also keeps the heads, and the other players follow in order. Money then changes hands per pitcher won.*

Quoits *Quoits are circular metal rings or horseshoes and they are cast at a peg (or hob), of which there are two, 18 yd (16.5m) apart, in clay. The quoit is cast so as to either land pierced by the hob or as near as possible to it. A narrow angle of flight enables it to embed in the clay. Players have two quoits, and score one point for the one nearest the hob (two points if both are nearer than the opponents' two) and three points for a quoit around the hob.*

Rope-pulling *This was like tug-o'-war, but often the two teams were either side of an obstacle like a stream. At Ludlow, the rope had a knob on each end, painted in the colours of the team taking the strain at the other end. To win, a team had to wet their knob in the stream.*

Knurr and spell *This game's stronghold is the moorland areas of Yorkshire and Lancashire. The knurr is a small boxwood ball 1 in (2.5cm) in diameter, the spell a spring, regulated by a thumbscrew, on a wooden base, and the pommel is a long stick with a padded handle and swollen end. The spring is released, propelling the ball upwards, and it is struck by the pommel at about chest height. The course is triangular, 250 yd (228.5m) long each side, staked out with 20 yd (18m) marks. One point is scored for each 20 yd (18m) mark passed by the knurr. The player scoring the most points after an agreed number of hits wins the game.*

Billeting *This is more skillful than knurr and spell, and like it can still be seen in the Norland area of North Yorkshire. The billet is a piece of wood, with a turned end, 3-4 in (7.5-10cm) long, which is balanced on the end of the striking stick. It is tossed in the air and struck before it falls to ground. If it is tossed so that it drops vertically, then struck in the centre, it will travel furthest – perhaps 50 yds (46m). The longest hit wins.*

Shinney and whipping *Shinney was a precursor of hockey. At Newarke, Leicester, the shinney game was followed by Whipping Toms setting about the players with whips, but only below knee level. Bellmen assisted them, but if a victim could grab a bellman the whipping stopped.*

Fives *Nowadays this game is confined to public schools, such as those at Eton, Rugby and Winchester, each version of which has its own characteristics. As a popular sport, fives was widespread in Durham in the 19th century. Basically the game involves hitting a ball with the hand against a wall, or in a three-wall recess, to force your opponent into error. Later a padded glove was used, and this gave way to the racquet the popularity of which eclipsed the original game.*

Prison bars *Two teams face each other with the members of a team linking hands. One member makes a break and tries to run to the opposite end without being touched or caught. A member (only one) of the opposite team tries to intercept. Then another makes a run and so on. A member touched joins the rival side. The winner is the team that finishes with the most members.*

Holly Boy and Ivy Girl *In this game boys made a corn dolly decorated with holly and girls made one decorated with ivy. Each puts their dolly in a hiding place. The boys try to find the Ivy Girls and the girls the Holly Boys. Those found are burned on a bonfire.*

Other Shrovetide 'sports' included dog- and bear-baiting, dog-tossing, cock-fighting and throwing at cocks, which children used to do with sticks. The white ball in bowls was called the cock.

Another tradition was 'Barring-out the Master' when children shut out their teachers from school and refused to admit them unless they were given an extra day's holiday. The last recorded instance was in 1938 in Tideswell, Derbyshire.

As with many days that were on the eve of an important change, whether it be to lifestyle or of the calendar, Shrove Tuesday was popular for divination. The more devout held church-clipping ceremonies, whilst those bent on sweeping away the present smashed their crockery.

Variable Dates

Shrove Saturday

In Oxfordshire this day was called Egg Feast Day or Egg Saturday or Brusting (bursting) Day. Eggs pickled for winter preservation were given as gifts; brusting pudding was a thick, crumbly pancake, also made in Lincolnshire.

Quinquagesima Sunday Shrove Sunday, The Sunday before the beginning of Lent

Shrove Monday Collop Monday

On this day remaining fresh meat was cut up into **Minced Beef Collops** *(see p.183 for recipe)*, or steaks, for salting or hanging up until Lent was over. In the mid-Pennines children would knock on doors and say 'Pray Dame, a collop', meaning a slice of bacon. The fat would be cut off and used the next day to cook pancakes. Collop and eggs (i.e. bacon and eggs) was a favourite meal in the North of England. The bacon was left to stand in hot water before toasting and the egg poached in vinegar and water.

In Cornwall, where pea soup was eaten instead of collops, it is called Peasen Monday. In the West Country the night of mischief is called Nickanan Night, or, in Devon, Dappy Door Night.

Shrove Tuesday Pancake Tuesday, The last day before Lent

This was the day when people confessed, in response to the curfew bell (pancake bell) rung in every parish, still to be heard in a few places today. After confessing their sins in church people were 'shriven'. As the last day before Lent it was a time of great festivity before the coming days of abstinence. Shops closed on the shriving bell, and pupils in some schools used to lock out their teachers (barring-out) and refuse to let them back in until granted an extra day's holiday.

Church-clipping, parishioners clasped hands and surrounded the church, was done, particularly in Somerset and Wiltshire where threading the needle was played at the same time.

Threading the Needle *Couples dance in meandering lines, taking it in turns to form an arch for the others to dance through.*

Pancakes *(see p.183 for recipe)*, in order to use up all the fat and butter in the house, truckle cheese, biscuits and fruit cakes are traditionally eaten. Pancake-tossing and pancake races, during which the pancake must be tossed a number of times, are held, as well as pancake-eating competitions. In Baldock, Hertfordshire people eat **Baldock Doughnuts** *(see p.183 for recipe)* instead of pancakes, and in Norwich **Coquille Buns** *(see p.183 for recipe)*. *Coquille* is French for shell (-shaped) and may have given rise to the modern American term 'cookie'.

Children and apprentices had a holiday and used to roam the streets (going a-shroving) singing Shrovetide songs and asking for pancakes or other little treats.

In Cornwall and the Scilly Isles, on Exmoor, and in the Brendon Hills, Shrove Tuesday Eve was Mischief Night. Boys with blackened faces would try to enter houses, throw broken crocks on the floor, and leave undetected. If discovered they would demand money or pancakes to desist. In Dorset and Wiltshire people threw their old crockery at doors – Lent Crocking – to request a pancake to be tossed back. In other parts it was called Lensharding.

Pancake Greaze (tossing), Westminster School, Little Dean's Yard   London

At 11am, boys attempt to retrieve whole a pancake tossed by the cook over the high bar of the Old School Room. The bar is 16ft (5m) off the ground. After the inevitable scramble the boy who gets the largest piece wins a guinea. This event is not open to the public.

WESTMINSTER SCHOOL IS OPPOSITE THE HOUSES OF PARLIAMENT.

Pancake Race, Olney   Buckinghamshire

The pancake bell is rung at 11:30am and 11:45 to warn women to start making their pancakes and at 1pm to summon them to the race. They must be over 18, have been resident for at least three months, and wear headscarves and pinafores. During the race from the pump in Market Square to the church the pancake must be tossed three times.

OLNEY IS BETWEEN MILTON KEYNES AND WELLINGBOROUGH ON THE A509.

Pancake Races, Winster, near Matlock   Derbyshire

There are separate races for men and women at 2pm between the Dower House and the Old Market House. You must bring your own pan and pancake.

TAKE THE A6 NORTH OUT OF MATLOCK AND TURN LEFT ON TO THE B5057, PAST WENSLEY.

Pancake Race, Stone, near Dartford   Kent

DARTFORD IS ON THE RIVER THAMES OFF JUNCTION 1A OF THE M25.

Pancake Day Races, Lincoln's Inn Fields   London

LINCOLN'S INN FIELDS IS JUST TO THE SOUTH OF HIGH HOLBORN.

Pancake Race, Whitby Pier   North Yorkshire

WHITBY IS ON THE COAST AT THE JUNCTION OF THE A171 AND THE A174.

Going a-shroving, Durweston   Dorset

Valentine Rickman, who died in 1925, bequeathed money so that local children could continue shroving and that flowers would always be on his grave. Now, children sing a shroving song whilst they give flowers to passers-by.

DURWESTON IS JUST NORTH WEST OF BLANDFORD FORUM ON THE A357.

Driving the Devil into the Sea, Clovelly, near Bideford   Devon

Boys drag cans through the village and down to the beach in the evening, making sufficient noise to drive out the Devil.

TAKE THE A39 WEST FROM BIDEFORD, PAST BUCK'S CROSS.

⚫ Shrovetide Tip-toeing, Gittisham, near Honiton — Devon

In the evening children tip-toe from house to house, asking for contributions.

TAKE THE A375 SOUTH FROM HONITON AND EXIT RIGHT TO GITTISHAM.

⚫ Cornish Hurling Match, St Columb Major and St Columb Minor — Cornwall

The match at St Columb Major lasts from 4.30pm until 8pm, with a rematch 11 days later.

Hurling *This furious Celtic game has superficial similarity to hockey, but players can catch the ball in the air and carry it for three paces, kick it, and hit it with hands or hurley – which is like a broad-ended hockey stick. The goal is like rugby goalposts. If the ball goes under the crossbar and between the uprights, three points are scored. If the ball goes over the crossbar and between the uprights one point is scored.*

TAKE THE A3059 EAST FROM NEWQUAY.

⚫ Court of the Company of Purbeck Marblers and Stonecutters, Town Hall, Corfe Castle — Dorset

This meeting starts at midday, for members only, and is followed by the Shrove Football Match. To join the Company an apprentice must pay 6s.8d (33p), a penny loaf and a quart of ale.

CORFE CASTLE IS BETWEEN WAREHAM AND SWANAGE ON THE A351.

⚫ Shrovetide Football, Corfe Castle — Dorset

This takes place after the Marblers Court, and after payment of the peppercorn rent of 1 lb of pepper to play on Owre Farm which is part of the pitch. The rent also ensures passage for the marblers' stone to the sea.

CORFE CASTLE IS BETWEEN WAREHAM AND SWANAGE ON THE A351.

⚫ Shrovetide Football, Shawcross, Ashbourne — Derbyshire

This game between the Up'ards and the Down'ards starts at 2pm, and continues on Ash Wednesday if there is no winner. The ball is cork-filled and the goals are two mills three miles apart, with a stream through the pitch. The ball may be kicked, carried or thrown. The earliest record of the game is in 1682.

ASHBOURNE IS BETWEEN DERBY AND LEEK, NORTH WEST FROM DERBY ON THE A52.

Right: Shrovetide Football, Corfe Castle, Dorset, 1951
Far right: Shrovetide Football at Ashbourne, Derbyshire, 1923

Shrovetide Football, The Pastures, Alnwick   Northumberland
This continues on Ash Wednesday if there is no winner.
ALNWICK IS ON THE A1 NORTH OF MORPETH.

Shrovetide Football, Rothbury   Northumberland
ROTHBURY IS ON THE B6344 PAST PAUPERHAUGH.

Shrovetide Football, Atherstone, near Nuneaton   Warwickshire
This lasts from 3pm until 5pm.
TAKE THE A444 NORTH OUT OF NUNEATON, THEN LEFT ON THE A5.

Shrovetide Football, Dorking   Surrey
DORKING IS BETWEEN GUILDFORD AND REIGATE ON THE A25.

Shrovetide Football, Sedgefield   Durham
The start is at 1pm.
TAKE THE A177 NORTH FROM STOCKTON-ON-TEES.

Shrovetide Football, Chester-le-Street   Durham
TAKE THE A167 OR A1(M) NORTH FROM DURHAM.

Shrovetide Football   Derby
DERBY IS AT THE JUNCTION OF THE A6 AND A38.

Egg Shackling, Stoke St Gregory and Shepton Beauchamp, Sedgemoor   Somerset
STOKE ST GREGORY IS EAST OF TAUNTON, PAST NORTH CURRY AND MEARE GREEN. SHEPTON BEAUCHAMP IS BETWEEN ILCHESTER AND ILMINSTER ON THE A303.

Shrove Tuesday Skipping, Scarborough   North Yorkshire
Thousands of people skip along a mile of the Foreshore Road.
SCARBOROUGH IS ON THE COAST BETWEEN WHITBY AND BRIDLINGTON ON THE A165.

Shrovetide Skipping at Scarborough, 1939

Lenten customs

Lent is the annual period of fasting for the 40 weekdays that immediately precede Easter. The six Sundays in the Lenten period are not fast days. Lent commemorates Christ's 40 days in the wilderness, but it comes at a time of the year when fasting was often necessary anyway because winter stores would by this time be running low. The word 'Lent' may come from the Anglo-Saxon *lengentide* referring to the lengthening of the hours of daylight, or it may be derived from the Saxon word for spring, *lenct*. Originally only one meal was eaten each day, and it could not contain meat, eggs, dairy produce or wine. As fish was permitted many Lent customs and recipes involved fish. Lent marriages were rare as sex was also prohibited.

Variable Dates

John Thake's Bequest, Clavering, near Saffron Walden   Essex
John Thake died in 1537, leaving a plot of land whose income was to be used to buy a barrel of red herrings and 720 white herrings for the poor of the village during Lent. The charity is still given but not in the form of herrings!

CLAVERING IS ON THE B1038 PAST WICKEN BONHUNT, SOUTH WEST OF SAFFRON WALDEN.

David Salter's Bequest, Farnham Royal   Berkshire
David Salter left provision in his will to buy herrings for the local poor, and a pair of kid gloves for the clergyman.

FARNHAM ROYAL IS BETWEEN SLOUGH AND BEACONSFIELD ON THE A355.

Jossing Block Money (in mid-Lent), Ightam   Kent
TAKE THE A25 EAST FROM SEVENOAKS.

Ash Wednesday The first day of Lent
For Christian's this is one of the two days of fasting and abstinence. Fish is generally eaten. Ashes are the symbol of sorrow, repentance and mourning, and penitents traditionally wore sackcloth and ashes. The ashes were sprinkled on their heads during the penitential service of the day, and

the unrepentant were cursed aloud. Some people made an ash cross on their foreheads, and children would carry an ash twig with its black buds symbolising mourning. Ashes and ash wood sticks have become symbols of this day. White was never worn on Ash Wednesday. Alms were traditionally given on this day.

Games of marbles are played, as in Sussex this day is the start of the marbles season, ending at noon on Good Friday. On Ash Wednesday Aunt Sallys (straw effigies dressed in women's clothes) were beaten or used for target practice. A possible source of this ritual is to be found in Cornwall where the figure was male and called Jack-a-Lent, thought to be an effigy of Judas Iscariot.

Fritters, fish, fish pie, **Lenten kedgeree** *(see p.184 for recipe)*, peas, **Frumenty** *(see p.184 for recipe)* and Hasty Pudding are traditional foods.

Cakes-and-Ale Sermon, Church of St Faith, Crypt of St Paul's Cathedral　　London
In his will of 1612 Alderman John Norton left money to the Stationers' Company for refreshments of cakes and ale on the day of their Ash Wednesday service. After partaking, the Company in their ceremonial livery parade to the Crypt of St Paul's Cathedral where the Chaplain of the Company gives the Cakes-and-Ale Sermon.
ST PAUL'S CATHEDRAL IS BETWEEN LUDGATE CIRCUS AND MANSION HOUSE.

The Thursday after Ash Wednesday Fritter Thursday
In the North of England this was known as Fritter Thursday because families would eat fried fritters of dough.

The Friday after Ash Wednesday
This was known as Kissing Friday in some northern areas, on which girls must receive uncomplainingly a kiss from any boy.

The second Saturday after Shrove Tuesday

Cornish Hurling Match, St Columb Major　　Cornwall
This is a rematch of the Shrove Tuesday match, starting at 4.30 pm.

Mothering Sunday Mid-Lent Sunday, The 4th Sunday in Lent, Laetare Sunday
Laetare means rejoice, and on this day Christians can relax from any self-imposed penitences. For a mid-Lent break servants were often given a holiday. Originally worshippers presented gifts to their Mother Church on this day. This was accompanied by church-clipping (clasping, embracing) which was a ceremony where people expressed their love for their church by joining hands around it and walking round it. Later the idea of honouring the mother of one's family sprang up, and young people were given the day off to do so.

Daughters made **Simnel cake** *(see p.184 for recipe)* – the name comes from the Latin *simila*, meaning 'fine flour' – and frumenty for their mothers, visited them if away from the family home (going a-mothering), and decorated their homes with violets, primroses, daffodils and other spring flowers. Nosegays of wild flowers were blessed in church and then presented to mothers. Mothers are relieved of all chores by their children. In the North of England the traditional culinary gifts were **Fig Pies** *(see p.184 for recipe)* with mulled ale.

Other foods eaten on this day are egg custard, comfits, lambs' tails, white sugar candies flavoured with caraway and spice, wafers and waffles.

Church-clipping at All Saints, Hastings　　East Sussex
HASTINGS IS ON THE COAST AT THE JUNCTION OF THE A21 AND A259.

Carling Sunday Passion Sunday, Care Sunday, The 5th Sunday in Lent
Northumberland Carlings *(see p.184 for recipe)*, Whirlin' Cakes, Passion Dock, and fig pies are eaten. Carlings are grey peas and were one of the approved foods to eat during Lent. This may be a survival of the ancient pagan custom of eating beans in commemoration of the dead, in this case

of the imminent death of Christ. The person getting the last carling in the dish will be the first to marry. Passion Dock is a pudding made from dock leaves, nettles, oatmeal and onions, mostly in Yorkshire. The reference to figs is to the alleged cursing of a barren fig tree by Christ on his triumphal entry to Jerusalem, but Fig Sunday is celebrated on the 4th, 5th or 6th Sunday in Lent in different regions of England.

Palm Sunday The Sunday immediately preceding Easter

Christians commemorate Christ's entry on a donkey into Jerusalem, where he was met by people waving palms. Crosses were made with branches and decorations of greenery were put up, particularly from catkin-bearing willows like sallow (or pussy willow). Palm could not then be grown in England so sallow became known as English Palm. Sprigs of sallow were worn in buttonholes. By a similar substitution daffodils did the job of the lily and were known as Lent Lilies. These customs date from at least the 5th century, were banned during the Reformation as idolatrous, but revived afterwards.

Pax Cakes or Buns (*Pax* is Latin for 'peace') were distributed after the church service. For a dessert on this day it is traditional to make a **Fig Pie** or **Pudding**, or **Pond Pudding** (*see p.184 for recipes*). Children also used to make liquorice water by mixing liquorice with well water, which on this day was regarded as 'holy'.

✛ Distribution of Pax Cakes, Hentland, King's Capel and Sellack, near Ross-on-Wye   Hereford and Worcester

After the day's church service, wafers bearing a picture of the Paschal Lamb and the words 'Peace and Good Neighbourhood' are distributed to the congregation. The accompanying free mug of ale was stopped by prudish Victorians. There was however money provided to continue the ancient tradition, left to the parish by Lady Scudamore in 1570. The pax cakes are round (4½ x ¼) and hard, and are issued from white linen-lined baskets by the vicar, with a message to forgive all those who may have been involved in any kind of quarrel or disputes in order to prepare oneself spiritually for Easter.

TAKE THE A49 WEST OUT OF ROSS-ON-WYE, RIGHT AT BRIDSTOW ALONG THE WYE.

Spy Wednesday Judas Wednesday, Dark Wednesday

This is so called to commemorate the activities of Judas Iscariot and the plot to betray Jesus.

Maundy Thursday Passover Night

This is the last day of Lent. Maundy means 'command,' referring to Christ's final command to his followers at the Last Supper. Christ washed the feet of his disciples at the Last Supper and commanded his followers to be humble and do likewise. Traditionally Heads of State and the Church washed the feet of the poor on this day, and gave gifts of cloth and food. The first English king to carry out the washing of feet was Edward II in 1326. Edward III in 1361 began the practice of giving alms to a number of poor people equal to his age, then 50. Nowadays the monarch distributes specially minted silver Maundy coins (1d, 2d, 3d, 4d) in purses to as many men and women as there are years in her age, and does so each year in a different cathedral town.

Churches were often cleaned on this day. Roast lamb is traditionally eaten on this day, served with bread not potatoes.

Distribution of the Royal Maundy,
originally in Westminster Abbey but now in a different cathedral annually
Attendance is by invitation only.

Marvyn Dole, Ufton Court, Ufton Nervet, near Reading
Berkshire

This traditionally mid-Lent dole, distributed from a hall window, consists of bread, linen and clothing for the poor of the village, as prescribed in the will of Lady Elizabeth Marvin who died in 1581. The dole was a token of her gratitude for the villagers' rescue of her when she got lost in a local forest.

TAKE THE A4 WEST OUT OF READING, LEFT AFTER SHEFFIELD BOTTOM, THROUGH SULHAMSTEAD.

The Travice Dole, Leigh
Greater Manchester

To keep his memory alive, Henry Travice ordained in his will of 1627 that 40 people had to pass over his grave (which is inside the church), and in return he left the sum of £10 to be divided by the local vicars amongst the people of the parishes of Leigh, Atherton and Tylesley. Now, three people cross his grave after the Maundy Thursday evening service.

TAKE THE A580 WEST OUT OF MANCHESTER, RIGHT ON THE A574 TO LEIGH.

Maundy Thursday

March

customs

March comes in like a lion and goes out like a lamb, so the old weather lore saying goes. The first of the field crops would be sown, and other spring preparations made in farm and garden, as the days lengthened on the approach of the vernal equinox. In such a busy month in the country there were relatively few celebrations or festivals. The improvement in the weather meant that more outdoor games could be played, and archery was generally started in March.

Fixed Dates

1st March St David's Day

St David is the patron saint of Wales who died this day in AD 589. He founded St David's Abbey in Pembrokeshire, known for its strict regime and life of austerity. He was said to have saved the monastery at Glyn Rhosyn from destruction by Irish invaders by converting them to Christianity. A daffodil is worn, and leeks are eaten.

Fleas appear on this day so rise at dawn, fling the windows open, and sweep the house from top to bottom, keeping all windows closed thereafter.

2nd March St Chad's Day

St Chad was the humble Bishop of Lichfield who died on this day in AD 672. Peas and beans are traditionally sown on this day.

3rd March St Winnol's Day

St Winnol was a West Country abbot from Brittany.

4th March St Adrian's Day

St Adrian was an Irish missionary murdered by Vikings on this day in AD 875.

5th March St Piran's Day

This Cornish saint, a 5th-century hermit from Perranzabuloe, near Newquay, is the patron of Cornish miners, who would not work on this day.

6th March St Baldred's Day

St Baldred was an 8th-century Lothian hermit.

7th March

This day marked the end of spring seed planting, and a celebration in the evening with fruit buns and spiced ale was called Hopper-Cake Night. A hopper is a seed basket.

9th March St Constantine's Day

St Constantine was a Cornishman who was martyred on Kintyre in Scotland in the 6th century.

11th March

Penny Loaf Day, Newark   **Nottinghamshire**

During the Civil War Hercules Clay dreamt that his house was burning down. He evacuated his family, and it transpired that soon the Roundheads did indeed destroy his house during the siege of Newark. In gratitude, Hercules left £100 to purchase penny loaves, shoes and boots for the poor of the town who turned up to listen to a sermon. The sermon still takes place, but the money has now run out.

TAKE THE A1 NORTH FROM GRANTHAM TO NEWARK.

12th March St Gregory's Day

St Gregory was the 6th-century pope who sent St Augustine on his religious crusade to Britain in AD 597.

The second Tuesday in March

The Bridewell Service, St Bride's Church, Fleet Street   **London**

This commemorates Edward VI's foundation of Bridewell Royal Hospital in 1553.

ST BRIDE'S CHURCH IS NEAR LUDGATE CIRCUS.

17th March St Patrick's Day, St Withburga's Day

St Patrick is the patron saint of Ireland. He was born in AD 389 in Northamptonshire, the son of a Christian Roman father, a tax collector, and a Celtic mother. He began the conversion of the Irish to Christianity. A shamrock is worn, to commemorate St Patrick's use of the three-lobed leaf to illustrate the Holy Trinity to King Loigaire. St Withburga was a 7th-century Norfolk nun.

18th March St Edward the Martyr's Day

King Edward was murdered near Corfe Castle, Dorset in AD 979, allegedly by Elfthryth so that her son Ethelred could claim the throne.

19th March St Joseph's Day

St Joseph lived in the first Century, a descendant of the king Judah. Girls seeking a good husband traditionally invoke St Joseph. This day is a lucky one to be born on but not to get married on.

20th March St Cuthbert's Day, St Herbert's Day

St Cuthbert was a 7th-century misogynist hermit on the Farne Islands, Northumberland, and St Herbert, a contemporary and friend, lived a similar life on an island in Derwentwater, Cumbria. They both died on 20th March AD 687.

21st March The Vernal Equinox

This day was celebrated by the Ancient Celts as the day when the Sun God Bran (alleged to be buried on Tower Hill, London) regains power over the forces of darkness and causes the days to lengthen thereafter. Druids celebrate this day on Tower Hill Terrace. Formerly this was St Benedict's Day, but that has been moved to 11th July. This is the last day on which to sow peas safely.

🎯 Kiplingcotes Derby, South Dalton, near Beverley — Yorkshire

Dating from 1519 this is the oldest flat race for horses in England. Men and women who weigh more than 10 stone (140lb/64kg) may ride the four-mile-course, though lighter riders may compete if they carry weights. Starting by a sandstone post a mile north of the old Kiplingcotes railway station, the course takes the horses across fields, a railway bridge and a road, to finish in a lane off the A163 between Market Weighton and Middleton-on-the-Wolds. The first prize is the interest gained on an investment of £365 made in 1618.

TAKE THE A164 NORTH OUT OF BEVERLEY, LEFT ON THE B1248, EXIT LEFT TO SOUTH DALTON.

✚ Oranges and Lemons Service, St Clement Danes Church, Strand — London

The bells chime the tune of the nursery rhyme at 9am, noon, 3pm, and 6pm. The service is at 3:30pm, after which the oranges and lemons that decorate the church are given to the children of the local primary school. In medieval times fruit porters would pay a toll at Clements Inn to carry their oranges and lemons through to Clare Market.

ST CLEMENT DANES CHURCH IS ON THE STRAND BETWEEN ALDWYCH AND THE ROYAL COURTS OF JUSTICE.

24th March Old New Year's Eve, St Gabriel's Day

This day was New Year's Eve until 1752 when the Julian Calendar was replaced by the Gregorian Calendar. New Year's Eve at that time became 5th April, the date that still marks the end of the financial year.

St Gabriel was the famous archangel, and there is evidence that the term 'angel' was applied to real people, devoted messengers of the faith, and not to supernatural beings.

25th March Old New Year's Day, Lady Day, Feast of the Annunciation of the Virgin

Christians celebrate the Annunciation, the day on which Mary was told by the Angel Gabriel that she was to be the mother of Christ. This was New Year's Day before 1752, on which there were many fairs. Lady Day was a Quarter Day, fixed for legal purposes, on which rents were due. The tax year still starts near this day.

The Oranges and Lemons service at St.Clement Danes Church, London, 1921

🐧 **Tichborne Dole, Tichborne Park, Tichborne, near Alresford**   Hampshire

The gift of flour (originally bread) to the villagers was established by Lady Mabella Tichborne in 1150. As she lay dying Mabella pleaded with her husband Sir Roger Tichborne, known for his reluctance to part with money, to set aside some land for the local poor. Sir Roger agreed on condition that the size of the plot be determined by how far Mabella could crawl before a burning faggot from the fire went out. The doubty lady crawled round 23 acres (9.5 ha), still known as The Crawls. The flour, from corn grown in The Crawls, is anointed before an open-air service commences, at which each adult receives one gallon (4.5l) and each child half a gallon (2.25l), issued from a wooden trough.

TAKE THE B3046 SOUTH OUT OF ALRESFORD, TURNING RIGHT TO TICHBORNE.

28th March St Alkeda's Day

St Alkeda was a Saxon princess and a nun. St.Alkeda was murdered in AD 800 by Norsewomen.

29th March St Gwynllyw and St Gwladys' Day

This is the only husband-and-wife team to share a saint's day. They lived in the 6th century in Gwent, Wales.

This day is the first of the three Borrowing Days. The last three days of March are said to have the weather typical of April, so, in terms of their weather, April 'borrows' them from March.

One day at the end of March

🏛 **Old Bolingbroke Candle Auction, Old Bolingbroke**   Lincolnshire

In the Council Chamber each year (formerly every 5th year, and in late December) a candle auction is held for the right to graze animals on Poor Folks' Close in the village. The proceeds which accrue from use of the land are given to the poor on St Thomas' Day, 21st December, a traditional day to give charity. The general public are not admitted to the auction.

TAKE THE A158 EAST OUT OF HORNCASTLE.

Shortly before Easter

👑 **The united guilds of the City of London annual service, St Paul's Cathedral**   London

The oldest of the London craft guilds dates from the 12th century, with 17 being formed in the last 50 years. Their association with the Church stems from one of their early functions to guarantee a decent burial to members. In return for a monopoly of trade they promised fair value; control of prices, wages, working conditions, competition and appointments; inspection and quality control; and punishments for poor workmanship and other malpractices. Most guilds have a distinctive livery, or uniform, and are known as City Livery Companies. They were governed by a Master, usually two Wardens, with a supporting Court of Assistants. Some also had Freemen and a Yeomanry. Entry was by patrimony (for a son of a liveryman), apprenticeship for a defined period, or redemption by payment. Liverymen were entitled to be Freemen of the City, and are the sole electorate for the annual appointment of Lord Mayor and Sheriffs. After approval by the Lord Mayor and Aldermen a new company may apply for a Royal Charter, the right to bear arms and a livery.

ST PAUL'S CATHEDRAL IS BETWEEN LUDGATE CIRCUS AND MANSION HOUSE.

Below is listed, in order of precedence, the Livery Companies, and those without livery, and the address of their Hall. If no Hall exists the address is that of the clerk or office of administration. Note that two companies annually rotate positions six and seven.

Livery Company		Hall or Office
1	Mercers' Company	Ironmonger Lane, EC2
2	Grocers' Company	Princes Street, EC2
3	Drapers' Company	Throgmorton Street, EC2
4	Fishmongers' Company	Fishmongers' Hall, EC4
5	Goldsmiths' Company	Foster Lane, EC2

	Livery Company	Hall or Office
6/7	Merchant Taylors' Company	30 Threadneedle Street, EC2
7/6	Skinners' Company	8 Dowgate Hill, EC4
8	Haberdashers' Company	Staining Lane, EC2
9	Salters' Company	Fore Street, EC2
10	Ironmongers' Company	Barbican, EC2
11	Vintners' Company	Upper Thames Street, EC4
12	Clothworkers' Company	Dunster Court, Mincing Lane, EC3
13	Dyers' Company	Dowgate Hill, EC4
14	Brewers' Company	Aldermanbury Square, EC2
15	Leathersellers' Company	St Helen's Place, EC3
16	Pewterers' Company	Oat Lane, EC2
17	Barbers' Company	Monkwell Square, Wood Street, EC2
18	Cutlers' Company	Warwick Lane, EC4
19	Bakers' Company	Harp Lane, Lower Thames Street, EC3
20	Wax Chandlers' Company	Gresham Street, EC2
21	Tallow Chandlers' Company	4 Dowgate Hill, EC4
22	Armourers' and Brasiers' Company	81 Coleman Street, EC2
23	Girdlers' Company	Basinghall Avenue, EC2
24	Butchers' Company	87 Bartholomew Close, EC1
25	Saddlers' Company	Gutter Lane, EC2
26	Carpenters' Company	Throgmorton Avenue, EC2
27	Cordwainers' Company	30 Fleet Street, EC4
28	Painter-Stainers' Company	9 Little Trinity Lane, EC4
29	Curriers' Company	43 Church Road, Hove, East Sussex
30	Masons' Company	9 New Square, Lincoln's Inn, WC2
31	Plumbers' Company	218 Strand, WC2
32	Innholders' Company	Dowgate Hill, EC4
33	Founders' Company	13 St Swithin's Lane, EC4
34	Poulters' Company	7-8 King's Bench Walk, Temple, EC4
35	Cooks' Company	49 Queen Victoria Street, EC4
36	Coopers' Company	13 Devonshire Square, EC2
37	Tylers' and Bricklayers' Company	6 Bedford Row, WC1
38	Bowyers' Company	7 Chandos Street, W1
39	Fletchers' Company	College Hill Chambers, EC4
40	Blacksmiths' Company	41 Tabernacle Street, EC2
41	Joiners and Ceilers' Company	8 West Heath Road, SE2
42	Weavers' Company	1 The Sanctuary, SW1
43	Woolmen's Company	192-198 Vauxhall Bridge Road, SW1
44	Scriveners' Company	4 Wilton Mews, SW1
45	Fruiterers' Company	1 Serjeants Inn, EC4
46	Plaisterers' Company	1 London Wall, EC2
47	Stationers' and Newspaper Makers' Company	Stationers' Hall, EC4
48	Broderers' Company	11a Bridge Road, East Molesey, Surrey
49	Upholders' Company	56 Kingsway, WC2
50	Musicians' Company	4 St Paul's Churchyard, EC4
51	Turners' Company	1 Serjeants' Inn, EC4
52	Basketmakers' Company	87-95 Tooley Street, SE1
53	Glaziers' Company	9 Montague Close, SE1
54	Horners' Company	365 Fulham Road, SW10
55	Farriers' Company	3 Hamilton Road, Cockfosters, N14
56	Paviors' Company	Cutlers' Hall, Warwick Lane, EC4
57	Loriners' Company	2-5 Benjamin Street, EC1

Livery Company	Hall or Office
58 Apothecaries' Society	Blackfriars Lane, EC4
59 Shipwrights' Company	Ironmongers' Hall, Barbican, EC2
60 Spectacle Makers' Company	Apothecaries' Hall, Blackfriars Lane, EC4
61 Clockmakers' Company	2 Greycoat Place, Westminster, SW1
62 Glovers' Company	Bakers' Hall, Harp Lane, EC3
63 Feltmakers' Company	53 Davies Street, W1
64 Framework Knitters' Company	51 Dulwich Wood Avenue, SE19
65 Needlemakers' Company	4 Staple Inn, Holborn, WC1
66 Gardeners' Company	College Hill Chambers, EC4
67 Tin Plate Workers' Company Alias Wireworkers	71 Lincoln's Inn Fields, WC2
68 Wheelwrights' Company	Greenup, Milton Avenue, Gerrards Cross, Buckinghamshire
69 Distillers' Company	1 Vintners Place, EC4
70 Patternmakers' Company	6 Raymond Buildings, Gray's Inn, WC1
71 Glass Sellers' Company	6 Eldon Street, EC2
72 Coachmakers' and Coach Harness Makers' Company	9 Lincoln's Inn Fields, WC2
73 Gunmakers' Company	48-50 Commercial Road, E1
74 Gold and Silver Wyre Drawers' Company	40A Ludgate Hill, EC4
75 Makers of Playing Cards Company	1 Serjeants Inn, Fleet Street, EC4
76 Fan Makers' Company	107-111 Fleet Street, EC4
77 Carmen's Company	81-87 Gresham Street, EC2
78 Master Mariners' Company	Victoria Embankment, WC2
79 Solicitors' Company (City of London)	Cutlers' Hall, Warwick Lane EC4
80 Farmers' Company	7-8 King's Bench Walk, Temple, EC4
81 Air Pilots and Air Navigators' Guild	30 Eccleston Street, SW1
82 Tobacco Pipe Makers' and Tobacco Blenders' Company	154 Fleet Street, EC4
83 Furniture Makers' Company	Grove Mills, Cranbrook Road, Hawkhurst, Kent
84 Scientific Instrument Makers' Company	9 Montague Close, SE1
85 Chartered Surveyors' Company	12 Great George Street, SW1
86 Chartered Accountants' Company	81-87 Gresham Street, EC2
87 Chartered Secretaries' and Administrators' Company	16 Park Crescent, W1
88 Builders' Merchants' Company	128 Queen Victoria Street, EC4
89 Launderers' Company	34 Broadhurst, Ashtead, Surrey
90 Marketors' Company	25 Pebworth Road, Harrow
91 Actuaries' Company	5 New Bridge Street, EC4
92 Insurers' Company	Hall of the Chartered Insurance Institute, 20 Aldermanbury, EC2
93 Arbitrators' Company	75 Cannon Street, EC4
94 Builders' Company	127 Thomas More House, Barbican, EC2

Companies without Livery	Hall or Office
Parish Clerks' Company	14 Dale Close, Oxford
Watermen and Lightermen of the River Thames	18 St Mary-at-Hill, EC3

Easter customs

Nowadays Easter is thought of as Good Friday until Easter Monday, but in times past the whole week was referred to as Easter Holy Week. The word 'Easter' is derived from the Anglo-Saxon goddess of the dawn and spring *Eostre*, equivalent to the Norse *Frigga*, and her festival. This festival in her honour was to celebrate renewed growth after the dormant period of winter. The egg was the symbol of the life force. Rabbits and hares are symbols of good luck and of fertility. In fact the Easter bunny is derived from the hare, the symbol of *Eostre* and also of the Moon goddess. Hare-hunting was done commonly on Easter Monday in the past.

Our modern celebrations are a fusion of these and the commemoration of Christ's resurrection. As it was traditionally a time of death and re-birth the Church was able to superpose the death and resurrection of Christ as the theme. Easter is sometimes called the Pasch or paschal season, meaning Passover. This refers to the Jewish Passover feast on 14th April celebrating the liberation of Egypt, but to Christians it has become synonymous with Easter. Many of our Easter foods are derived from those eaten at Passover, such as lamb, eggs, cake, bread and wine.

In keeping with the spirit of renewal, new clothes were often bought for Easter, including a new bonnet. for the women

The destruction of winter was symbolised years ago in Ashton-under-Lyne, Lancashire by the Riding-the-Black-Lad ceremony in which a dummy dressed in black was destroyed and burnt. This is reminiscent of the burning of the Shrove Tuesday Holly Boy. Village crosses were decorated with holly (holly-bussing).

Many traditional games and dishes exist in various parts of the country. There is egg-rolling at Preston, Scarborough and Barton-upon-Humber. Sports included handball, foot-races, stoolball, barley-brake, battels or river jousting and Tilting the Quintain.

Barley-brake *A piece of ground is divided into three parts, the middle part being called 'Hell'. A man and woman, holding hands, stay in Hell, while the others try to run through without being intercepted. Anyone who is caught, stays in Hell to help catch the others as they again try to run through the middle part.*

River Jousting *A pole was set in fast-flowing water with a shield attached. Contestants in boats (no oars allowed) drifted down river and tried to lance the shield and break their lance without falling in. Two boats with rescuers stood off nearby.*

Tilting the Quintain *A quintain is a post with a crossbar, free to swivel, on top. On one end of the bar is a shield, and from the other is suspended a sandbag. The tilter rides up with a lance, and when the shield is struck the sandbag swings round, and can strike a slow-witted or unskilful rider. The only surviving example in England stands on the village green at Offham, Kent.*

The sport of lifting or heaving is traditionally practised in Northern England. A chair is decorated with white ribbons and flowers and taken round the houses. Each takes it in turns to sit in it and be lifted by four others. First the men lift the women, then the women lift the men.

Village men and boys used to give simple plays or performances to collect money and eggs for Easter. This was called pace-egging.

Tansy Pudding *(see p.185 for recipe)*, **Cheese Cake** *(see p.185 for recipe)*, pudding-pies, baked custards, roast lamb and roast veal are among the traditional dishes eaten.

Variable Dates

Good Friday

On this solemn day Christians commemorate the crucifixion of Christ. Traditionally bells begin tolling at 3pm, the reputed hour of Christ's death, as still done at Ayot St Peter in Herefordshire. Altars were cleared of all adornments and no decorations except yew were allowed in the church, yew symbolising mourning. Before the Reformation some churches even took down their crucifix, and replaced it on Easter Sunday. Good Friday was considered a lucky day on which to be born.

No meat is eaten, but fish is allowed. Until the 16th century every Friday and Saturday were fish-only days, after that it was Friday only by individual choice. **Hot Cross Buns** *(see p.185 for recipe)* are traditionally eaten for breakfast, and because of their association with luck and prosperity some are hung from the rafters to protect the household from evil, sailors from shipwreck, clothes from moths and corn from mice. Originally these buns were pagan offerings, made in the shape of a bull with a cross to represent the horns. Or it may be that the cross represents the four quarters of the moon. The Church adopted the bun as Good Friday fare.

People were generally suspicious and fearful on this day, and brought branches of rowan into the house to ward off evil. This day was second in importance to Hallowe'en for many witches. Blacksmiths never shod horses on this day because they would not drive in nails, fishermen would not fish and no clothes were washed for fear they would drip blood.

Tilting the Quintain at Offham Green, Nr Wrotham, Kent

In former times Judas effigies were exhibited in the streets and burned afterwards much as Guy Fawkes effigies are today, the last surviving area to do this being Dingle in Liverpool's docklands. At dawn in the predominantly Catholic dockland area children made the effigies and took them round the houses, shouting 'Judas is a penny short of his breakfast!' to get pennies thrown to them. Later the Judas effigies were burnt on street bonfires. It may be that this custom is a Church substitution for an older pagan ritual of the burning of a scapegoat. In contrast, there were also parades with effigies of Christ nailed to the cross, reminiscent of those in Catholic countries of Europe and in Latin America.

Good Friday was a common day to hand out dole or other bequests left to the poor in wills.

Planting seeds is traditional, particularly peas, beans and potatoes. This is the only propitious day on which to move bees.

Traditional Good Friday games are marbles, skipping (for example, at Brighton, East Sussex and Linton and Hadstock in Cambridgeshire), and spinning tops.

🕭 Giving the Widows' Sixpence and the Butterworth Dole, St Bartholomew the Great, Smithfield   London

Originally, a now forgotten donor left money to be placed on a gravestone and poor widows had to step over the stone to collect the money. This may have been a vestige of a sin-eating ceremony, where poor people were paid to consume the sins of the departed so they could ascend to heaven without such encumbrances. The ceremony has been replaced by the Butterworth Dole after a bequest by Joshua Butterworth in 1887. The current income of 62 pence cannot reasonably be divided between the stated 21 widows, so hot cross buns are now given to local children at 11:30am before the Good Friday service.

THE CHURCH IS IN CLOTH FAIR OFF WEST SMITHFIELD.

🕭 Hanging up the Hot Cross Bun, 'The Widow's Son', 75 Devons Road   London

A former landlady used to hang up a bun every Easter in memory of her sailor son who failed to return from a voyage in 1788 after writing to ask that a bun be put aside for him. The tradition continues every year, when a sailor is invited to add another bun to those suspended in a net from the ceiling. More are then handed out to the customers.

DEVONS ROAD IS THE B140 LINKING THE A102 AT BROMLEY-BY-BOW WITH THE A1205.

Picking up sixpences from tombstones at St Bartholomew's, London

Uppies and Doonies Ball Game, Workington
Cumbria

This is a kind of football match, with the goals at Workington harbour and Workington Hall, a mile (2.5km) apart, between the two halves of the town. It was originally contested between miners and dockers, and also takes place on Easter Tuesday and the following Saturday.

WORKINGTON IS ON THE COAST ON THE A597.

British Marbles Championship, Tinsley Green, near Crawley
West Sussex

Of the many games of marbles that have grown up over time the one used here is called Ring Taw, where a tolley (shooting marble) is used to knock the other marbles out of a 6ft (2m) ring.

Ring Taw Marbles *Forty-nine marbles are placed in the centre of a sanded, circular, concrete circle 6 ft (2m) across. A ¾ in (2cm) glass tolley is flicked with the thumb to try and knock as many marbles out of the circle as possible, but leave the tolley inside. If successful the shooter goes again, otherwise the tolley stays until the turn comes round again. In championships only 13 marbles are put in the circle.*

LEAVE THE M23 AT JUNCTION 10 TOWARDS CRAWLEY ALONG CRAWLEY AVENUE.

Egg rolling, Holcombe Hill, Bury
Greater Manchester

BURY IS NORTH OF MANCHESTER, AT THE JUNCTION OF THE A56 AND A58, JUST OFF THE M56.

Orange-rolling, Pascombe Pit, Dunstable Downs
Bedfordshire

DUNSTABLE IS TO THE WEST OF JUNCTION 11 OF THE M1.

Maids' Money, St Mary's Church, Reading
Berkshire

READING IS AT THE INTERSECTION OF THE A4 AND A329.

Good Friday Skipping, Alciston
East Sussex

TAKE THE A27 EAST FROM LEWES.

Easter Eve Holy Saturday

Easter baskets are made, often out of a withy bread basket. Hard-boiled eggs (pace or paschal [passion Lamb] Eggs) are decorated or rolled down slopes to see which will go furthest. All whose eggshells remain intact will have good luck. Egg-rolling was thought by Christians to symbolise the rolling away of the stone which closed Christ's tomb.

Cumberland Pasch Eggs are made by dipping eggs in hot water for a few moments, then marking name, age or a decorative design with the end of a tallow candle. Immersing in cochineal or other dye colours the unwaxed surface. In Liverpool and elsewhere eggs were dyed yellow by being boiled in onion skins.

To dye an egg, hard-boil in salty water to which a plant dye has been added: pasque flowers to give a green colour; furze, broom or whin flowers to give yellow; cochineal or beetroot for pink; onion skins for yellow to brown.

Wrapping petals or leaves around the egg and tying it in cloth will create dyed patterns.

A branch with buds about to flower is taken indoors and decorated with hanging symbols of rebirth (decorated blown eggs, chicks, lambs, bunnies and other babies, spring flowers) as an Easter Tree.

Boys played a game like conkers but using an egg in the palm of the hand. An egg which smashes another is called 'a cock of one, two', and so on. A gentler game is egg tapping (Jauping pasche-eggs) where the egg is held in a clenched fist and the opponent's fist is tapped. Players take it in turns to try to crack the opponent's egg but leave their own whole. An egg treasure hunt was also a popular game.

Pace Egg Plays are spring rites, of a similar character to Mummers Plays, and were once common in North West England, particularly in Cumbria, Rochdale, Burnley and Fylde, near Blackpool, and in west Yorkshire and parts of Cheshire. Groups of young men and boys would enact dramas, often involving St George, of formalised battle, death and revival of the dead by a comic doctor. As after Mumming Plays alms were collected. In Cumbria and North Yorkshire the costumed Jollyboys went round singing a song, asking for eggs and beer.

Well-worship and water spirits are associated with Easter Eve and Easter Day, a pagan survival integrated into later ritual.

Making a Withy Bread Basket *Basket-making is known to be more than 9,000 years old, and in England the commonest material used is the withy or osier willow, grown principally in Somerset today. Shoots are cut and sold in bundles called bolts, of which there are three grades. Green rods are the cheapest as they have not been stored for seasoning. Brown rods are cut in winter and stored, so are of higher quality. The top quality rods are white rods, which are cut when the plant is growing and stacked in water to keep them supple. In each case the bark is stripped off before use. The main lengths are Tacks (3 ft/90 cm), Short-Small (4 ft/120 cm), Long-Small (5 ft/150 cm) and Threepenny (6 ft/180 cm), although shorter lengths can also be bought. Before use soak the rods in water, at least half an hour per foot (30.5cm), and then stand on their butt ends in a sheltered dark place to drain for half an hour. Then cover with hessian or an old blanket for about one hour per foot (30.5cm), after which they will be ready to use. Do not expose them to draughts or sunlight whilst in storage.*

The main tools needed are: secateurs, a sharp knife, a bodkin for creating a route through the basketwork for an inserted rod, and a pair of snip-nosed pliers for pulling rods through. The stages in creating a bread basket are: first, make a base (called a slath) using a weaving technique called pairing, then insert stakes as uprights, and finally weaving the walls around them. Designs can be obtained from the many specialist books on basketwork.

Pace-egging, Far and Near Sawrey, Ambleside, Grasmere

Cumbria

This is a procession and alms collection by the local Jollyboys.

THE SAWREYS ARE SOUTH OF AMBLESIDE ON THE B5285.

Pace-egging Play, Calder Valley School, Mytholmroyd

West Yorkshire

The boys of the school have resurrected the play formerly performed in nearby Midgley, where the detail of the tradition was best maintained, particularly the beflowered and beribboned headdresses. From Good Friday the boys tour the local villages, including Heptonstall, Midgley, Todmorden, Luddenden, and then Halifax.

MYTHOLMROYD IS WEST OF HALIFAX ON THE A646.

A re-enactment of the Pace-Egging Play, Midgley, 1939

Nutters Dance by the Britannia Coconut Dancers, Bacup   Lancashire

The performers give a unique display of coconut dancing, garland dancing and clog dancing in their costumes of short white skirts, black breeches, clogs and white-plumed hats. In keeping with the pagan belief that spells would be more effective if the perpetrator were in disguise the dancers have blackened faces. The 'coconuts' are like castanets, and are fixed to their palms, belts and knees, to be sounded as they are led through the streets by the Whipper-in, who whips the winter away. The dance starts at 9am and ends at the neighbouring village of Stacksteads. Possibly the tradition originally hailed from the village called Britannia, just to the south of Bacup.
BACUP IS NORTH OF ROCHDALE ON THE A671 THROUGH WHITWORTH.

William Hubbard's Bequest, St Mary-in-Arden Churchyard, Market Harborough   Leicestershire

In his will of 1774 William Hubbard left one guinea to establish the custom of singing hymns over his grave on this day, which the choir and congregation duly do.
TAKE THE A508 NORTH FROM NORTHAMPTON TO MARKET HARBOROUGH.

Easter Sunday

Christians commemorate joyfully Christ's resurrection from the dead. Traditionally a family day, it was customary to witness the rising sun. Children used to take a cup with sugar or peppermint in it to a well, fill it with water and drink. This was called 'rinsing'. Throwing egg shells (with bent pins and pebbles) into the well would make a wish come true.

In keeping with the themes of rebirth and renewal, eggs (disallowed in Lent) were eaten for breakfast and an item of new clothing was worn today, particularly a hat or pair of gloves. The Easter Egg, symbolising the return of spring and the continuance of life is regarded as a good luck token and given as a present, usually one made of chocolate since the 19th century. In the past hens' eggs dyed and/or finely decorated were given, or confectionery eggs made of marzipan, fondant or sugar. After the Christian Church absorbed the pagan festivities the egg came to symbolise resurrection. Decorated eggs of many different materials are now made as gifts.

In Lostwithiel, Cornwall, Easter festivities were once presided over by a character similar to the Lord of Misrule called the Mock Prince.

Lamb, duck, **Easter Biscuits** *(see p.185 for recipe)*, Simnel Cake, cheesecake and tansey pudding are traditionally eaten, as well as a number of regional delicacies such as Dock Pudding (made from Passion Dock) in Cumbria and Pudding Pies (a pie filled with currants and custard) and Cherry Beer in Kent.

Distribution of the Easter Dole, Ellington   Cambridgeshire

This dole may be claimed by a traveller who sleeps in the village for at least one night. Distribution sometimes takes place on Easter Monday.
ELLINGTON IS ON THE A14 WEST OUT OF HUNTINGDON, PAST BRAMPTON.

Battersea Park Carnival Parade   London

This parade is in fond memory of the habit of Victorian ladies of showing off their new spring bonnets in the park. It features flowers from the Scilly Isles and ladies in fanciful hats.
BATTERSEA PARK IS BETWEEN THE CHELSEA (A3216) AND ALBERT (A3031) BRIDGES.

Easter Monday

Easter Monday was traditionally a time of enjoyment. Men lift women on this day, either using a chair decorated with flowers and ribbons, or crossing their arms, grasping wrists, with the woman sitting in the 'cradle'. The men take off the women's shoes first. Either three lifts are done or the chair is turned three times. Afterwards the men claim a kiss or a fine of one shilling.

Egg-rolling was the commonest pastime. Sometimes hard-boiled, sometimes raw, the object was to see which egg rolled furthest without breaking. The broken shell must not be left behind lest witches use it to work malicious spells against the former owner, as they are alleged to do if they acquire other human debris such as nail clippings, hair cuttings and bits of discarded clothing.

Other traditional Easter Monday games are handball, stoolball, skittles, archery, football, bowls, marbles and river jousting. Hare and stag hunts were held on this day.

Bread and cheese, Biddenden Cakes, hare pie (normally contains beef), ale, and loaves are among the traditional foods eaten.

Handball *Similar to soccer except that the ball can be caught, thrown, bounced or struck with the palm, but not kicked except by the goalkeepers in their goal-circles, which players must not enter.*
Stoolball *This game originated in the south of England, possibly in Sussex. It is a precursor of cricket, and is said to have been played by milkmaids, hence the stool. A bowler bowls underarm at a stool, and the batter tries to hit the ball with the hand. There is a batter at each end of the pitch and their exchange of ends when the ball is hit scores a run. The rest of the scoring is similar to cricket.*
Skittles *Nine hornbeam skittles (or pins) stand on circular metal plates on a hornbeam platform, in a diamond with one in the centre. Three 'cheeses' (flat disks of lignum vitae) are pitched at the skittles. A point is scored for each pin downed, with another go if all are down. A set of throws is a 'chalk';a game consists of three chalks.*

Pace-egg Rolling, Avenham Park, Preston
Lancashire
PRESTON IS ON THE M6 BETWEEN WARRINGTON AND LANCASTER.

Pace-egg Rolling, Fountains Abbey, near Ripon
North Yorkshire
TAKE THE B6265 WEST FROM RIPON, THEN LEFT AT ALDFIELD ON AN UNCLASSIFIED ROAD.

Pace-egg Rolling, Selby
Yorkshire
SELBY IS SOUTH OF YORK ON THE A19.

Distribution of the Easter Dole (or Maids' Charity), Biddenden
Kent
This is a food dole of bread, cheese, tea and Biddenden Cakes. The cakes have two female figures on them and are distributed either from the parish church or the Old Workhouse at 10am. They are paid for by the rent from 20 acres of land left to the parish by Elizabeth and Mary Chulkhurst, two Siamese twins born in 1100 who died in 1134.
TAKE THE A28 WEST OUT OF ASHFORD, RIGHT ON THE A262.

Hare Pie Scramble and Bottle Kicking Match, Hallaton
Leicestershire
A woman who was saved from a bull by a hare darting across its path bequeathed a piece of land outside Hallaton to the rector on condition he made and distributed a hare pie and bottles of ale. The match afterwards, for a bottle of ale, is between Hallaton and Medbourne and actually

involves kicking three small barrels, not bottles, over one or other parish boundary. The contest starts at 2:15pm, and involves three separate attempts to score with the barrels, two of which contain ale, the other being empty.

TAKE THE B664 NORTH EAST OUT OF MARKET HARBOROUGH, THEN LEFT AT MEDBOURNE.

Coal Carrying Championships, Gawthorpe, near Dewsbury — West Yorkshire

Although not strictly a folk festival – it began in 1963 – it is at a time of the year when lifting is traditional. Men carry 121 lb (55kg), women 44lb (20kg) along an inclined course of just under a mile (2.5km).

GAWTHORPE IS ON THE A638 BETWEEN DEWSBURY AND JUNCTION 40 OF THE M1.

Harness Horse Parade, Regent's Park Inner Circle — London

This is the time to see our beautiful large breeds of working horse, resplendent in their brasses and other decorations, pulling private and commercial vehicles.

REGENT'S PARK IS IN MARYLEBONE NW1.

Morris Dance Festival, Thaxted — Essex

TAKE THE B184 SOUTH EAST FROM SAFFRON WALDEN.

The Great Shirt Race, Bampton-in-the-Bush — Oxfordshire

TAKE THE A4095 SOUTH WEST FROM WITNEY.

Easter Tuesday

Women lift men on this day, either using a decorated chair or crossing their arms, grasping wrists, with the man sitting in the 'cradle'. The women take off the men's shoes first.

Issuing the Twopenny Starvers, St Michael's Church, Bristol — Avon

Originally the poor of the city could only afford black bread, so once a year white bread was given as a treat, after a special service. Now, buns, called Twopenny Starvers, are given to 500 children.

BRISTOL CAN BE REACHED ON THE M4 AND M5.

The Morris Dancers of Thaxted, Essex, 1952

Hocktide customs

The Sunday after Easter is the beginning of Hocktide, and was a time of feasting, fun and games. The origin of it is obscure, and some sources point to only the Monday and Tuesday as constituting Hocktide. It may be that the main purpose of Hocktide was to collect tolls, rents and dues, that is, from those 'in hock'. The collection often involved the reluctant being lifted up and turned upside down so that their money fell out. This may well have given rise to the Hock game of 'lifting', done by men on women on Hock Monday and by women on men on Hock Tuesday.

Notable surviving Hocktide celebrations are those happening at Hungerford, Berkshire, and also at Randwick, Gloucestershire.

Variable Dates

The Friday after Easter

📅 **Election of Hocktide Court officials, Hungerford**   **Berkshire**

At the Macaroni Supper (macaroni, cheese and watercress) in the John o'Gaunt Inn the officials of the Hocktide Court are elected for the year. The offices are Portreeve, Constable, Bailiff, Water Bailiffs, Overseers of the Port Down, Tithing Men, Ale-tasters, Blacksmith and Bellman. The inn is named after John of Gaunt, who granted the town the rights to use certain grazing land and fishing banks. His hunting horn, which used to be blown to open the first new court session, is still in existence, but the one now used, the Lucas Horn, dates from 1634. The court session opens at 8am on Hock Tuesday.

HUNGERFORD IS AT THE JUNCTION OF THE A4 AND A338.

Hock Sunday Low Sunday

This is the name given to the Sunday immediately following Easter, and is sometimes considered the start of Hocktide. This day has acquired other names in the past. Quasimodo Sunday is a reference to the first line of the Introit to the Hock Sunday service 'Quasi modo geniti infantes', and the traditional reading of the biblical story of the talking ass has led to its acquisition of the name Balaam's Ass Day.

The Monday after Easter Tuesday Hock Monday

At Hocktide money was raised for charity by groups of men (usually on the Monday) and women (usually on the Tuesday) 'tripping up and binding' passers-by and demanding money for their release. Men allowed free passage to women who substituted a kiss for a coin. After the Reformation when binding was banned, ropes and chains were put across roads instead, in order to stop passers-by.

Horn, oranges, hot punch, hot pennies and horseshoes are all associated with Hocktide.

The Tuesday after Easter Tuesday Hock Tuesday

Hocktide Court and Festival (Tutti Day), Hungerford — Berkshire

Hungerford Hocktide officials are elected at the Hocktide Court the previous Friday, and at 8am their term of office begins. The elected officials appoint Tuttimen – 'tutty' means bunch of flowers or nosegay – who carry decorated poles with an orange on top. A more likely derivation of their name is 'tithe-men', as it was their job in the past to collect rents. They are accompanied by the Orange Scrambler, in feathery hat, who trades an orange for a kiss or a penny fine from women in the street. Originally there was a Hocktide penny-tithe. At the Court's lunch, important guests are initiated by the 'Shoeing of the Colts' ceremony, where they are grabbed and up-ended so that horseshoes can be nailed to their shoes. The blacksmiths desist when the guest cries 'Punch!'. Afterwards oranges and hot pennies are showered on the children outside. This Court and Festival is the only extensive surviving Hocktide ceremony.

HUNGERFORD IS AT THE JUNCTION OF THE A4 AND A338.

2nd Wednesday after Easter

The Spital Sermon, Church of St Mary Woolnoth, Lombard Street and King William Street — London

This sermon is preached to Governors of Christ's Hospital and the Bridewell Royal Hospital, in the presence of the Lord Mayor of London and representatives from the Corporation of London.

THE CHURCH IS OPPOSITE THE BANK OF ENGLAND.

Hocktide Festival, Hungerford, Berkshire

April
customs

April is the month when the cuckoo arrives to herald spring, but because it is also a month of uncertain weather, there is much weather lore for this month. It begins with All Fools' Day, which may be seen as a time to let off steam after the hardships of winter. Land lettings continued because some auctions were still held according to the old calendar. Spring cleaning, including sweeping the chimneys, was being done and this applied also to churches which replaced their floor covering with new hay or rushes. After the celebrations on St George's Day thoughts turned to divination and death as St Mark's Day loomed, only to change again as preparations for May Day occupied the last days.

Fine-weather sports could often be played in April. In Berkshire, cudgel-play, quarter-staff and single-stick were popular; in the Fens, pole-leaping; in Kent and Sussex, cricket; in the North of England, football; and in Cumbria, Cornwall and Devon, wrestling.

Quarter-staff *The quarter-staff was 8 feet long, grasped in the middle with one hand, with the other placed between the middle and the end where needed. The object was usually quoted as 'to break the head' of the opponent, as it was for similar combat sports.*

Cricket *Before the modern game evolved there were two stumps 1ft (75cm) high with a single bail 2ft (1.5m) long. Between the stumps was a hole. The bat was curved. To claim a run the batter had to put the bat in the hole before a fielder could place the ball in it.*

Variable Dates

Early April

🎫 **Candle Auction, Tatworth, near Chard**   Somerset
A pin is not used in the candle; the bidding ceases when the flame sputters out.
TATWORTH IS JUST OFF THE A358 SOUTH OF CHARD.

Twice yearly, in April and October

🎫 **The Great Barmote Court, Moot Hall, Wirksworth**   Derbyshire
This and the High Peak Court are England's oldest surviving industrial courts, dating from their

establishment by Edward I in 1288 after the Inquisition of Ashbourne. This Court regulates the lead-mining industry in the Low Peak.

FROM ASHBOURNE TAKE THE B5035 NORTH EAST AND EXIT RIGHT AFTER CARSINGTON.

Fixed Dates

1st April April Fools' Day

All Fools' Day may originally have been a celebration to mark the end of the spring equinox and is at least as old as the 2nd century, or it may have been the end of New Year celebrations on the old calendar – when New Year's Day was where 25th March is now. Coming after Lent, there may also have been an element of celebration that the fasting was at an end which has merged with the pagan end-of-winter festivities. A further ingredient may be that the foolery originally represented the mocking of Christ before his death. Also, it is known that the festival of the Celtic god of humour, Lud, was held in the spring.

People are sent on fool's errands, or have pranks played on them, but this must cease at 12 noon. Examples of fools' errands – often to apprentices – are –'Buy a new bubble for a spirit level.' – 'Buy a packet of sky hooks' – 'Buy some elbow grease'– 'Buy a glass hammer' – 'Buy a left-handed screwdriver'– and 'Buy a bottle of pigeon's milk'. The apprentices were also asked to go to the stores and ask for a long stand! Pennies were stuck to the ground, and tempting items left lying around but attached to a fine thread, which was used to whisk them away when someone tried to pick them up. Books were balanced on classroom doors, and it seemed that almost every shoelace was claimed to be undone.

3rd April St Richard's Day

It is said that in the 13th century the brine-pits at Droitwich, Hereford and Worcester, dried up, and that Richard of Chichester made them flow again. Thereafter, the local people celebrated the event at the brine-pits, but now do so in Vines Park by the statue of St Richard.

✿ **Celebration of the Restoration of the Brine-pits, Droitwich**   **Hereford and Worcester**

DROITWICH IS ON THE A38 BETWEEN WORCESTER AND BROMSGROVE.

April 1st – Having a spree with one that's obnoxious in your neighbourhood

5th April St Derfel's Day
St Derfel was the 6th-century Abbot of Bardsey, who was originally one of King Arthur's knights.

Placing the quill in the hand of John Stow's Statue, Church of St Andrew Undershaft, Leadenhall Street   London
John Stow, formerly a tailor, became a historian and chronicler of London in the 16th century. His *Survey of London* is a valuable work for it was the first comprehensive study of London and pre-dates the Great Fire of London. In recognition of his services, a memorial service is held once every three years, (due March 1999, 2002, etc) attended by the Lord Mayor and his Sheriffs, at which a new quill is placed in the hand of his statue.
THE CHURCH IS OPPOSITE THE LLOYD'S BUILDING.

6th April Old Lady Day

Letting the 'White Bread' Meadow, Bourne, near Spalding   Lincolnshire
The Monday after Palm Sunday has also been the day when this strange combination of boys' foot race and auction is held. The runners cover a 100 yd (30.5m) stretch and back, over and over again, and if no bids take place during a stretch then the auction finishes and the highest bidder secures the lease. Afterwards everyone takes a meal of bread, cheese, onions and beer. The custom originated with the will of Richard Clay in 1770 who left the meadow so that its income could pay for bread for the local needy of Eastgate.
TAKE THE A151 WEST FROM SPALDING, OR THE A15 NORTH FROM PETERBOROUGH.

7th April St Brynach's Day
Little is known of the ancient Welsh king, Brynach.

The Saturday following Old Lady Day

Candle Auction (Land auction by candlelight), Tatworth, near Chard   Somerset
At a private meeting of the Stowell Court bidding for the use of Stowell Mead, a water meadow and watercress bed, takes place by candlelight. Bidding finishes when a tallow candle is burned out. Afterwards a supper of bread, cheese and watercress is eaten.
TATWORTH IS ON THE A358 JUST SOUTH OF CHARD.

The Stow Ceremony: Placing a quill in the hand of John Stow's statue, London

11th April St Guthlac's day

St Guthlac was a soldier in the 8th century who became a monk at Repton, Derbyshire. Later he lived out the rest of his life as a hermit in Crowland in the Lincolnshire fens.

13th April Rush-Bearing

This is one of many rush-bearing days when the rush flooring of the local church and houses underwent their annual change, a custom which dates from Saxon times. Everyone dressed up in white, bedecked with flowers, and paraded to church in decorated horse-drawn carts.

In the Middle Ages rushwork became a popular craft, and carpets, floor mats, table mats, baskets and other items were woven.

Making a Rush Mat *The best rush to use is the flowering rush, Juncus effusus, which is found by slowly-flowing rivers and lakes. Cut near to the base and tie into bundles (called 'bolts'), keeping the stems straight. Keep in a dark, cool, dry, draughty place so they can dry out naturally. When you are ready to use them, draw stems out from the bolt by the butt end, lay them out on a lawn or path and sprinkle with water, turning so that they get evenly damp. Roll in gently in hessian or an old blanket and leave to cure for four hours. Then use. Any not used within about two days may get sticky and need drying and dampening afresh. Designs can be obtained from the many specialist books on rushwork.*

14th April St Tibertius' Day

Nothing is known for certain about the life of St Tibertius. This is known as First Cuckoo Day in Sussex, and was the date of the Cuckoo Fair in Heathfield, East Sussex.

16th April St Magnus' Day

St Magnus was a 12th-century Norwegian Jarl who was martyred in the Orkney Isles.

17th April St Donan and his Companions' Day

St Donan was a 7th-century Irish follower of St Columba on Iona, who left to found a monastery and commune on Eigg, where they were tragically all murdered by local people following a land dispute.

19th April St Alphege's Day

St Alphege was an 11th century Archbishop of Canterbury, captured and murdered by Vikings.

20th April

The Cuckoo Fair at Tenbury, Hereford and Worcester was held on this day.

21st April St Beuno's Day

St Beuno was a Welshman, from Gwynnedd, who was reputed to be able to effect remarkable cures, often using the water from the well at Clynnog.

23rd April St George's Day

In the 13th century, replacing Edward the Confessor, St George became the patron saint of England, but little is known about him save that he lived in the 4th century and died at Lydda, Palestine. Knighthoods of the Order of the Garter are bestowed on this day. Although a red rose is often associated with this day, the saint's colour is in fact blue, after the colour of the original garter, and it is traditional to wear something blue. St George appears in many Mummers' Plays at Easter and Christmas. He is the patron saint of Norwich, Norfolk and this date was called Mayor's Day. A feature of the procession and town festivities was an elaborately costumed dragon, called 'Snap', which can be seen in replica on the second Saturday in July in the Lord Mayor's Street Procession. The oldest surviving Snap costume can be seen in Norwich Castle Museum.

The Cuckoo Fair at Orleton, Hereford and Worcester was held today.

✸ **St George's Day Fair, Bewdley**   **Hereford and Worcester**
TAKE THE A456 WEST FROM KIDDERMINSTER.

◉ St George's Day Fair, Penrith — **Cumbria**

PENRITH IS OFF JUNCTION 40 OF THE M6 (A6).

◉ St George's Day Fair, Hatfield — **Hertfordshire**

TAKE THE A1(M), JUNCTIONS 2, 3 OR 4.

🏛 Court Baron of the Burgesses of the Manor of Lichfield
(St George's Day Court), Lichfield — **Staffordshire**

LICHFIELD IS BETWEEN BIRMINGHAM AND BURTON-ON-TRENT ON THE A38.

24th April St Mark's Eve

This was considered an evening for divination, particularly for those seeking a partner. In Lincolnshire, Satan was said to be abroad. Animals could talk and fern seed ripened and dispersed – the Devil's Harvest.

On this day in Yorkshire people tried to find out who would die in the next three years. They would sit on their church porch between 11:00pm and 01:00am for three years running and on the third year apparitions of those who were to die the following year would come to church. In other areas people would go into the churchyard for this period of three hours and hope to see the spirits of those who would die in the next year, but if they fell asleep this fate would be theirs.

Anyone born on this day is alleged to be able to see spirits.

25th April St Mark's Day

St Mark was one of the four Evangelists, who wrote one of the four Gospels, and is said to have founded Venice.

Scatter ashes on the hearth at midnight on the Eve and this morning a footprint will be revealed. Whosoever's foot fits the print will marry into the household. Other divination customs relate to this day, including some which would reveal to girls an image of their future sweetheart.

Farmers never ploughed on this day, as it was feared that one of the horses would die within the year. The boundaries of the parish of Alnwick, Northumberland were ridden on this day, the route going through a pond called Freeman's Well.

27th April St Sitha's Day

Little is known about this female saint, still less for certain.

The last Sunday in April

✠ Tyburn Walk, near Marble Arch — **London**

This is a pilgrimage, by Roman Catholic clergy, from St Sepulchre's Church, by the site of old Newgate Prison, to the site of Tyburn Gallows near Marble Arch. Many Catholic martyrs were hanged on the gallows, Tyburn Tree, after taking this walk from Newgate. The tree was felled in the late 18th century, and Newgate Prison was demolished in 1902. The Old Bailey now stands on the site of the former prison. The bell which was rung at midnight on the eve of each execution can be seen in St Sepulchre's Church.

Along the route is St Etheldreda's Church, Ely Place in which can be seen statues of four martyrs and a stained glass window showing four bodies hanging from Tyburn Tree.

MARBLE ARCH IS AT THE MEETING OF BAYSWATER ROAD AND OXFORD STREET.

28th April St Vitalis Day

St Vitalis lived in the 3rd century, but little is known about her.

On this day the Romans held their *Floralia* flower festival in honour of the Goddess Flora. The use of flowers and greenery in May Day decorations may have originated in *Floralia*.

29th April St Endellion's Day

St Endellion was a 6th-century Cornish saint, and her shrine is near Wadebridge.

30th April May Day Eve, Beltane, Walpurgis Night

This is the ancient Celtic Feast of Bel (or Beltane), which began when the winter sun died.

Walpurgis Night is an important witches' festival. Malevolent fairies were abroad and people protected their houses with crosses made from rowan wood and with elder leaves. This is the most unlucky day of the year on which to be born.

In later times houses were decorated with branches of sycamore or may. Blue, yellow and pink flowers were used in decorations.

In the North of England villagers went May Birching. After dark they would creep round and hang a branch on a house which signified the character of the occupant. Lime meant 'prime', pear meant 'fair', thorn meant *scorn*, holly meant 'folly', briar meant 'liar', nut was for a 'slut', and gorse for a 'whore'. Rowan, whose old name was wicken, meant 'chicken', in those days considered a term of affection.

Hobby Horse Parade, Minehead and Dunster   Somerset

This event starts at midnight (Warning Eve) and continues until 3rd May (Booting Day). There are two Hobby Horses, the older Sailor's Horse, kept at the quay, and the Town Horse kept in The Old Ship Afloat public house.

In the morning the parade is in Minehead and in the afternoon at Dunster. The Town Horse is accompanied by costumed teazers called 'Gullivers' whose job it is to persuade villagers to give money. Traditionally on Booting Day women are 'held down' by the Hobby Horse, touched ten times with its head, and then they are made to dance with it.

THESE TOWNS ARE BOTH ON THE A39 ON THE NORTH SOMERSET COAST.

Padstow Hobby Horse, Padstow   Cornwall

This starts at midnight, when the whole town comes alive. The two 'Obby 'Osses are the Blue 'Oss, representing the town's teetotaller group which contributes its funds to charity, and leaves from the Institute at 10am, and the older Red (formerly Black) 'Oss whose supporters use contributions for jollification, which leaves from the Golden Lion Inn at 11am. 'Oss and Teazer weave about, and any who dance with the 'Oss will be blessed with good fortune in the coming year. Any woman who gets caught under the frame of the 'Oss will become pregnant before the year is out. The Padstow May Carol is sung to welcome the summer.

TAKE THE A39 WEST OUT OF WADEBRIDGE, RIGHT ON TO THE A389 PAST LITTLE PETHERICK.

The Hobby Horse, Dunster, Somerset, 1925

Rogationtide customs

The Rogation Days are the Monday, Tuesday and Wednesday before Ascension Thursday. Rogationtide starts five weeks after Easter. The Litany of Saints was chanted as the clergy and villagers visited fields, ponds, meadows and coastal waters to ask for Divine blessing on all growing things. Rogation means 'beseeching' or 'asking', or an 'outdoor litany'. Services are traditionally held in the fields and on the coast or in harbours. It is possible that two Rogation themes developed from pagan spring fertility rites and from two Roman festivals: the blessing of crops at Ambervailia and the beating of bounds at Terminalia, a May festival in honour of the God of Boundaries Terminus.

Processions around the parish boundaries are commemorated by Beating the Bounds, which seems to be a survival of the pagan ritual to awaken the sleeping earth. In the past boys were actually beaten with willow wands to instill in them where the boundaries were. They were also required to traverse any obstacles on the boundary, such as climb over houses, crawl through hedges or culverts and wade through ponds. Many surviving Beating the Bounds ceremonies are on Ascension Day but some remain in Rogation Week. On the Lichfield gang (walk) today elm boughs are carried, and this ceremony has both the beating and water connections. In some ceremonies the dragon personified the infernal spirit to be driven out of the parish.

Rogation Days are sometimes called Cross Days, because of the cross carried at the head of the procession, or Gang Days in the North of England where walking the boundaries is called ganging. Gospel Oaks were planted at the places where the procession stopped to pray for good crops. On these walks charity was distributed to the poor.

At Crompton, Lancashire the gang route goes across a reservoir, through an outlet tunnel, then over the roof of the King's Arms at Grains Bar. At St Mary Redcliffe, Bristol the course of an underground spring is followed on a Saturday in October. At St Mary's, Leicester the Beating of the Bounds was every three years, as it still is at the Tower of London. The Beating of the Bounds at St Dunstan's-in-the-East Church is by boys of St Dunstan's College, Catford, London.

Boundary changes have made some traditional routes impractical or impossible and a reduced symbolic walk and blessing are now substituted. This is the case at Oddington, Oxfordshire. At Cannington, near Bridgwater, Somerset the boundaries are no longer beaten, but the walk is still held and the fields blessed. Many ceremonies have lapsed. St Clement Danes, London, now the church of the RAF, no longer has bounds to beat.

Every May the cherry orchards in Newington, Kent were blessed. Blessing the boats now takes place at North Shields and Cullercoats, Tyneside on the Late Spring Bank Holiday. At Hastings, Sussex the Blessing of the Sea has been moved to a Sunday in May. Blessing the Sea ceremonies were also held at St Leonards, Folkestone, Whitstable, and Whitby. Harvest-of-the-Sea services were held at Brixham and Flamborough. Blessing the waters and shipping took place at Southampton. Some of these have recently been revived in one form or other.

Traditionally, water is drunk and fresh produce eaten at Rogationtide.

Variable Dates

✠ The Beating of the Bounds at the Manor and Liberty of the Savoy   London

The area between the Strand and the Embankment was once administered by a Court Leet of the Duchy of Lancaster. Before that it was the manorial land of Peter, Count of Savoy, who was given it by Henry III in the 13th century. Twelve boundary markers survive, and the Court Leet now meets once every five years for the sole purpose of appointing a Jury to beat the bounds. They are accompanied by the choir of the Queen's Chapel. At the markers choirboys are up-ended and bumped on a cushion.

THE NEAREST UNDERGROUND STATIONS ARE CHARING CROSS AND EMBANKMENT.

✠ Beating the Bounds   Leicester

This takes place once every three years.

LEICESTER IS AT THE JUNCTION OF THE A6 AND A47.

✠ Beating the Bounds, Cannington, near Bridgwater   Somerset

The bounds are no longer beaten, but they are still walked and the fields are blessed.

TAKE THE A39 WEST OUT OF BRIDGWATER.

⬤ Riding and perambulation of the borough boundaries, Richmond   North Yorkshire

The corporation, as Lord of the Manor , has the duty to undertake the circuit under a charter granted by Elizabeth I in 1576.

RICHMOND IS WEST OF THE A1. TAKE THE A6108 FROM SCOTCH CORNER.

Beating the Bounds, Cannington, Somerset

Beating the Bounds, Plymstock

Blessing of the crops at Shipton Cliffs, 1935

Rogation Sunday
The 5th Sunday after Easter, The Sunday immediately preceding Ascension Thursday

Blessing the Fields, Hever   Kent
TAKE THE B2028 EAST FROM LINGFIELD, THEN AN UNCLASSIFIED ROAD TO HEVER ON THE LEFT.

The Blessing of the Cherry Orchards, Newington   Kent
This is an example of a post-World War I revival of a crop blessing, which is not related to parish
boundaries, and a number once existed in southern England.
TAKE THE A2 SOUTH EAST FROM LONDON, JUST PAST RAINHAM.

Blessing of the Waters, Mudeford, near Christchurch   Hampshire
After a service at All Saints' Church a procession headed by the choir and a band gangs (walks)
down to the quay, where prayers are said and hymns sung. The vicar rows out to sea with a fisherman and blesses the waters, leaving a small cross floating in the sea.
MUDEFORD IS ON THE COAST OFF THE A337 JUST EAST OF CHRISTCHURCH.

Rogation Monday

Bidding for grazing rights, Wishford Magna church, near Salisbury   Wiltshire
This may date from the 16th century, and is an auction for the grazing rights on two pieces of
land, Bonham's Mead and Abbey Mead, from 1st November until 12th August. The bidding starts
at 8 pm at the church gates, the church door key being used as a gavel, and finishes at sunset.
Locally the ceremony is known by the misnomer of the Midsummer Tithes.
TAKE THE A36 NORTH OUT OF WILTON, THEN LEFT TO WISHFORD MAGNA.

Wilkes Charity Perambulation, Leighton Buzzard   Bedfordshire
TAKE THE A4146 SOUTH FROM MILTON KEYNES.

Rogation Tuesday The Tuesday before Ascension Day

Rogation Wednesday Ascension Eve

Horngarth or Planting the Penny (Penance) Hedge, Whitby

In the past, for this ceremony oak, elm and willow were decorated with flowers and ribbons, and wild boar was eaten. This reflects the origins of the custom in 1159 when Ralph de Percy, William de Bruce and a man called Allatson, whilst hunting in Eskdale Forest, chased a boar into a hermitage. The hermit refused to allow the hunters to enter, so they beat the hermit within an inch of his life. The Abbot of Whitby was summoned, and the hermit begged him to be forgiving. The abbot confiscated the hunters' lands, but leased them back on the assurance that they committed an annual penance on this day. The penance was that they should cut wood to make a fence in Whitby harbour, using penny knives, of sufficient strength to survive three high tides. If the fence collapsed their lands were forfeited. If the tide was so high that the erection of the fence was impossible then the men were excused for that year.

The land now belongs to the Hutton family who maintain the tradition. The Manor Bailiff presides and gives three blasts on an 800-year-old horn when the hedge is complete (by 9am) and shouts 'Out on ye!' three times. The latter was originally cried by the lady of the manor, and the charge was formerly read out by the Town Crier.

WHITBY IS ON THE COAST AT THE JUNCTION OF THE A171 AND THE A174.

Ascension Day The 40th day after Easter

Ascension Day is always a Thursday. Christians commemorate the ascension of Christ into heaven, 40 days after his resurrection.

Ascension Day is associated with beating of bounds and with customs emanating from pagan water- or well-worship. The Church and civil authorities tried for centuries to ban well-worship, and only succeeded to the extent that the importance of water to life was made the focus of many ceremonies, and at others a saint came to be attached to the well and was in turn made the focus of attention. With its religious accoutrements the decoration (or 'dressing' as it is usually called) of wells survives, particularly in the Peak District of Derbyshire. Traditionally clothes were never washed on this day, lest someone dies as the clothes are drying. Bringing a leafy hawthorn branch indoors today will protect the family from accidents.

Well-dressing in Derbyshire at Ascension Tide, particularly at Tissington, Tideswell, Wirksworth, Buxton, Ashford and Eyam, and also at Bisley, Gloucestershire and Endon, Staffordshire, is now a religious ceremony of blessing local wells. The tradition of thanksgiving certainly

Planting the Penny Hedge, Whitby, North Yorkshire, 1966

Well Dressing, Tissington, Derbyshire, 1923

dates back to the Black Death when many villages were spared because of their pure water, but it may date further back to a Christian adaptation of the Roman flower festival *Fontinalia* to honour the spirits of streams and fountains. The wells are covered with boarded frames of damp soil, on which pictures are created with natural materials such as flowers, berries, leaves and moss.

Formerly at Nantwich, Cheshire the salt-workers decorated the brine-pit.

Willow wands with blue ribbons and nosegays; newly minted shilling, a meal of hot rolls, butter and radishes are all associated with Ascension Day.

✠ Beating the Bounds, Lichfield Cathedral   Staffordshire

This ceremony has elements of water worship as well as the traditional beating of bounds. In the morning branches of lime are pushed through all the letter boxes of houses in the Cathedral Close. At 10:15am, clergy and choir, carrying elm boughs, walk to six boundary points, some of the old cathedral enclosure, some marking sites of now disused wells. After the perambulation, back at the cathedral, the choristers dip their branches into the font.

LICHFIELD IS BETWEEN BIRMINGHAM AND BURTON-ON-TRENT ON THE A38.

✠ Beating the Bounds, St Michael's Church, Northgate   Oxford

After the 9am service, the procession starts on its journey along the boundary, through shops, including Marks and Spencer, through college grounds, through Broad Street market cellars and over a wall at St Peter's College. At each boundary stone, which is chalked and beaten with bamboo canes, a sermon is read.

OXFORD IS AT THE JUNCTION OF THE A40 AND A34.

✠ Well dressing, Tissington   Derbyshire

Six wells are dressed in the village.

TISSINGTON IS JUST OFF THE A515, PAST FENNY BENTLEY, NORTH OF ASHBOURNE.

✠ Well Dressing, Bisley, near Stroud   Gloucestershire

This is one of the few such well-dressing traditions outside Derbyshire, started in 1863 by the Reverend Thomas Keble after restoring the village wells.

BISLEY IS TO THE WEST OF STROUD, ON AN UNCLASSIFIED ROAD.

✿ Love Feast (or Celebration of the Gospel Elm), Wicken — Northamptonshire

In 1587 the two hamlets of Wyke Dyve and Wyke Hamon, which had a long history of rivalry over many matters, decided to unite under the name of Wicken. In hopes of future harmony a Love Feast was instituted, and its annual commemoration, with cakes and ale, takes place on this day. Parishioners gather under the elm in the centre of the village for a short service, during which the hundredth psalm is sung, and then everyone adjourns to the local hotel to indulge in the feast.

TAKE THE A422 NORTH EAST FROM BUCKINGHAM AND EXIT LEFT TO WICKEN.

◉ Beating the Bounds of the City of London and its Liberties — London

This was formerly done on one of the Rogation Days, when the Beadle actually bumped charity schoolboys on the walls carrying lead boundary markers, and if there was no marker he thrashed them with willow wands. Today boys carry wands and merely thrash the boundary markers with them.

◉ The Beating of the Bounds at the Tower Liberty — London

The Tower of London stands in grounds called the Tower Liberty. Every three years (due 1999, 2002, etc) at 6:30pm after Evensong a procession of the Chief Yeoman Warder, Yeomen in full ceremonial dress carrying pikes, Tower Chaplain and choirboys carrying willow wands walk to each of the 31 boundary stones. At each the Chaplain cries, 'Cursed be he who removeth his neighbour's landmark!', whereupon the Chief Warder says to the choirboys, 'Whack it boys, whack it!', which they do with gusto.

THE TOWER OF LONDON IS ON THE RIVER THAMES BY TOWER BRIDGE.

◉ The Beating of the Bounds of All Hallows-by-the-Tower Parish — London

The beaters of the bounds of this parish meet the beaters of the bounds of the Tower Liberty at a disputed marker at Tower Hill, where the Lord Mayor of London makes an appearance to symbolically challenge the Governor of the Tower.

ALL HALLOWS-BY-THE-TOWER PARISH IS ON BYWARD STREET, LONDON EC3

Beating the Bounds at the Tower of London 1906

May customs

To rural folk, May heralded the start of summer, when people looked forward to what passes for fine weather in England, fresh produce and blooms, new relationships and outdoor sports and entertainment. May Day was formerly one of the biggest festivals of the year, but because of calendar and public holiday changes and the movement of events to Bank Holidays, May customs have become spread out over several weeks. Many rituals had elements of fertility-, tree- and water-worship, and of cleansing of body and soul, with floral decorations common. Also, superstition, supernatural beliefs and divination abounded at this important change of season and work routine. It should be remembered that Lemuralia, the Roman equivalent of Hallowe'en was early in this month.

Seasonal need for farm labourers and fisheries workers increased, more hiring fairs were held. The fisheries were blessed. For sweeps it was the end of the busy season, but for many tradespeople the busy period was about to start, as days lengthened and weather improved. Sports were the same as April.

At the end of the month came the royalist honouring of Oak Apple Day to mark the restoration of the monarchy and, with it, festivals banned by the Puritans.

Variable Dates

The Great Barmote Court for the Joint Liberty of Stoney Middleton and Eyam **Derbyshire**
STONEY MIDDLETON IS ON THE A623. EYAM IS JUST TO THE NORTH OF STONEY MIDDLETON.

Blessing the Sea, Whitby **North Yorkshire**
WHITBY IS ON THE COAST AT THE JUNCTION OF THE A171 AND THE A174.

On a Sunday in May

Dunkirk Veterans' Service, Church of St Lawrence Jewry, Gresham Street **London**
GRESHAM STREET IS THE B128, LINKING ALDERSGATE STREET WITH THE BANK OF ENGLAND.

Blessing the Sea, Hastings **East Sussex**
HASTINGS IS ON THE SOUTH COAST OF ENGLAND AT THE END OF THE A21 FROM LONDON.

1st May **May Day**

Prior to the Restoration the advent of the merry month of May was a time of great celebration, when summer was welcomed by men blowing on cow-horns. Girls rose early to bathe their faces in the May morning dew, which was held to have curative and beauty properties. Blankets soaked in May dew were thought to be able to cure sick children wrapped in them. Wells are able to grant wishes on May Day. The Pin Well, Wooler, Northumberland was traditionally visited by lovers. Fairies are abroad today so don't leave your baby unattended lest it be kidnapped and replaced by a changeling. May was the least popular month to get married in, as the offspring of a May bride are doomed to bad luck. Similarly, animals born in May were thought to be obstinate and troublesome.

Fishermen have many May Day superstitions. Fenland fishermen would never push their boats out on this day lest they see the ghosts of their dead colleagues. In Sussex, however, the first catch on May Day brought good luck. Broom-makers never worked on May Day for to turn a branch into a broom on this day was very unlucky.

Erection of a maypole (an ancient fertility symbol and representation of the sacred tree of life) and dancing, garlands and posies of spring flowers are traditional on this day, although celebrations are often transferred to the May Bank Holiday. Permanent maypoles stand in Welford-on-Avon (70 ft 21.5m), Warwickshire; Temple Sowerby, Cumbria; Barwick in Elmet (100 ft 30.5m), near Leeds, West Yorkshire; Ickwell Green, Bedfordshire, Paganhill (94 ft 128.5m), near Stroud, Gloucestershire; Belton, near Oakham, Leicestershire; Wellow, near Ollerton, Nottinghamshire; Gawthorpe, near Wakefield, West Yorkshire. Just after the Restoration a maypole 134 ft (41m) high was erected in the Strand, London. St Andrew Undershaft Church in the City of London is so called because its south door was in the shadow of the Aldgate maypole in Leadenhall Street. This maypole was a victim of the frequent Puritan purges in 1517. In former times people used to try to steal the maypole from another village, as this was tantamount to acquiring the good luck that was embodied in the maypole. At some time in the month traditional May dances are held at Elstow, Bedfordshire; Chislehurst, Kent; Offham, Kent; Kingsteinton and Lustleigh, Devon. Other May Day festivities are held at Charlton-on-Otmoor, Oxfordshire; Flore near Weedon, Northamptonshire; and Shrewsbury, Shropshire.

Originally ring dances were performed around the maypole, the ribbon-plaiting dance now seen dates from the 19th century. May Garlands were hoops or pyramids decorated with flowers, greenery and ribbons. May carols were sung and money collected. Young men would wear linen shirts on which their sweethearts had embroidered patterns or sewn ribbons and bows. This tradition led to the dress of May and garland dancers.

Blessing the sea, Hastings, 1947

Raising of the Maypole

Children also made May Dolls to put inside the garlands, or they would put the dolls in a decorated box, cover them with napkins and ask people to pay to lift the napkin for luck. This tradition of May Dolls was most common in the south of England, surviving longest in Edlesborough, Buckinghamshire (where mother and child dolls were put inside the wreath or bowery – possibly representing Mary and Jesus) and Bishopsteignton, Devon.

The flower called May is hawthorn blossom – its collection, along with the maypole (of birch or pine), garlands of flowers and branches of blackthorn was called 'going a-maying', to the accompaniment of horns blowing. Sometimes these were collected on May Day Eve, and in this way the fertilising powers of nature were brought into the home. Hawthorn was sacred to Persephone, Goddess of Spring, and its flowering in ancient times signaled the time to start the Celtic festival of Beltane. Later in the day a young girl would be crowned Queen of the May, and children would dress dolls as the Lady of the May. These aspects of the May celebrations echo pre-Christian tree- and nature- worship and the commemoration of the resurrection of Attis, lover to Kybele, Goddess of Flowers and Fruitfulness. The crowning of the May Queen (and May King or Green Man) is a relic of the Kybele and Attis myth. Another possible origin of the May Queen is the image of Flora, the Roman Goddess of Spring. Oliver Cromwell banned May ceremony, which was extremely boisterous, but Charles II restored it.

Sweeps' and milkmaids' processions were held on this day. The character Jack-in-the-Green featured in the processions, the symbol of the renewal of life. He is a man dressed all over with greenery. Morris dancing (Black Face, Cotswold, North West Clog, Border), and other styles of dancing such as Mollie dancing, long sword dancing, clog dancing, garland dancing, step dancing, and stave dancing are all to be seen on this day. In parades common characters are Mummers, Guisers, Hobby Horse, the Teazer, All Sorts, the Fool or Whiffler, and folk characters such as Robin Hood, Maid Marian and so on. Horses and carts were decorated with flowers, greenery and ribbons. May Fairs were held, at which archery competitions were popular.

Bonfires were lit on this day, and people would jump through the flames. Farmers would even drive their cattle through them. These bonfires originated with the Celtic rituals of Beltane when fires were lit to purify the earth and drive evil spirits away. Bones were burnt because of their foul smell – hence the word 'bonfire'.

Perhaps the only village in England which has an unbroken history of pagan May ritual is Longdendale, Derbyshire, where wells are decorated, bonfires lit and anthropomorphic images erected.

May Day was a Celtic Quarter Day.

Junket (*see p.185 for recipe*) and spiced **Gingerbread** (*see p.185 for recipe*) are traditionally eaten on May Day, and also **Egg custard** (*see p.185 for recipe*). Nipple Cakes were eaten in the past. They had bumps on top which were pulled off one by one and thrown over the shoulder. A prayer was said to protect family and livestock.

May Cup (*see p.186 for recipe*) is a drink traditionally offered to visitors and travellers on May Day.

✠ **Decorating the Rood Screen with a Garland, Charlton-on-Otmoor**   Oxfordshire

A huge garland is constructed, and just before 10am the seven oldest children in the village carry it to the church, singing May carols. Once there the garland is sprinkled with holy water and placed on the 15th-century rood screen. A small box wood cross is placed under the large cross which is atop the screen. At the conclusion of the service maypole dancing and other festivities are held in the village.

TAKE THE A34 NORTH EAST FROM OXFORD, RIGHT ON THE B4027, LEFT AT ISLIP.

🎭 **Bringing in the May, Wilton, Salisbury**   Wiltshire

WILTON IS JUST WEST OF SALISBURY ON THE A30.

✠ **Singing the May Carol from the top of Magdalene College Tower**   Oxford

Robed choristers from Magdalene Church School welcome the May with this Latin hymn (*Te Deum Patrem Collimus*) at 6am. The bells are then rung and in the streets below Morris dancing and other street entertainments start.

OXFORD IS AT THE JUNCTION OF THE A40 AND A34.

✠ **Hymns and Carols at the Bargate, Southampton**   Hampshire

These are sung at 6 am by pupils of King Edward VI School, traditionally from the roof, but now from the lawn as the roof cannot be accessed.

BARGATE IS IN THE CENTRE OF SOUTHAMPTON, WHICH IS AT THE JUNCTION OF THE M3 AND M27.

✺ **May Fair, Boston**   Lincolnshire

BOSTON IS ON THE A16 NORTH OF SPALDING.

✺ **May Fair, Hereford**   Hereford and Worcester

HEREFORD IS AT THE JUNCTION OF THE A49 AND THE A438.

🎭 **May Queen of London Festival, Hayes Common**   Kent

THIS IS ON THE A232 BETWEEN KESTON MARK AND WEST WICKHAM.

🎭 **May Festival, Elstow**   Bedfordshire

ELSTOW IS JUST SOUTH OF BEDFORD ON AN UNCLASSIFIED ROAD OFF A5134.

🎭 **May Day Revels, Welford-on-Avon**   Warwickshire

TAKE THE B439 WEST FROM STRATFORD-UPON-AVON, THEN LEFT ON AN UNCLASSIFIED ROAD.

🎭 **Maypole Dancing, Wadworth**   South Yorkshire

WADWORTH IS SOUTH OF DONCASTER ON THE A60.

♘ **Tilting the Quintain, Offham**   Kent

TAKE THE A25 EAST FROM SEVENOAKS, THEN RIGHT AFTER WROTHAM HEATH.

♛ **Riding the Bounds, Berwick-on-Tweed**   Northumberland

BERWICK-ON-TWEED IS ON THE COAST ON THE A1 JUST SOUTH OF THE SCOTTISH BORDER.

May Bank Holiday

This is usually the first Monday in May.

🎭 **Jack-in-the-Green Festival, Hastings**   East Sussex

This Jack-in-the-Green is conical in shape, ten ft (1m) tall with a floral crown on top. He is awakened at dawn with a dance on a nearby hilltop, and after the festivities he is symbolically slain by cutting off his crown. Pieces of the crown are prized as souvenirs.

HASTINGS IS ON THE SOUTH COAST OF ENGLAND AT THE END OF THE A21 FROM LONDON.

Royal May Day, Knutsford, Cheshire

Sweeps' Procession and May Festival at Rochester   **Kent**

May Day at Rochester is full of excitement and variety. There are street performers of all kinds, displays of Morris and other folk dancing, guisers, stalls and plenty of traditional delicacies to buy. The procession, in the early afternoon, is headed by Jack-in-the-Green, awakened at dawn by a dance on a nearby hilltop, and includes chimneysweeps and boys dressed as sweeps' climbing boys. Before the Climbing Boys Act of 1868, May Day was a sweeps' holiday, after the busy period in early spring following the winter.

ROCHESTER IS ON THE NORTH KENT COAST ON THE A2.

May Festivities, Ickwell Green   **Bedfordshire**

This 400-year-old event is held on Old May Day and on the last Saturday in May. It starts with a dawn raid on the maypole by Morris Men. At 1pm the main celebrations start. A May Queen is elected. The Morris dancers are accompanied by two Moggies, with blackened faces, and carrying brooms. They perform antics for the crowds and ask for money.

TAKE THE B658 SOUTH OF SANDY, THEN RIGHT AT UPPER CALDECOTE.

Whit Walk, Bradford   **West Yorkshire**

Formerly held at Whitsuntide, this walk is now a race over 31 miles (50km), from Bradford, through Ilkley and Otley, back to Bradford.

BRADFORD IS BETWEEN LEEDS AND HALIFAX, WITH ILKLEY AND OTLEY JUST TO THE NORTH.

The Saturday nearest May Day

Royal May Day and Sanding the Streets, Knutsford   **Cheshire**

In addition to the traditional May Day activities, a Sanding Ceremony is held. Sand decorations are made in the streets by passing different coloured sands through funnels to trace the designs. Traditionally this was done outside a bride's home before her wedding day.

TAKE THE A537 WEST FROM MACCLESFIELD.

2nd May Elevation of the Cross

On this and succeeding days during May Week many hiring fairs were held for the seeking of seasonal employment by farm labourers. The folk song Brigg Fair tells of one such. The workers would show an implement of their trade, and hope to conclude a deal with the employer paying them a kind of transfer fee called 'earnest money'.

Eve of the Finding of the Cross by St Helena (in 326), Colchester   **Essex**

St Helena was the daughter of the British king, Coel (Old King Cole).

COLCHESTER IS BETWEEN CHELMSFORD AND IPSWICH ON THE A12.

3rd May St Helena's Day, Rood Day, Discovery of the Holy Cross

'Rood' is another word for 'cross' or 'crucifix'. This day commemorates the discovery of the 'true cross' in AD 326 by St Helena, daughter of the British king, Coel (Old King Cole), and mother of Constantine the Great.

The Sunday after Holy Cross Day

Pig's Face Feast, Avening, near Stroud — Gloucestershire

This feast commemorates the building of the local church in 1080 and takes place every second year, on the Sunday after Holy Cross Day. Meat from a wild boar's head is served in sandwiches, followed by fruit.

TAKE THE A46 SOUTH OF STROUD, THEN LEFT ON B4014.

The first weekend in May

May Celebrations, Gawthorpe, near Wakefield — West Yorkshire

GAWTHORPE IS ON THE A638 BETWEEN DEWSBURY AND JUNCTION 40 OF THE M1.

The first Sunday in May

Randwick Wap, St John the Baptist's Church, Randwick, near Stroud — Gloucestershire

This is the first part of a two-part Hocktide custom which starts at 11:15am with an outdoor service during which two large cheeses are blessed. They are then rolled three times round the church, anticlockwise. One is then eaten, whilst the other is retained for the second part of the custom on the second Saturday in May.

RANDWICK IS ON AN UNCLASSIFIED ROAD NORTH WEST OF STROUD.

7th May St John of Beverley's Day

St John, from Harpham, near Bridlington, Humberside was the 7th-century healer believed to protect Beverley Minster. Water from St John's Well in Harpham is said to have curative powers.

The Tuesday nearest 7th May

Blessing St John's Well, Harpham — Humberside

A service is held at the well, decorated with flowers for the occasion, and the well is blessed.

HARPHAM IS BETWEEN DRIFFIELD AND BRIDLINGTON, JUST SOUTH OF THE A166.

8th May St Michael's Day, St Indract's Day

The Feast of the Apparition of St Michael is celebrated in Cornwall where St Michael is the patron saint of Helston.

St Indract was an Irishman who lost his life in Somerset in AD 700 whilst on route back to Ireland with grain for those starving after a poor harvest. Saxon raiders thought he was carrying valuables.

Furry Day, Helston — Cornwall

If the 8th May falls on a Sunday or Monday, Furry Day is celebrated on the preceding Saturday. 'Furry' is thought to derive from the Old English *fery* meaning feast day of a patron saint. The Early Morning Dance is performed first after the Mayor starts the proceedings at 7am from the Guildhall. The alternative word 'Faddy' is from the Cornish for 'sycamore', as sycamore branches are waved in the Hal-an-Tow which starts at 8:30 am from St John's Bridge. This may be a surviving example of a crop fertility dance, but has some features of Mumming. The Furry Song that accompanies the parade refers to St George and the Dragon, St Michael, Robin Hood and Little John, and Aunt Mary Moses. The Children's Dance starts at 10:15am from the secondary school. The main Furry Dance starts at the Guildhall at noon, and is for couples in formal dress. Men wear morning coats, silk hats and lily-of-the-valley bouttonnieres, and women wear garden party hats, long gloves, summer frocks and lily-of-the-valley corsages. The line of pairs of dancers weaves in and out of houses, bringing the occupants good luck. The last dance is at 5pm and this one is for everyone to join in whatever they are wearing.

HELSTON IS ON THE A394 BETWEEN FALMOUTH AND PENZANCE.

Nearest Sunday to 8th May Chestnut Sunday

✦ Chestnut Sunday, Hampton Court   Middlesex

This is a traditional outing to Bushy Park to see the triple avenue of chestnut trees planted in the reign of William III.

HAMPTON COURT IS ON THE RIVER THAMES WHERE THE A309 MEETS THE A308.

9th May

On this day was the Roman festival of *Lemuralia*, when the spirits of the dead walked the earth. It was similar to Hallowe'en. The Church tried to remove all vestiges of the commemoration from May festivities, but the avoidance of marriage in May remained for a long time.

10th May

✦ Beaconsfield Fair   Buckinghamshire

BEACONSFIELD IS JUST OFF THE M40 AT JUNCTION 2.

The second Saturday in May

⊞ Randwick Wap, Randwick, near Stroud   Gloucestershire

This is the second part of the two-part Hocktide custom which starts at 1pm at the War Memorial. After a parade in 18th- and 19th-century costumes a Wap Mayor and Wap Queen are elected. 'The Runnick Weavers' Song' is sung. Accompanied by the High Sheriff, Sword Bearer and Mop Man – who sprays onlookers with water – the Wap Mayor and Wap Queen are carried shoulder high to the village pond where the Mayor is tossed in. The Mayor's Song is sung. Later the two engage in a cheese-rolling competition with the saved cheese and some wooden ones, having three goes. The real cheese is then eaten.

RANDWICK IS ON AN UNCLASSIFIED ROAD NORTH WEST OF STROUD.

The second Sunday in May

The game of Battledore and Shuttlecock/Shuttlefeathers was played on this day in the old West Riding of Yorkshire, originally for divination.

Battledore and Shuttlefeathers *This forerunner of badminton involved just hitting the shuttlecock upwards as many times as possible, to score a higher number of consecutive strikes than your opponent.*

11th May Old May Day Eve

It is bad luck to pick blackthorn on this day, as it is guarded by fairies.

12th May Old May Day, Garland Day, St Pancras' Day

As many people moved to a new job at this time (Flitting Day), possibly originating from a hiring fair, it was after a holiday. Cheese-making started on this day and cows were put out to pasture.

Fragrant roses, cowslips, lilies and wood violets are among the flowers used in garland-weaving. Cowslip balls were suspended, or tossed in the air and caught in the manner of battledore and shuttlefeathers. A similar game was played through the garland hoop.

✦ Garland Day, Abbotsbury, near Weymouth   Dorset

In the past when there was a local mackerel fishing fleet, this custom was a combination of blessing the fleet and waters and a May celebration. Garlands were taken to the boats in a procession,

blessed and taken out to sea by the fishermen to be left as an offering on the water. This marked the beginning of the fishing season. Nowadays after 'bringing in the may' and making the garlands, the parade goes to the War Memorial and church, but some garlands are thrown out to sea.
TAKE B3157 WEST OUT OF WEYMOUTH, PAST PORTESHAM.

Stow Fair, Stow-on-the-Wold　　　　　　　　　　　　　　Gloucestershire
The charter for this fair was granted in 1476 by Edward IV. This is the first of two dates on which the fair is held. As a horse fair it is much frequented by gypsies and travellers, but originally it was a sheep fair.
STOW-ON-THE-WOLD IS AT THE JUNCTION OF THE A424 AND A429.

13th May

Blessing the fishing boats, Abbotsbury, Chesil Bank　　　　　　　Dorset
No fishing boats exist here now, so three garlands on wooden frames, made and carried by children (organised by one local family), are paraded through the village and laid on the War Memorial.
TAKE B3157 WEST OUT OF WEYMOUTH, PAST PORTESHAM

14th May Pag Rag Day
In some areas this was a similar day to Flitting Day, when seasonal workers packed their belongings into a handcart or backpack and moved to their next job.

15th May St Dympna's Day
St Dympna was the daughter of a 6th-century Celtic monarch. She was murdered by him when she refused to take her mother's place in his bed after the death of her mother.

The first new moon in May
This was the favoured time to hold a Toad Fair. Since ancient times the Toad Man (hence the surname Todman) travelled the area telling fortunes and holding divination sessions. He would cast a handful of toad bones on to the ground and read the pattern they made. Also at Toad Fairs would be healers and quacks, plying their trades and selling folk remedies and concoctions. The last surviving Toad Fair was at Stalbridge in Dorset in the early 19th century.

Garland Day at Abbotsbury, Dorset

The Sunday nearest the 16th May

⊕ **Blessing the Waters of the Well, Church of St Mary and St Walstan, Bawburgh**   **Norfolk**
The waters of St Walstan's Well are said to heal any organ and to be able to restore lost genitals.
Farmers took their cattle to the well to ensure good health. Today a simple blessing ceremony is
performed. The local fair is also held.
BAWBURGH IS WEST OF NORWICH ON THE B1108.

17th May St Madron's Day
St Madron was a Cornish saint from the village near Penzance that bears his name.

The Wednesday nearest 18th May

⊕ **Dunting the Freeholder, Newbiggin-by-the-Sea, near Morpeth**   **Northumberland**
The bounds were formerly ridden, but today the ceremony involves walking round the old common on Newbiggin Moor. At the Dunting (Bumping) Stone on the moor new freeholders are
bumped three times on the stone.
NEWBIGGIN-BY-THE-SEA IS BETWEEN BLYTH AND LYNEMOUTH, TO THE EAST OF THE A189.

19th May St Dunstan's Day
St Dunstan lived in Mayfield, East Sussex in the 10th century and is the patron saint of blacksmiths. It is said that the good luck symbolism of horseshoes arose when St Dunstan was
approached by the Devil to have his hooves shod. He drove a nail deep into the Satanic foot, and
then extracted a promise from the Devil, in return for extracting the nail, that he should never
enter a building where a horseshoe is nailed outside. However, the horseshoe had magical associations long before Christianity, having the shape of the crescent moon and being made of iron –
which repels witches and fairies. Beer and apples are traditionally consumed on this day.

The third Thursday in May

⊕ **Weighing the Mayor, The Guildhall, High Wycombe**   **Buckinghamshire**
The Mayor and other officials are paraded through the streets before being publicly weighed in a
chair suspended from a tripod and scale. The Town Crier announces the weights, checked by the
Inspector of Weights and Measures, and the previous weights. Any reductions are cheered as they
are taken to be the result of honest toil and sweat. Increases in weight are jeered as being the con-
sequence of idleness.
HIGH WYCOMBE IS JUST NORTH OF JUNCTION 4 OF THE M40.

⊕ **Throwing the Kitchels (after the election of a new mayor), Guildhall, Harwich**   **Essex**
The new Mayor carries out the 300-year-old ritual of throwing buns (called Kitchels) to those
gathered at the Guildhall at noon.
HARWICH IS A COASTAL TOWN ON THE A120 EAST FROM COLCHESTER.

20th May St Ethelbert's Day
Ethelbert was an 8th-century king of East Anglia, who was murdered by order of King Offa of
Mercia to stop him marrying Offa's daughter Ælfrith.

21st May St Collen's day
St Collen was a 7th-century hermit who lived at the foot of Glastonbury Tor.

✳ **Henry VI Memorial Meeting, Wakefield Tower, Tower of London**   **London**
Representatives of Eton College and King's College, Cambridge, both founded by Henry VI, meet
at the spot where he was murdered in 1471. Lilies from Eton and roses from King's College are laid.
THE TOWER OF LONDON IS ON THE RIVER THAMES BY TOWER BRIDGE.

23rd May

⚜ Mayoring Day, Rye   East Sussex

Traditionally held on 23rd May, after the election of a new Mayor, it now takes place on either the early or late Spring Bank Holiday. After a new Mayor is elected a service is held at St Mary's Church, and then at 11am the new Mayor throws hot pennies, to the value of £20, from the top floor of the Town Hall, for all, mainly children, to scramble for.

RYE IS NEAR THE COAST AT THE JUNCTION OF THE A259 AND A268.

Late Spring Bank Holiday

This is usually the last Monday in May.

⚜ Blessing the Boats, North Shields and Cullercoats   Tyneside

This former Rogationtide ceremony has been absorbed into the North Shields Fish Quay Festival.

NORTH SHIELDS IS ON THE NORTH BANK OF THE RIVER TYNE ON THE A187. CULLERCOATS IS FURTHER EAST BY THE MOUTH OF THE RIVER, NORTH OF TYNEMOUTH ON THE A193.

🎪 May Celebrations, Wellow, near Ollerton   Nottinghamshire

WELLOW IS JUST SOUTH OF OLLERTON ON THE A616.

💃 Morris and Hooden Horse celebrations, Charing, near Ashford   Kent

This former Whitsun celebration starts at 11am at Charing Church, when the East Kent Morris Men and the Hooden Horse, with its snapping jaws, entertain the crowd before doing likewise at Westwell.

CHARING IS ON THE A20 NORTH WEST OF ASHFORD.

✳ Well-Dressing, Endon   Staffordshire

This has all the traditional May festivities, including crowning the May Queen; she tastes the water from the well, said to have curative powers and tug-o'-war and tossing the sheaf are played.

TAKE THE A53 NORTH EAST OF STOKE-ON-TRENT, THEN LEFT ON B5051.

Tossing the Sheath *A sheath or sack of straw is tossed over a bar, which is then raised for another round. Competitors drop out when they fail to clear the bar, until only the winner remains.*

⚙ Cheese-rolling, Cooper's Hill, Brockworth   Gloucestershire

Originally at Whit, these cheese-rolling races have been held since medieval times. Competitors must register in advance. Starting at 6pm, there are four races, and those who win can keep the wood-encased cheeses that they catch.

BROCKWORTH IS ON THE A436 SOUTH EAST OF GLOUCESTER.

Court of Arraye of Men and Arms and Greenhill Bower, Lichfield　　Staffordshire

This was formerly held on Whit Monday, firstly is in deference to an ancient statute, of 1176, which required every able-bodied man to present himself in armour and armed for combat, even if the armour and weapons had to be home-made. In the 15th century an additional burden was added, 12 suits of chain mail and two suits of knight's armour. King James I annulled the statute, but it continued as a local custom. At 10am at the Guildhall the Mayor carries out the inspection of the 'troops', and this custom then joins with the Greenhill Bower, a May festival dating back to the time of the 7th-century king Oswy. Garlands, decorated poles, the crowning of the Bower Queen, processions and games all feature.

LICHFIELD IS BETWEEN BIRMINGHAM AND BURTON-ON-TRENT ON THE A38.

Kingsteinton Fair, Kingsteinton　　Devon

Traditionally, a ram is roasted at this fair, which was once held on Whit Tuesday. The custom originated long ago when a ram was sacrificed at Fairwater Spring after it ran dry. The flow of water resumed and the practice has been kept up ever since.

TAKE THE A380 NORTH OUT OF TORQUAY.

The Tuesday after Late Spring Bank Holiday

Setting up the Maypole, Barwick-in-Elmet　　West Yorkshire

This takes place every three years (due in 1999, 2002, etc). Formerly the maypole, claimed to be the tallest in England, was taken down every three years at Easter and re-erected on Whit Tuesday, with a fair and celebrations. Three Pole Men are elected to supervise the erection of the pole, made of two spliced larch poles. Four garlands are fixed halfway up, hung with bells attached to red-white-and-blue ribbons. For the climax, a villager climbs the pole and spins the fox weathervane.

TAKE THE A64 NORTH EAST OUT OF LEEDS, THEN RIGHT ON AN UNCLASSIFIED ROAD.

The Friday after Late Spring Bank Holiday

Cotswold Olimpick Games, Dover's Hill, Chipping Camden　　Gloucestershire

Formerly held on the Friday after Whitsun, it is at least 500 years old. The earliest name of someone associated with the Games is that of Robert Dover. Events included wrestling, leaping, skittles, football, pitching the bar, men playing at cudgels, throwing the iron hammer, handling the pyke, leaping over the heads of men kneeling, hunting the hare (which was not killed), cock-fighting, horse racing over a mile course, back-sword play, walking on hands, jumping in sacks, shin kicking and many others. Some of these are still staged, including tug o' war and climbing the greasy pole. The games start at 7:30pm with the firing of a gun mounted on a wooden castle.

TAKE THE A44 SOUTH EAST OF EVESHAM, THEN LEFT ON THE B4081.

The Saturday after Late Spring Bank Holiday

The Scuttlebrook Wake, Chipping Camden
Gloucestershire

This is essentially a May festival, named after the brook that runs picturesquely through the town. It start at 2:30pm with a Morris side – formerly a shire horse – pulling a cart on which ride the May Queen elect and her entourage to the town square. The old Queen crowns the new, and then traditional May celebrations follow.

TAKE THE A44 SOUTH EAST OF EVESHAM, THEN LEFT ON THE B4081.

25th May St Aldhelm's Day
St Aldhelm was a 7th-century Bishop of Sherbourne in Dorset, founder of Malmesbury Abbey. He is remembered as one of the first to write in English, at a time when Latin was the normal literary medium.

26th May St Augustine's Day
St Augustine was sent by Pope Gregory to England in AD 596 to convert the people to Christianity. After converting King Ethelbert of Kent, he supervised the building of the first Cathedral in England, at Canterbury, in AD 601. He was appointed its first Archbishop.

27th May St Bede's Day
The 8th-century Anglo-Saxon scholar and historian known as the Venerable Bede is best known for his work *Ecclesiastical History of the English People*, a collection of biographies of the faithful of the time.

The last weekend in May

The Ancient Scorton Silver Arrow Tournament, Scorton
North Yorkshire

Whilst this archery contest at the oldest sports club in Britain cannot strictly be classified as a folk ceremony, it is however noteworthy for having long-bow events and the history of the club dates from 1673.

LEAVE THE A1 AT CATTERICK AND TAKE THE B1263 EAST TO SCORTON.

A revival of the Ancient Cotswold Games, Glostershire

29th May Royal Oak Day, Oak Apple Day

The house is decorated with oak branches in commemoration of Charles II's escape from the Roundheads by hiding in an oak tree on 6th September 1651 after the Battle of Worcester. The oak tree was in the grounds of Boscobel Hall, Boscobel, Staffordshire. He had hidden in a secret room the previous night. Charles took the throne on 29th May 1660, and this day was celebrated with all the gusto that the Puritans of Cromwell's Commonwealth had condemned.

The wearing of a sprig of oak on this day indicated one's loyalty to the restored king, and non-wearers were likely to be set upon. Children challenged others to reveal their oak sprig, and if they did not their bottoms would be pinched. Hence this day became known as Pinch-Bum Day. In parts of the country where oak-apples are called shick-shacks the day is called Shick-Shack Day. It may well be that the royal associations with this day hide a tradition of tree-worship that is very much older. Beer is drunk and **Plum Puddings** *(see p.186 for recipe)* are eaten at the Royal Hospital in Chelsea, founded by Charles II on this day.

� Royal Oak Day, Royal Chelsea Hospital, Hospital Road   **London**

The Founder's Day Parade of Chelsea Pensioners marks the founding of this hospital for old and wounded soldiers by Charles II in 1682. They cover the statue of Charles II with oak greenery, and wear oak leaves on their uniforms.

THE HOSPITAL IS JUST NORTH OF CHELSEA BRIDGE.

✾ Oak Apple Day Celebrations, Lord Leycester Hospital   **Warwick**

WARWICK IS BETWEEN STRATFORD-UPON-AVON AND LEAMINGTON SPA.

✾ Oak Apple Day Celebrations, Guildhall, Worcester   **Hereford and Worcester**

WORCESTER IS ON THE A44.

🌳 Garland Day, Castleton   **Derbyshire**

The crowning of the Garland King, reminiscent of Jack-in-the-Green, is an ancient and unique ceremony. The procession starts at 6pm. He, on horseback, wears a wooden bell-shaped frame decorated with leaves and flowers, followed by the Queen – both in Stuart costume, a silver band and girl dancers dressed in white. At St Edmund's Church about 9pm the garland is hauled to the tower's highest point, and the girls do the Castleton Morris dance by the maypole in the market place to the music of the band. The King lays the Queen's bouquet at the War Memorial.

TAKE THE A625 EAST OUT OF CHAPEL-EN-LE-FRITH.

🏛 Preservation of Wood-Cutting Rights in Grovely Forest,
Wishford Magna, Salisbury   **Wiltshire**

The procession to Grovely Forest takes place at first light accompanied by the sound of horns. Branches of oak are collected; those with many oak-apples are particularly sought after. Four women then lead a small group to Salisbury Cathedral to present oak branches and firewood to the Dean at 10am.

At noon there is a procession to the church tower where an oak bough is hoisted. It is called the 'Marriage Bough' and is thought to bring fecundity to couples married at the church during the coming year.

TAKE THE A36 NORTH OUT OF WILTON, THEN LEFT TO WISHFORD MAGNA.

🌳 Arbor Day, Aston-on-Clun, near Ludlow   **Shropshire**

A large black poplar in the village is dressed with flags attached to long poles, to remain until the following year. The custom was certainly in force in the late 1780s when local squire John Marston married Mary Carter, but it may also hearken back to the time when local childless women decorated the tree in honour of the Fertility Goddess Bride. Carrying twigs from the tree was thought to aid fertility. Many Carter's descendants continued to give money to support the custom until her estate was sold in 1951, the local parish providing funds thereafter.

TAKE THE A49 NORTH WEST OUT OF LUDLOW, THEN LEFT ON THE B4368.

Laying a wreath on Charles II's statue, All Saints Church — **Northampton**

The garland of oak-apples is laid at noon, originally as a tribute to Charles II who provided the wood to rebuild the town after it burnt down in 1675.

NORTHAMPTON IS AT THE JUNCTION OF THE A43 AND A428.

The Saturday nearest 29th May

Commemoration of the Battle of Neville's Cross, Durham Cathedral — **Durham**

An anthem is sung from each of three sides of the tower to commemorate this battle, which was actually fought between David II of Scotland and Edward III of England on 17th October 1346 ! The west side is not used as a mark of respect for a chorister who once fell from there.

TAKE THE A177 NORTH FROM DARLINGTON.

The Hearts of Oak Friendly Society Club Walk, Fownhope, near Hereford — **Hereford and Worcester**

Members of this society carry staffs decorated with oak-apples when they go on this annual walk.

TAKE THE B4424 SOUTH EAST OUT OF HEREFORD.

Langport and Huish Episcopi Club Walk, near Taunton — **Somerset**

TAKE THE A358 SOUTH EAST OUT OF TAUNTON, THEN LEFT ON THE A378.

30th May St Walstan's Day, St Hubert's Day

St Walstan was a farm labourer in 11th-century Norfolk, though of noble birth. The water from his well at Bawburgh is reputed to have curative powers, particularly for cattle.

St Hubert was a former Bishop of Maastricht in Holland.

Charles Dickens Festival, Rochester — **Kent**

This festival lasts for four days and celebrates the strong associations of Charles Dickens with the town and its environs. Visitors are invited to dress in mid-19th century clothes and to join in the many costumed characters to be seen around the festival. The City of Rochester Society organises a traditional craft fair and walking tours.

ROCHESTER IS ON THE NORTH KENT COAST ON THE A2.

Royal Oak Day, Chelsea Hospital, London 1960

A revival of Oak Apple Day, Hertfordshire, 1967

Whitsuntide Customs

Whitsuntide, or just Whit, starts seven weeks after Easter Sunday. It is the week from Whit Sunday until the day before Trinity Sunday. In earlier times, after the devotions of Whit Sunday, the week took on a holiday atmosphere and featured sport, games (e.g. skipping, handball, foot races, cheese-rolling, bagatelle, archery, wrestling, tug-o'-war, cudgelling, climbing a greased pole for a leg-of-mutton prize), merrymaking, Morris dancing, Mystery and Miracle plays (such as the famous Chester Plays), biblical dramas and special foods. At Bury St Edmunds, Suffolk women played trap, bat and ball, a game similar to knurr and spell. Fairs, fetes, pageants, horse parades and carnivals were also held in Whit week. Fairings (packets of sugared almonds, gingerbread and the like) were sold to young men for their sweethearts. Large fairs included the Corby Pole Fair (still held every 20 years), the Whitsuntide Fair at Truro, Cornwall, and the Whit Fair, Manningtree, Essex where a whole ox was roasted.

Whit Walks, particularly popular on Whit Friday, may have originally been Rogationtide Beating-the-Bounds ceremonies, but were adopted by Friendly Societies and promoted as healthy activities. Large numbers used to participate in Manchester and Salford. The Friendly Societies also ran Sick Clubs, to which members contributed in case illness befell one of them, and organised Club Feasts. These were a type of insurance company. These were strictly teetotal, and may have been deliberately promoted to oust the popular, but raucous, Whitsun Ale festivities. The North of England galas with their processions and banners built on these traditions.

Birch branches, flowers, rushes, cheesecakes (not the modern sort but curd tarts made from egg, sugar, fruit, rum and beastlings or colostrom), **Banbury Cakes** *(see p.186 for recipe)*, Top Cakes (topping of egg white and sugar), gooseberry pudding, roast veal, pikelets, home-cured ham, bread, and tea with thick cream or rum are all associated with Whit.

Many Whit celebrations have been moved to the Late Spring Bank Holiday at the end of May.

Trap, Bat and Ball *This game probably originated in Suffolk, and is played by two teams (of even number up to 20) on a pitch 21 yd (19.2m) long and 13 ft 6 in (4m) wide. One team bats, the other fields, as in cricket. A batter, using a bat like a table-tennis bat, stands at one end of the field and the ball is projected upwards from the trap, which has a see-saw mechanism. The ball is struck with the bat, in an attempt to get it between two 7ft (2m) high white posts at the other end of the grass pitch. This makes an unconfirmed run. Then, the bowler, from between the posts, bowls underarm to try to hit the small white flap at the front of the trap with the ball. If successful the batter is out, if not the run is con-*

firmed. In another variation, if the ball travels past distance markers, points are scored. A batter is out if the ball is caught, or is missed three times, or if a fielder throws the ball and hits the trap.

Bagatelle *Similar in principle to billiards, bagatelle is played on a table with a slate bed covered with green cloth. Balls are struck with a cue, as in billiards. In the bed are nine indentations, numbered 1 to 9, one in the centre and eight in a circle around it. Just below the indentations is the spot for the black ball and at the near end of the table another spot for the striking ball. There are four white striking balls and 4 red, each player having turns with all eight balls. The object is to strike the black so that both striking ball and black land in indentations and score points. Black scores double and a game is 120 points. If the black is missed, or the striking ball rebounds back beyond the halfway mark, then that striking ball is removed from the table for that turn.*

Variable Dates

The Pole Fair, Corby   Northamptonshire

This takes place every 20 years; the next is due in 2002. The roads leading to the fair are manned so that no one passes without paying. Any man refusing to do so is hoisted on to a pole and taken to the stocks. Women are taken in a chair. These may be the only stocks still in use anywhere in England.

CORBY IS ON THE A6003 NORTH OUT OF KETTERING, AT THE JUNCTION WITH THE A427.

The Wednesday before Whit Monday
(and Wednesday nine days after the Summer Bank Holiday)

Swearing on the Horns, Old Wrestlers Tavern, North Road, Highgate   London

It is said that this custom began as a protection racket, when giving money and swearing allegiance to the horn-bearers was protection against further interference. Nowadays the oaths are light-hearted and oath-takers receive a certificate from the mock judge naming them as a 'Freeman of Highgate', the money going to charity. This used to be held every May and September.

NORTH ROAD IS THE B519, JUST OFF THE JUNCTION OF THE A1 AND THE A1000.

In the stocks at Corby Pole Fair, Northamptonshire

Whit Saturday

✤ Well Dressing, Wirksworth **Derbyshire**

Wirksworth, a small market and limestone quarrying town, once the most important lead mining centre in Derbyshire, has nine wells, which need a large number of natural items to decorate.

FROM ASHBOURNE TAKE THE B5035 NORTH EAST AND EXIT RIGHT AFTER CARSINGTON.

Whit Sunday The 50th day or 7th Sunday after Easter Pentecost

Whit Sunday falls on the same day as the Jewish Feast of Pentecost when Jews celebrate the giving of the Ten Commandments on Mount Sinai. 'Pente' means fifty, as Pentecost is 50 days after Easter. Christians commemorate the descent of the Holy Spirit upon the heads of 3,000 apostles who were baptised on this day and given the gift of tongues. A white dove appeared. Whitsun is so called after the white garments worn by those baptised and confirmed on this day. Open-air services were once common on this day. For indoor services the church would be decorated with greenery and flowers and rushes strewn on the floor. On Whit Walks, religious processions, the tradition of wearing white is kept alive. Chapels in the North of England in the past used to organise Whit Treats for Sunday Schools.

The Whitsun-Ale was a feast for parishioners organised by the church, followed by dancing and sports. The improving weather was and encouragement to hold the festivities outdoors, there being a lack of large buildings in which to hold such parish events and a risk of fire in those such as barns which did exist. Sometimes a Lord and Lady of the Ale were elected. Apart from their own brewed ale the churches served special cakes and buns, cheesecake and baked custard. The Whitsun-Ale festivities traditionally oblige men to do women favours or give them treats. They had the character of May festivals, but also included music and dancing, sports and games, Miracle Plays and organised hunts. Money raised went to the upkeep of the church buildings.

Children born on this day were thought likely to die very soon, hence the practise of putting the baby through a mock burial a few days later, and resurrecting it, changing to the new 'birthday', so that the baby would not be known as a Whitsun baby.

The traditional Whit Sunday meal is roast duckling and peas followed by **Gooseberry Pie** (see p.186 for recipe), tart or pudding.

Rush Sunday, St Mary Redcliffe Church, Bristol · Avon

The nave is carpeted with rushes, and the rest of the church decorated with flowers, for this morning's service in the presence of the Mayor.

BRISTOL CAN BE REACHED ON THE M4 AND M5.

Scrambling for Bread and Cheese, St Briavels, Forest of Dean · Gloucestershire

After the evening service a dole of bread and cheese is distributed from the church wall by a forester. This tradition is thought to have started when the Earl of Hereford removed the ancient right of the villagers to take wood from the forest. The Earl's wife pleaded for the right to be reinstated, and the Earl agreed on condition that she was willing to ride around the area to which the right applied – naked.

To the Earl's surprise she accepted the condition and rode naked around an area now known as the Hudnalls, where the villagers can gather wood to this day. In recognition of her sacrifice the villagers instituted a collection of a penny a year from each for the poor, later to be replaced by the bread – and – cheese dole.

TAKE THE B4228 NORTH OUT OF CHEPSTOW.

Whit Monday

This was the most popular day for Whit games and dancing, particularly Morris dancing, but many sides have since moved their performances to the Late Spring Bank Holiday. In Kent the Hooden Horse accompanied the Morris dancers. Syringa, rose, lilac are traditionally used for decorations on this day.

Morris Dance Festival, Thaxted · Essex

This is the traditional date for this festival, but in recent years it has been held on the last weekend in May. The local Morris side acts as host and organises dance tours for visiting sides around the immediate area.

TAKE THE B184 SOUTH EAST FROM SAFFRON WALDEN.

Bampton Morris, Bampton-in-the-Bush · Oxfordshire

This traditional date may be moved permanently to Spring Bank Holiday Monday, so popular is this; the only festival to have an unbroken history. There are three local sides. A cake impaled on a sword is carried round, and to take and eat a piece is to invite good luck.

TAKE THE A4095 SOUTH WEST FROM WITNEY.

Headington Quarry Morris, Headington · Oxfordshire

This side was formerly composed of quarry-men and builders, and they have a tradition of performing a mummers' play and of sword-dancing as well as Morris dancing.

HEADINGTON IS ON THE A40 ON THE NORTH EAST EDGE OF OXFORD.

Ancient Fair, St Ives · Cambridgeshire

The character granting the fair is actually older than the town, it being granted by Henry I in 1110 to St Benedict of Ramsey and St Ive of Slepe. The town grew up around the fair, which became one of the largest in the country by the 13th Century, lasting the 40 days before Pentecost. Now it lasts just one day.

ST IVES IS ON THE A1123 EAST OF HUNTINGDON.

Anglican Whit Walk · Manchester

There are Whit Walks in several locations throughout the city, originally these were Sunday School outings where the children adorned their white clothes with fresh flowers and carried colourful banners.

Anglican Whit Walk, Salford · Greater Manchester

SALFORD IS ON THE WESTERN EDGE OF MANCHESTER, ON THE A57.

🏛 Flitch of Bacon Trial, Great Dunmow

Essex

This takes place every leap year, on Whit Monday or on a Saturday in late June. Each year a husband and wife can claim a flitch of bacon if they can prove that they have not quarrelled since the day of their marriage. A mock court cross-examines the couples, in a custom thought to have originated in the 13th century.

A similar event took place in Little Dunmow in and before 1751, and also in Saffron Walden and Ilford, all in Essex. A Flitch Trial at the manor house in Wychnor, near Burton-upon-Trent, Staffordshire, where a layman had to convince the court he was happily married, or a priest convince of his devotion to his religious duties, appears never to have resulted in the award of a flitch! A wooden flitch still hangs in the manor hall to represent the unclaimed award.

The original date for the Trial was the first Monday in August, every second year. One was last held in 1955.

GREAT DUNMOW IS ON THE A120 EAST OF BISHOP'S STORTFORD.

🏛 Selling of the Keep of the Wether, The Nag's Head, Enderby

Leicestershire

'Keep' means 'hay crop', from a field called the Wether, which is auctioned by a custom established by John of Gaunt in about 1380. A silver coin is passed from hand to hand, and the only person who can bid is the one holding it. The money raised goes towards a celebration dinner.

TAKE THE B4114 SOUTH WEST FROM LEICESTER, THEN RIGHT ON THE B582.

✠ Pilgrimage to the Shrine of Our Lady of Walsingham, Little Walsingham

Norfolk

The wells are reputed to have healing properties. The shrine was founded in the 11th century, and has been a place of pilgrimage since medieval times.

TAKE THE B1105 NORTH FROM FAKENHAM.

Whit Tuesday

☺ Dicing for Bibles, St Ives

Cambridgeshire

In 1675 Dr Robert Wilde, a Puritan, left £50 in his will to purchase a piece of land whose generated income should be for the purchase of Bibles, which were to go to the winners of a game of dice, to be rolled on the altar. The land became known as the Bible Orchard. Every Whit Tuesday evening at the local church six girls and six boys go dicing for Bibles, but now on a table, not the altar. In 1880 the Bishop of the diocese insisted that the altar could not be used to roll dice, so a table was placed in the aisle. The participants, supervised by the vicar, are now six church of England and six non-conformist children, which perhaps would explain not having met with the approval of the Puritan founder of the charity.

ST IVES IS ON THE A1123 EAST OF HUNTINGDON.

Whit Friday

This was the most popular day for Whitsun walking, which may have developed from boundary walking.

✠ Whit Walk and Brass Band Contest, Saddleworth Moor   Greater Manchester

After the walk comes the Brass Band Contest, held in the evening.

THE A635 RUNS THROUGH THE MOOR.

The Saturday after Whitsun

✠ Scuttlebrook Wake, Chipping Campden   Gloucestershire

This was once a very boisterous and noisy celebration but it is now a more gentile affair. At 2.30pm Morris Men pull a cart through the town (the brook now runs through culverts under the High Street) on which rides the May Queen attendants and page. The May Queen is crowned in the town square, and then there is maypole dancing and performances by Morris sides.+

TAKE THE B4035 EAST FROM EVESHAM.

The Second Saturday after Whitsun

🎧 May Celebrations, Wellow, near Ollerton   Nottinghamshire

WELLOW IS JUST SOUTH OF OLLERTON ON THE A616.

Whit Friday celebrations at Saddleworth, Manchester

Trinity Customs

Trinity is the 8th Sunday after Easter Sunday, the first after Whitsun, and the following Monday. Few Trinity traditions survive, and even fewer actually still held on their original date. Southwold Trinity Fair, Suffolk, has moved to the first Monday in June. Trinity customs survived longest in Oxfordshire as the Oxfordshire Lamb Ales, with a remnant still to be seen at the Trinity Monday Fair at Kirtlington.

Variable Dates

Trinity Sunday The 1st Sunday after Pentecost,
The 57th day after Easter, The 8th Sunday after Easter

Christians celebrate the mystery of the Holy Trinity, and Mystery Plays were often staged. It was customary in some parts to dress the pews of the local church with hay on Trinity Sunday. The last surviving examples were probably at Shenington, Oxfordshire and Clee-in-Grimsby, Humberside.

Stuffed chine-and-bread pudding made with currants, as well as fruit peel, suet, eggs and milk were traditionally eaten, also cheese cakes.

Trinity Monday

✹ Trinity Monday Fair, Kirtlington   Oxfordshire

In former times there were three ceremonies called the Oxfordshire Lamb Ales, at Kirtlington, Eynsham and Kidlington, where a lamb was ceremoniously paraded through the streets, subjected to a chase and other indignities, then slaughtered and paraded again on a pole. It would be eaten the following day, being made into mutton pies, the head, unfleeced, going into a Head Pie, whose portions were prized as good luck talismans. A Bower was erected of a framework covered in greenery, symbolising the Trinity. Nowadays only traditional fairground activities are engaged in. In nearby Kidlington, whose celebrations have lapsed, young girls had their hands tied behind their backs, by the thumbs, and chased a lamb, trying to catch it with their teeth. The hapless animal was then slaughtered, defleeced and paraded on a pole, to be eaten the following day.

KIRTLINGTON IS BETWEEN WITNEY AND BICESTER ON THE A4095.

Corpus Christi customs

Variable Dates

Corpus Christi The Thursday after Trinity Sunday

Corpus Christi is the Thursday after Trinity Sunday when Christians celebrate the presence of Christ in the bread and wine of the Eucharist, and the doctrine of transubstantiation. 'Corpus Christi' means 'the body of Christ'.

In times past the Host was borne in stately procession through the streets, and biblical dramas (elaborate Miracle or Mystery Plays) were performed by guilds from high partitioned carts called *pagiante* (hence pageant) in the wealthy religious centres like Chester, York, Wakefield, Coventry and Durham. Miracle Plays and Mystery Plays are one and the same thing. They were performed by Town Guilds, and featured the whole biblical cycle from Creation to Doomsday. 'Mystery' means 'Trade', and each trade guild was responsible for one scene or act. Comedy and rhyming couplets were used to popularise the presentation. Chester, York, Wakefield and Coventry still stage the plays, but no longer at Corpus Christi, and not each year.

Corpus Christi fairs were held in many parts, of which the best known was at Coventry, with its remembrance of Lady Godiva's famous naked ride through Coventry market. Godgifu was the wife of an 11th-century Earl named Leofric, who brutalised and overtaxed his subjects. Godgifu pleaded with him to be merciful, and his response was to agree on condition that she make the ride for which she has been remembered ever since.

The Corpus Christi carol is no longer sung, and the extensive celebrations still to be seen today in Catholic countries have long since disappeared in England.

Election of Master of the Skinners' Company and procession from Skinners' Hall in Dowgate Hill to the Church of St Mary Aldermary, Queen Victoria Street London

DOWGATE HILL IS BY THE SIDE OF CANNON STREET STATION.

The procession is led by boys from Christ's Hospital School, including those awarded scholarships by the Company, and includes the newly-elected Master, Clerk, two Beadles and members of the Court of the Company. All carry posies, originally as an attempt to mask the foul stench of the streets.

June customs

Outdoor activities, work and play, dominate June, the lightest month in England. There were many fairs, particularly horse fairs. June was when sheep-shearing took place – the end being marked by much celebration by the shearers. Another trade was marling, the excavation from pits of a soft alkaline clay soil called 'marl', which was spread over agricultural land. When the season ended, or a the pit was exhausted, it was decorated with flowers and greenery and celebrations followed.

Hay-making began in mid-June, both on owned land and on land for which seasonal bids were made at auctions or lots were drawn, signalling the gradual turning of the agricultural season as Midsummer, with its bonfires and celebrations, approached. This was a time like May Day when folk memories dictated custom, as trees were decorated and anointed, people leapt through flames to purify themselves, and minds were put to telling fortunes and seeking signs about future events.

Churches and social clubs held walks in June, and it was also a time for well-dressing, church-clipping and rush-bearing/hay-strewing to renew traditional floor coverings in churches. Athletic competitions, such as running, leaping, sack races and archery were popular. There were also fun events, including whistling competitions (for the clearest whistler, and for the whistler who could keep going when others tried to make him/her laugh), Jingling and Catching the Pig's (greased) Tail.

Jingling *Players collect in a large roped-off circle. All are blindfolded except the catcher, or Jingler, who carries a bell in each hand to advertise his position to the others. The blindfolded players chase the Jingler, who tries to evade capture for a specified time.*

At the end of June the tanneries closed at the end of their season of bark stripping and processing. This would be marked with feasting and festivities, such as at the Tanbark Festival at Cricklade, Wiltshire at which a Mummers' Play was performed. At the end of the cherry-growing season, towards the end of the month, there were festivities and fairs.

Variable Dates

The Bideford Bridge Foot Race   Devon
This takes place early in the month. Competitors try to run across the bridge over the River Torridge before the church clock strikes 8.
TAKE THE A39 WEST OUT OF BARNSTAPLE.

⊚ Town Criers' Competition, Pewsey, near Marlborough   **Wiltshire**
TAKE THE A345 SOUTH OUT OF MARLBOROUGH.

✸ Belton Horse Fair, near Loughborough   **Leicestershire**
TAKE THE A6 NORTH OUT OF LOUGHBOROUGH, THEN LEFT ON THE B5324.

✹ The York Mystery Plays   **York**
These are held as part of the city's Arts Festival every three or four years (due 1999, 2002, etc).
YORK IS AT THE JUNCTION OF THE A19 AND A64.

✹ Morris Dancing, Abingdon   **Oxfordshire**
TAKE THE A34 SOUTH OUT OF OXFORD.

Fixed Dates

1st June St Wistan's Day, St Wite's Day

St Wistan was a 9th-century Saxon prince who was murdered by his cousin for his religious opposition to his cousin's incestuous intentions towards his widowed mother, the Queen of Mercia.

St Wite's tomb is in Whitchurch Canonicorum church in Dorset, but nothing is known about her for certain. An offering of cake and cheese at this tomb is made by those seeking relief from their afflictions.

❂ Duck Feast, Charlton   **Wiltshire**
This feast is in honour of Stephen Duck, former Keeper of the Queen's Library to Caroline, wife of George II. He allegedly committed suicide by jumping into the Thames in 1756 because of the stress caused by accusations of an affair with Queen Caroline. It is also alleged that Lord Palmerston was his friend, and that it was he who gave land in trust for an annual memorial feast, held at The Cat public house.
TAKE THE A342 WEST FROM UPAVON.

2nd June St Elmo's Day

Little is known for certain about St Elmo, who gave his name to St Elmo's Fire, the glow resulting from the electrical discharges seen on ships' mastheads or around church steeples during a storm.

The first Monday in June

✸ Trinity Fair, Southwold   **Suffolk**
This three-day fair formerly started on Trinity Sunday, and is known from as far back as 1489. In the morning the Mayor of the town visits Southwold Primary School to give the children Trinity Money, and then opens the fair.
TAKE THE A12 NORTH OUT OF SAXMUNDHAM, THEN RIGHT ON THE A1095.

4th June St Petroc's Day

St Petroc was a 6th-century Cornishman who founded the monasteries at both Padstow and Little Petherick.

5th June St Boniface's Day

St Boniface was born Winfrith in Crediton, Devon in AD 675. He wrote the earliest known Latin Grammar, and became a missionary in Europe, where he was murdered in D 754.

The first Thursday in June

❂ Neston Women's Club Walk, Wirral   **Cheshire**
TAKE THE A540 NORTH WEST OUT OF CHESTER, THEN LEFT ON TO THE B5135 TO NESTON.

The first Friday in June

❀ **Sick Club Procession, Stoke Abbott** **Dorset**

Skittles, shove-ha'penny and other sports are played.

TAKE THE A3066 NORTH OUT OF BRIDPORT, LEFT ON TO THE B3163 AT BEAMINSTER,
THEN LEFT ON AN UNCLASSIFIED ROAD TO STOKE ABBOTT.

Shove Ha'penny *The ha'penny, or halfpenny was a coin in the old currency, although the game is often played with metal disks of the same size. The board is a rectangle of hardwood (24 in [61cm] by 14 1⁄2 in [37cm[) covered with slate, squared at the playing end and semi-circular at the other. Across the board are marked lines 1 1⁄4 in (3cm) apart dividing the board into nine beds. Along each long side is a strip 1 1⁄4 in (3cm) wide for marking with chalk the positions of disks which are slid along the board. This is a game of skill and co-ordination. Each player has five disks. A disk is placed so that it overlaps the starting edge, and it is struck with the palm or the ball of the thumb so that it ends up in a bed. Opponents' disks may be moved by one's own disk. The object is to try and fill beds, which can be done in any order. A bed with three of a player's disks claims it for that player, and any opposing disks are also credited to that player. A game is called a 'horse', and a match is the best of three horses.*

The first Saturday in June

❀ **Chawleigh Friendly Society Club Walk, Chawleigh, near Molton** **Devon**

This begins at 11:30am at the Royal Oak Inn. The Society began in 1869 and is still functioning.
TAKE THE A377 NORTH WEST OUT OF EXETER, THEN RIGHT ON TO THE B3042.

The Thursday before the 2nd Wednesday in June

✿ **Appleby Horse Fair, Appleby** **Cumbria**

This is the largest traditional horse fair remaining, and the largest annual gypsy gathering in the country. Licensed by James II in 1685, the horse preparation and trading takes place on four sites: The River Eden where the horses for sale are washed; Long Marton where the fairgoers camp; Fair Hill where the bartering takes place; and Holme Fair Meadow where horses are raced and bet on.
TAKE THE A66 EAST OUT OF PENRITH.

7th June St Meriasek's Day, St Colman's Day

St Meriasek was a 6th-century Cornish saint, whose protection was traditionally sought by tin miners. St Colman was from Ulster.

8th June St William's Day

St William was the nephew of King Stephen and an Archbishop of York in the 12th century.

9th June St Columba's Day

St Columba was the Irish missionary who established the first monastery on the Scottish island of Iona in the 6th century.

May Day Festivities, Shillingstone   Dorset

SHILLINGSTONE IS ON THE A357 NORTH WEST OUT OF BLANDFORD FORUM.

11th June St Barnabas' Day, Feast Day

St Barnabas lived in the 1st century. He is often shown in medieval art carrying a hay-rake, as today is the traditional day on which hay-making (Haysel) begins.

Before the calendar change this was the longest day of the year. Garlands of sweet-scented flowers were made on this day to decorate homes and church.

Old St Barnaby Fair, Macclesfield   Cheshire

MACCLESFIELD IS AT THE JUNCTION OF THE A537 AND THE A523, DUE WEST OF BUXTON.

13th June St Anthony's Day

St Anthony was a lay preacher who lived in the 13th century in Padua, Italy.

The second Saturday in June

Trooping the Colour, Horse Guards' Parade   London

This parade, on the monarch's official birthday, was first held in 1755, and has happened regularly since 1805. Its original purpose was to ensure that troops regarded the colours around which they should rally in battle. It is done by one of the five regiments of Foot Guards, the Grenadier, Coldstream, Scots, Irish and Welsh Guards. The Queen now takes the salute in a phaeton. (The two mounted regiments of the Household Cavalry are the Life Guards and the Blues and Royals.)

HORSE GUARDS' PARADE IS ON THE WESTERN SIDE OF ST JAMES'S PARK.

Trooping the Colour rehearsal, Horse Guard's Parade, London

15th June St Vitus and Companions' Day

St Vitus lived in the 4th century. He has become associated with the nervous condition St Vitus' Dance (Sydenham's Chorea). On the day he was martyred two others met a similar fate, Crescentia and Modestus.

17th June St Nectan's Day, St Botolph's Day

St Nectan was a 6th-century Devonian. St Botolph came from Boston (Botolph's Town) in Lincolnshire.

St Nectan's Procession, St Nectan's Well, Hartland Point   Devon

It is said that when St Nectan was murdered he carried his head across the Point and dropped it in the well, spilling blood which caused foxgloves to spring up. To mark the day Mass is held at the well and a procession of children carrying foxgloves walks the traditional route.

HARTLAND POINT FACES THE ISLE OF LUNDY IN THE BRISTOL CHANNEL.

18th June Waterloo Day

The Duke of Wellington's Quit Rent, Stratfield Saye Manor, near Basingstoke   Hampshire

To keep his manor, the Duke must pay a Quit Rent of one tricolour flag to the reigning monarch on this day before noon. The flag is a replica of the one captured at Waterloo in 1815, and it is, after the presentation, displayed above the Duke's bust in the Guard Room at Windsor Castle, Berkshire. In the evening is a banquet in the Waterloo Chamber, by special invitation only, in honour of the victory. The chamber is decorated in the Duke's military colours of blue and yellow.

TAKE THE A33 NORTH EAST OUT OF BASINGSTOKE, THEN LEFT AT RISELEY ON AN UNCLASSIFIED ROAD.

19th June Feast of St Edmund

Saturday on or before 20th June (some say 19th June, the Feast of St Edmund)

Election of the Morris Mayor of Ock Street, Abingdon   Oxfordshire

The residents of Ock Street vote for one of the local Morris side to be Mayor or Squire of the side for the year. The result is given at 4pm.

Ox horns and roast ox are associated with the ceremonial ever since the Squire of the side won a pair of ox horns after a dispute at the local fair in 1700, where traditionally an ox was roasted.

TAKE THE A34 SOUTH OUT OF OXFORD.

Right: The Mayor of Ock Street, Abingdon, Oxfordshire
Far right: The Abingdon Morris Dancers with the Mayor of Ock Street

20th June St Alban's Day, St Govan's Day

St Alban was the first Celtic Christian martyr, having been put to death at Holmeshurst Hill, Verulamium, north of London under the orders of Diocletian at the beginning of the 4th century because he renounced Roman Gods.

St Govan, who lived on St Govan's Head in Dyved, Wales, is said to be one and the same as Sir Gawain of King Arthur's Round Table.

✪ Rose Service, St Alban's Cathedral, St Alban's   Hertfordshire

Children offer roses at the saint's shrine, and after being blessed the roses are scattered on the floor. This is said to represent the opening of rose buds on Holmeshurst Hill at this time when St Alban was murdered.

ST ALBAN'S IS BETWEEN HEMEL HEMPSTEAD AND HATFIELD ON THE A1057.

The Saturday before the longest day (usually the third Saturday in June)

✪ Bawming the Thorn, Appleton Thorn, near Warrington   Cheshire

'Bawming' means 'anointing' or 'decorating'. This ceremony has been moved from 5th July, Old Midsummer Day. The hawthorn tree in the village is honoured by decorating it with ribbons and garlands. A procession and gala follows. This is essentially a May rite with its roots in tree worship. The original thorn tree is said to have been a cutting of the Glastonbury Thorn.

APPLETON THORN IS JUST OFF JUNCTION 20 OF THE M6, WEST ON THE B5356.

The Sunday nearest 20th June

✪ Commemoration Service, All Saints' Church, Steetley Chapel, near Worksop   Nottinghamshire

This service commemorates the restoration in 1880 of the former chapel as a church after it fell into disuse when most of the village population was wiped out by the Black Death. The service starts at 3:15pm.

THE CHAPEL IS OFF THE A619 ONE AND A HALF MILES WEST OF WORKSOP.

21st June The Summer Solstice

Astronomically this is the day that the sun climbs highest in the sky and shines for longest, but midsummer day is traditionally the 24th June. Groups calling themselves Druids regularly try to gain access to Stonehenge in Wiltshire to perform at dawn what they claim are ancient rituals, but there is no evidence that these are in any way authentic (in contrast to the Beltane Festival at Peebles, Borders, in Scotland).

22nd June St Thomas More's Day, Old St Barnabas' Day

St Thomas More was a Catholic martyr who was executed in 1535 by order of Henry VIII for refusing to recognise the King's authority over the Church.

At the St Barnabas Horse Fair in Boroughbridge, North Yorkshire, a favourite with the crowds was Barnaby Tart, which was a lemon-curd tart.

✪ Coin Throwing, Midsummer Fair   Cambridge

LEAVE THE M11 AT JUNCTIONS 11, 12, 13 AND 14 FOR ROADS INTO CAMBRIDGE.

23rd June Midsummer Eve, St John's Eve

Many surviving customs have their origins in ancient sun worship and purification rites. Bonfires are lit in memory of the Druid Baal fires. Children join hands and leap through the embers to symbolise growth of corn and harvest abundance. Farmers drove their animals through the embers to protect them from disease. Ancient druidic divination practices survive in midsummer rites such as sowing hempseed in the churchyard at midnight, dropping melted lead into water, and sticking a black velvet cushion full of pins then hanging it at night in a right-foot stocking – all for the

purpose of glimpsing one's future mate. Rural people associated the night with superstitious belief in fairies, spirits and ghosts of the past. A garland of St John's Wort, picked at dawn, and fixed to the door will protect the household from fairies. The Federation of Old Cornwall Societies lights a chain of bonfires across the county, and children leap through the flames for luck, a survival of an ancient purification rite. The remarkable custom of Rolling the Cartwheel down Mel Tor, by villagers from Leusdon, Devon unfortunately ceased in the 1960s.

As on St Mark's Eve (24th April) it was thought that divination ceremonies tonight could reveal who would soon die.

Well-dressing, Buxton   Derbyshire
TAKE THE A6 NORTH WEST FROM MATLOCK.

Haxey Hood Game Elections, Haxey, Isle of Axholme   Lincolnshire
The King Boggon and committee of 12 are elected to prepare for the game on Plough Monday.
HAXEY LIES BETWEEN GOOLE AND GAINSBOROUGH ON THE B1396, JUST OFF THE A161

St Cleer Bonfire, Liskeard   Cornwall
This fire is crowned with a broomstick and is lit to keep witches away for the year. A sickle with a newly cut oak handle is thrown into the flames to ensure fertility for farmers and fields alike.
TAKE THE A38 WEST OUT OF LISKEARD.

Lighting the first Midsummer Bonfire, Carn Brea   Cornwall
Carn Brea is a granite tor between Camborne and Redruth, and is the signal for the others to be lit in a chain through Sennen, Sancreed Beacon, Carn Galver, St Agnes Beacon, St Cleer to the River Tamar. Each fire is blessed by a local clergyman in the Cornish language, and herbs and wild flowers are burnt. People leap across the embers for good luck and to drive away evil.
CARN BREA IS JUST TO THE SOUTH WEST OF REDRUTH ON AN UNCLASSIFIED ROAD.

The Saturday before the Saturday nearest 24th June

Well-dressing, Ashford-in-the-Water   Derbyshire
TAKE THE A6 EAST FROM BUXTON.

24th June Midsummer Day, Nativity of St John the Baptist

The prophet St John preached in the wilderness of Judaea and baptised his converts in the River Jordan. This day has always been a time of outdoor celebration. The exterior of the house is decorated with greenery, fires are lit and men jump through the flames for good luck, a vestige of ancient purification rites which often involved fire. The ashes of the midsummer fire are used to tell fortunes and foretell the future. All stay up beyond midnight.

The devil is said to appear if you run backwards seven times round Chanctonbury Ring, Steyning, West Sussex at midnight.

Cornish tin miners always had a holiday today.

The wildflower St John's wort, or chase-devil, was traditionally picked on Midsummer Day as it was believed to protect from evil and cure many ailments. In some areas rowan had similar beliefs attached.

St John the Baptist's birthday was moved to this date from January, and a few bits of folklore and Christmas tradition were moved with it; hence the ass's head worn by Bottom the Weaver in A *Midsummer Night's Dream*. St John's Day was always associated with water and many communities celebrated this day by dressing their wells.

Midsummer Day was a Quarter Day.

In Dartmoor, Devon there was a tradition of erecting platforms in trees and dancing on them, a remnant of ancient tree worship, perhaps.

Boughton Horse Fair, Northamptonshire began on this day, and lasted until 26th June.

Ceremony of the Fresh-Pluck't Rose, Mansion House   London

A freshly plucked red rose, in commemoration of Sir Robert Knolly's 14th-century fine for building a footbridge between his two houses, across Seething Lane, without permission, is presented to the Lord Mayor of London at the Mansion House by the churchwardens of All Hallows-by-the-Tower. The church stands on the site of one of Knolly's houses.

MANSION HOUSE IS AT THE JUNCTION OF VICTORIA STREET AND CANNON STREET.

Payment of the Rose Rent, The Crown and Thistle   Leicester

Each year the landlord pays the Mayor his annual stipend of four old pence and a damask rose.

LEICESTER IS AT THE JUNCTION OF THE A6 AND A47.

Election of Sheriffs and other officers by the Liverymen of the Guilds,
Common Hall, Guildhall   London

The elections take place in the guilds' own halls and the sheriffs-elect go in procession with the Lord Mayor, other Liverymen and City officers from Mansion House to Guildhall to be presented with their chains of office.

THE GUILDHALL IS JUST OFF GRESHAM STREET (B128)

Midsummer Day Rituals, Stonehenge   Wiltshire

This formerly took place on 21st June, the summer solstice. Enquire first about public access to this historic site.

STONEHENGE IS 2 MILES WEST OF AMESBURY, BETWEEN THE A303 AND A344.

Baschurch Ladies' Club Walk   Shropshire

TAKE THE A5067 NORTH FROM SHREWSBURY TO BASCHURCH.

The Saturday nearest 24th June

Well-dressing, Youlgreave   Derbyshire

TAKE THE A6 NORTH WEST FROM MATLOCK, THEN LEFT ON THE B5056.

Well-dressing, Tideswell   Derbyshire

TAKE THE A6 EAST OUT OF BUXTON, THEN LEFT ON THE B6049.

The Sunday nearest Midsummer Day

⚫ **Flookburgh Fair, Flookburgh, near Grange-over-Sands**   **Cumbria**
This fair grew up around the local fluke-fishing industry.
TAKE THE B5277 WEST FROM GRANGE-OVER-SANDS.

The Sunday following Midsummer Day Wakes Sunday

✋ **Winster Wakes Sunday, Winster, near Matlock**   **Derbyshire**
Wakes Sunday cakes and home-brewed ale or wine are consumed.
TAKE THE A6 NORTH WEST FROM MATLOCK, THEN LEFT ON THE B5057.

25th June St Non's Day

St Non was from Altarnum, Cornwall.

26th June St Anne's Day

The Pershore Fair, Worcestershire was held on this day, after the local harvest of cherries.

28th June St Peter's Day Eve

✠ **Rush-bearing, Barrowden**   **Leicestershire**
TAKE THE A47 WEST FROM PETERBOROUGH, THEN LEFT ON AN UNCLASSIFIED ROAD AFTER TIXOVER.

The Thursday nearest 28th June

⚫ **Jankyn Smith's Charity, St Mary's Church, Bury St Edmunds**   **Suffolk**
On his death on 28th June 1481 Jankyn Smith left money for a Mass on this anniversary and for cakes and ale for the clergy. A sermon is now given in his name in January; the residents of the local almshouses attend, receiving a shilling and refreshments
BURY ST EDMUNDS IS ON THE A45 EAST FROM NEWMARKET.

The last Saturday in June

✠ **Well-dressing, Bakewell**   **Derbyshire**
TAKE THE A6 NORTH WEST FROM MATLOCK.

✠ **Well-dressing, Hope**   **Derbyshire**
TAKE THE A625 WEST FROM SHEFFIELD, PAST HATHERSAGE.

✠ **The Glastonbury Pilgrimage, Glastonbury abbey**   **Somerset**
A procession and services are held in and around the ruins of the Abbey.
TAKE THE A39 SOUTH WEST FROM WELLS TO GLASTONBURY.

The last Saturday in June

▦ **Bromsgrove Court Leet, Bromsgrove**   **Hereford and Worcester**
A Court of ale-tasters, bread-weighers, and other standards officers is presided over by a Balliff.
BROMSGROVE IS AT THE JUNCTION OF THE M5 AND M42 (JUNCTION 4A).

The last weekend in June

⚫ **Bilston Carnival, Hickman Park, Bilston, near Wolverhampton**   **West Midlands**
This wakes was moved from November and retains some of the original features of wakes.
TAKE THE A41 SOUTH EAST FROM WOLVERHAMPTON.

29th June St Peter's and St Paul's Day

St Peter the Apostle reputedly lived and preached in Rome, and is buried in St Peter's Basilica. Hay-strewing of churches was commonly done in the south east Midlands on this day, and the Sunday nearest to it was called Hay Sunday. Unfortunately, the hay-strewing at Braunstone, Leicestershire has ceased. In many places rush-bearing was done, and it is equally regrettable that rush-bearing at Haworth, West Yorkshire is no longer done.

✠ **Rushbearing, Warcop, near Brough**   **Cumbria**

If the 29th is a Sunday this procession and service take place the day before. Girls bear a floral crown, with a wicker frame, and boys bear a cross made of rushes tied with red ribbons. The procession starts in the centre of the village at 2pm; at 3pm service a local rush-bearing hymn is sung.

TAKE THE A66 NORTH WEST FROM BROUGH, THEN LEFT ON AN UNCLASSIFIED ROAD TO WARCOP.

The last Monday in June

❋ **The Plague Feast, Hepworth, near Holmfirth**   **West Yorkshire**

This, with festivities, starts at 2pm to mark the deliverance of survivors the plague in 1665.

HEPWORTH IS SOUTH OF HOLMFIRTH ON THE B6106.

The Sunday following St Peter's Day

✠ **Hay-strewing, St Peter and St Paul's Church, Wingrave, near Aylesbury** **Buckinghamshire**

This custom is still observed, though not as a public ceremony.

TAKE THE A418 NORTH EAST FROM AYLESBURY, THEN RIGHT AFTER ROWSHAM ON AN UNCLASSIFIED ROAD.

✠ **The Rush Sermon, St Giles' Church, Farnborough**   **Kent**

TAKE THE A21 SOUTH FROM BROMLEY, THEN RIGHT ON TO THE B2158.

✠ **Blessing of the Sea, St Peter's Church, Folkestone**   **Kent**

At 3 pm, a service is held at the harbour to bless the fishermen, boats and sea.

FOLKESTONE IS ON THE COAST AT THE END OF THE M20 FROM LONDON.

The Winster Morris Dancers 'Witch' celebrates Wake Sunday, Winster, Derbyshire

July customs

July was a similar month to June in many ways, as the continuing light and clement weather allowed similar agricultural activities to proceed apace. Seasons for various produce would soon be concluded and preparations made for the harvest. At the start of July were many Cherry fairs, marking the end of the picking season, particularly in Hampshire, Hereford and Worcester, and Warwickshire and Hertfordshire. In contrast, the oyster fishing season was just starting.

Fairs, rush-bearing/hay-strewing, church-clipping and well-dressing were still happening somewhere, and also this month saw many open-air services and pilgrimages, though in the latter case one must resist suggesting that the fine weather was more of a factor than the devotional reasons for the journeys.

July sports included cricket; club-ball, a precursor of cricket the rules of which have not survived; stoolball; trap, bat and ball; golf or golf, played with a crooked club (or staff, or bandy); pall-mall; and tennis, which grew out of fives.

Pall-mall *The object of this game is to use a long-handled mallet to drive a ball through a suspended iron hoop in the fewest strikes. The game has superficial similarities to both polo and croquet.*

Variable Dates

Early July

Miracle Plays, Chester   Cheshire

Takes place in early July, every three or five years. The last one was in 1997, but always check first. Miracle Plays are referred to in the section on Corpus Christi customs and those at Chester date from 1422. The single play developed into a 3-day cycle of plays, which like the other city plays, made an important contribution to the development of drama and its use to present religious themes to an illiterate audience.

CHESTER IS AT THE JUNCTION OF THE A55 AND A41.

Gooseberry Fair, Tollesbury   Essex

TOLLESBURY IS ON THE B1023.

John Huntingdon's Pea-picking Charity, Sawston　　　　　　　　　　Cambridgeshire

In his will of 1554 John Huntingdon bequeathed land and money to his wife for the express purpose of planting 2 acres (.80 ha) of white peas, the harvest of which was to be given to the poor.
TAKE THE A10 SOUTH WEST FROM CAMBRIDGE, THEN LEFT ON TO THE A1301.

Mid-July

Well-dressing, Cutthorpe, near Chesterfield　　　　　　　　　　　　Derbyshire
TAKE THE B6051 NORTH WEST FROM CHESTERFIELD, THEN LEFT ON THE B6050.

Well-dressing, Heath, near Chesterfield　　　　　　　　　　　　　　Derbyshire
TAKE THE A617 SOUTH EAST OUT OF CHESTERFIELD, PAST TEMPLE NORMANTON.

Well-dressing, Ault Hucknall, near Chesterfield　　　　　　　　　　Derbyshire
TAKE THE A617 NORTH WEST OUT OF MANSFIELD, THEN LEFT AFTER PLEASLEY.

Well-dressing, Glapwell, near Chesterfield　　　　　　　　　　　　Derbyshire
TAKE THE A617 SOUTH EAST OUT OF CHESTERFIELD, PAST DOE LEA.

Well-dressing, Pilsey, near Bakewell　　　　　　　　　　　　　　　Derbyshire
TAKE THE A619 NORTH OUT OF BAKEWELL, THEN EXIT RIGHT TO PILSEY.

The Tweedmouth Feast, Berwick-on-Tweed　　　　　　　　　　　Northumberland
This event is held on a Thursday. The Tweed is a salmon river and one of the events is the crowning of the Salmon Queen. A local speciality is Salmon Kettles, a dish of locally caught salmon followed by gooseberry tart and a cup of tea. A fair, parades and other events are also held.
BERWICK-ON-TWEED IS ON THE COAST ON THE A1 JUST SOUTH OF THE SCOTTISH BORDER.

Late July

St Anne's Well Pilgrimage, Bristol　　　　　　　　　　　　　　　　　　Avon
BRISTOL CAN BE REACHED ON THE M4 AND M5.

The Coventry Miracle Plays, in the ruins of the old Cathedral　　　　　Coventry
These are held every three years, and are due next in 1999, 2002, etc.
COVENTRY CAN BE REACHED BY DRIVING SOUTH FROM JUNCTIONS 2 OR 3 OF THE M6.

The Venison Warrant Gift, Mansion House　　　　　　　　　　　　　London
The Lord Mayor of London is the recipient, twice a year, of a gift of venison under the terms of the 15th-century Venison Warrant. This started when Dick Whittington lent Henry V money to finance the wars in France, and was so impressed by the victory at Agincourt that he declined repayment. As a gesture of gratitude the King instituted the Venison Warrant, four bucks in July and four does in December.
MANSION HOUSE IS AT THE JUNCTION OF VICTORIA STREET AND CANNON STREET.

Fixed Dates

1st July St Serf's Day

St Serf was a Scottish saint, one of whose pupils, St Mungo or Kentigern, is better known. The huge Cherry fair at Odiham, Hampshire was held on this day to mark the end of the cherry-picking season. The pickers had a reputation for drunkenness and riotous behaviour at this celebration and this led to moves to ban such events in the cherry-growing counties of Hampshire, Hertfordshire, Hereford and Worcester and Warwickshire. These fairs however, have all ceased to take place today.

The first Monday in July

The Lot-meadow Drawing custom at Yarnton, Oxfordshire is now moribund, having survived since Norman times until 1978. Meadows by the River Thames were leased by drawing lots in the form of 13 wooden balls (made of holly wood) on which are inscribed the names of the 11th-century lot-holders. Hay-making no longer takes place here, but the last officials (Meadsmen) retain their titles as they are hereditary, and the balls are preserved.

The Friday nearest 1st July

Walk Day, Warrington   **Cheshire**

WARRINGTON IS AT THE JUNCTION OF THE A56 AND A57.

1st Saturday in July

Bodmin's Heritage Day, Bodmin   **Cornwall**

On the Friday before this day, ale-tasters visit local houses to invite them to taste a locally made ale (made the previous October) and make a donation. On Heritage Day itself the highlight is the Bodmin Ride, when riders carry garlanded poles in procession through the town. This originated as an annual tribute to the monks of St Benet's Priory, Lanivet.

BODMIN IS WEST OF LISKEARD AT THE JUNCTION OF THE A30 AND A38.

Rushbearing, St Theobald's Church, Great Musgrave, near Brough   **Cumbria**

At 2:15pm the procession of children carrying rush crowns leaves the Village Institute for the church.

TAKE THE B6259 NORTH FROM KIRKBY STEPHEN, THEN LEFT TO GREAT MUSGRAVE.

The first or second Saturday in July

Admiralty Court of the City of Rochester, Rochester   **Kent**

Since the 15th century the Mayor of Rochester has also had the title Admiral of the Medway. The court officials (the Admiral, the Aldermen of the City and a jury of Freemen of the river) in their

The custom of selling the grass on Yarnton Meadows, Oxfordshire

regalia meet in a barge off Rochester pier to regulate the oyster fisheries in the River Medway, according to the Act of Parliament of 1729, and to swear in new Bailiffs for the year.
ROCHESTER IS ON THE NORTH KENT COAST ON THE A2.

✢ Rush-bearing, St Mary's Church, Ambleside — Cumbria

The church is strewn with rushes. Wooden frames shaped like crosses, harps and orbs with woven rush designs are carried like standards in a procession. It starts at 2:30pm, and it stops in the Market-place for the singing of a rush-bearing hymn. Afterwards there are refreshments, including local gingerbread, and games.

Rushbearing is most common in the area of Cumbria that was formerly Westmorland, and is usually done by girls dressed in white and adorned with ribbons and flowers.
AMBLESIDE IS ON THE A591 NORTH WEST OF WINDERMERE.

The first Sunday in July

✳ Alport Castles Love Feast, Alport — Cumbria

This takes the form of a secular communion, in which bread and wine are replaced by ordinary refreshments. This is the only surviving love feast pilgrimage in England.
TAKE THE A6 NORTH WEST OUT OF MATLOCK, THEN LEFT ON THE B5056, AND RIGHT ON AN UNCLASSI-FIED ROAD TO ALPORT.

The second Sunday following St Peter's Day

✢ Hay-strewing Ceremony, Glenfield — Leicestershire

TAKE THE A563 NORTH WEST FROM LEICESTER AND GLENFIELD IS ON THE EDGE OF THE CITY.

4th July Old Midsummer Eve, St Martin o' Ballymus' Day

St Martin o' Ballymus was a Scottish saint.

ⓜ Midsummer Bonfire, Whalton, near Morpeth — Northumberland

Such fires (Beltane or Bale fires) were originally lit in honour of the Sun God. This is an exciting occasion involving Northumbrian pipers and other musicians, Morris dancers, Sword dancers and dancing round the bonfire.
TAKE THE B6524 SOUTH WEST FROM MORPETH.

5th July Old Midsummer Day, St Morwenna's Day

St Morwenna was a 7th-century Irish saint who became a hermit in Burton-upon-Trent, Staffordshire. It was believed that childless couples should sacrifice a pig to her.

Vintner's Company Procession, London

The Thursday following the Feast of the Translation of St Martin (4th July)

🚶 Procession of the Worshipful Company of Vintners, City of London   London

The procession goes from the Vintners' Hall in Upper Thames Street to the Church of St James, Garlickhithe. Broom-men, who are wine partners in white smocks and top hats, with besoms to sweep the way clear, and the carrying of nosegays remind us of the stench and rubbish which once characterised London streets. This tradition is at least 700 years old.

UPPER THAMES STREET (B132) GOES FROM BLACKFRIARS STATION TO LONDON BRIDGE.

7th July St Thomas à Becket's Day

After being made Archbishop of Canterbury Becket vigorously defended the rights of the Church against the Crown, and was put to death by order of Henry II in Canterbury Cathedral. Henry VIII had his shrine destroyed and declared that he was no longer to be regarded as a saint. No specific celebrations now occur on this day, which was last celebrated in the Stogumber district of the Quantock Hills, Somerset, the West Country always being a stronghold of his supporters.

The 2nd Wednesday in July

👶 St Peter's Fair and Pretty Maids' Charity, Holsworthy   Devon

In 1841 the Reverend Thomas Meyrick, brother of the rector, left money to be invested in government stock, the interest to go annually to the most worthy, quiet, handsome, regular-church-attending, single, female under 30 years of age. The task of those funding someone who matches this combination of virtues is not to be envied, and the one chosen is concealed in Holsworthy parish church until noon, to emerge from the tower door. She is chosen and kept behind the church doors until noon, when the Portreeve escorts her round St Peter's Fair – which was started at 8am by the Town Crier.

HOLSWORTHY IS BETWEEN BIDEFORD AND LAUNCESTON ON THE A338.

The second Saturday in July

✠ Well-dressing, Dore   South Yorkshire

This village was formerly in Derbyshire, and it has resurrected this tradition each year from 1959 as a way of emphasising the local feeling that in spirit at least, they are in Derbyshires.

DORE IS ON THE A621 SOUTH WEST OF SHEFFIELD.

The Sunday after the 7th July

✻ Kilburn Feast, Kilburn, near Thirsk
North Yorkshire

This local custom lasts four days and has a number of events which take place in the locality. An open-air sermon starts the proceedings; there is a race to the Kilburn White Horse; and the climax is a procession in which a 'Mayor' and 'Mayoress' (actually a man in drag) extort money from the villagers by fining them for completely ridiculous reasons.

TAKE THE A170 EAST FROM THIRSK, THEN RIGHT AFTER SUTTON-UNDER-WHITESTONECLIFFE.

9th July St Everild's Day

St Everild was born in Wessex in the 7th century and eventually founded a nunnery near Ripon, North Yorkshire.

11th July St Benedict's Day

In the 6th century St Benedictine founded the Benedictine order of monks.

13th July St Mildred's Day

St Mildred was the daughter of King Ermenburga of Thanet, Kent. She died in AD 700.

15th July St Swithin's Day

By tradition, whatever the weather on this day, so it will remain for 40 days. St Swithin was a 9th-century Bishop of Winchester who died in AD 862. When on this day in AD 971 his remains were removed to a shrine in the Cathedral a torrential thunderstorm broke and lasted for forty days. It was said that he was weeping at the moving of his bones. So began the legend. The number 40 is found in several references such as the length of time the biblical flood lasted and Jesus's stay in the wilderness. A 40-day limit applied to fines and rights of sanctuary. The significance of the number 40 is not clear.

◉ Proclamation for the Seamer Fair, Seamer, near Scarborough
North Yorkshire

The fair is no longer staged, but the reading of the Proclamation still takes place.

TAKE THE A6 SOUTH FROM SCARBOROUGH, THE RIGHT ON THE B1261.

The reading of the proclamation at the Seamer Fair, North Yorkshire

The Sunday nearest St Swithin's Day

✠ **Hay-strewing, St Swithin's Church, Old Weston, near Huntingdon**   **Cambridgeshire**
Originally the hay came from a field left to the church for the purpose of providing hay for this
ceremony on its Feast Day, but now the hay comes from elsewhere.
TAKE THE A604 WEST OUT OF HUNTINGDON, THEN RIGHT ON THE B660.

17th July St Kenelm's Day
St Kenelm was the young son of the 9th-century Mercian king, Kenulf.

19th July St Margaret's Eve

✸ **Little Edith's Treat, Piddinghoe, near Newhaven**   **East Sussex**
A treat is given to local children on the anniversary of the death of little Edith Croft, who died in
1868, aged 13 months. Elizabeth Croft, Edith's grandmother, set up an endowment to provide
funds for local children to enjoy tea and sports on this anniversary, though local donations are now
necessary to maintain the custom.
PIDDINGHOE IS ON AN UNCLASSIFIED ROAD NORTH OUT OF NEWHAVEN.

The Tuesday and Wednesday after 19th July

✸ **Honiton Fair (glove), Honiton**   **Devon**
The Town Crier opens the fair with a traditional proclamation, carrying the gilded leather glove on
a garlanded pole. Hot pennies are then thrown for children to scramble for.
HONITON IS AT THE JUNCTION OF THE A30 AND THE A35.

The Tuesday before the third Wednesday in July

✸ **Lammas Fair (glove), Exeter**   **Devon**
The 900-year old-fair is held no longer, but the Mayor still reads the proclamation, and a pole
from which is suspended a stuffed white glove decorated with flowers and ribbons is erected as it
was for the fair. The glove symbolised the Crown's protection of the peace. These proceedings are
now part of the Exeter Festival.
EXETER IS AT THE JUNCTION OF THE A30 AND M5.

20th July St Margaret's Day, St Uncumber's Day

St Margaret was said to be the daughter of a prince, but was brought up as a shepherdess and became a Christian. Her feast day was remembered longest in Gloucestershire, and it was customary to serve plum dumpling – called **Heg Peg Dump** *(see p.186 for recipe)* – on this day. 'Peg' is a pet form of the name Margaret.

St Uncumber, or Wilgefortis, was martyred when she refused to surrender her chastity.

22nd July St Mary Magdelene's Day

St Mary Magdelene was the first to see Jesus after his resurrection.

The third Saturday in July

Corby Highland Games, Corby   Northamptonshire

Former Scottish steel – workers started the Games, and they are still held with all the traditional events.

CORBY IS ON THE A6003 NORTH FROM KETTERING.

The third Sunday in July

Mapplewell and Staincross Sing, Staincross Junior School, Staincross, near Barnsley   South Yorkshire

This is one of the few surviving community sing-songs, dating from 1887. A fair is also held on this day.

TAKE THE A61 NORTH OUT OF BARNSLEY, EXIT LEFT TO STAINCROSS.

The third full week in July (Monday to Thursday)

Swan-upping, River Thames from Sunbury to Pangbourne   Surrey to Berkshire

Mute Swans have been royal birds since the 14th century, with the exception of those in the charge of the Vintners' and Dyers' Livery Companies. Each year, starting at Sunbury, Swan Markers in a procession of rowing boats seek out the swans, turn them upside down (upping) and check to see if their beaks have been nicked. Royal bills are not nicked, Vintners' birds have two nicks, Dyers' one. Cygnets are marked accordingly, with those of mixed parentage divided between pen and cob, an odd one given the cob's marking. At Windsor Castle the crews salute the Queen by shouting 'Her Majesty the Queen, Seigneur of Swans!' After completing the stretch to Pangbourne, the red-jerseyed Queen's Swanherd and crew, the green-liveried Vintners' and blue-liveried Dyers' Markers hold a banquet at which one of the dishes is roast cygnet.

SUNBURY IS AT THE JUNCTION OF THE M3 AND A308. PANGBOURNE IS ON THE A329 WEST OF READING.

25th July St James' Day, Grotto Day, St Christopher's Day

St James was a fisherman asked by Jesus to become one of his disciples. He preached with St John, and was martyred in AD 43 in Jerusalem. St James is buried at Santiago de Compostella in Spain, and pilgrims used to carry scallop shells as drinking vessels on their journey. Shell grottoes have been built in his honour, on 5th August which is Old St James' Day.

Oysters *(see p.186 for serving suggestions)* are traditionally eaten on this day, for it is said that those who do so will never want for money during the year. It marks the beginning of the oyster season, which on the old calendar was 5th August.

St Christopher is the patron saint of travellers, but as little is known about his life, the origin of this association is unclear. He is known to have been martyred in Asia Minor, possibly in the 5th Century, as a church in Bithynia, Turkey was dedicated to him in around 450 AD.

Blessing the Oyster Fishing Boats, St Reeves' Beach, Whitstable   Kent

This is one of the older established blessings, dating from the early 19th Century.

TAKE THE A290 NORTH FROM CANTERBURY.

✞ **St Christopher's Day Blessing, Church of St Michael Paternoster Royal, College Hill**   London

COLLEGE HILL IS BETWEEN MANSION HOUSE AND CANNON STREET STATION.

✿ **Ebernoe Horn Fair, Ebernoe, near Petworth**   **West Sussex**

This event takes place on 25th July or the previous day if the 25th is a Sunday. A horned black ram, donated by Lord Egremont, is roasted and an inter-village cricket match held, the horns going to the winning team. Horned ram's heads were once fertility symbols.

PETWORTH IS ON THE A272 WEST OF PULBOROUGH. EBERNOE IS TO THE NORTH, PAST BALLS CROSS.

☻ **John Knill's Charity (Dancing round John Knill's Needle), Worvas Hill, St Ives**   **Cornwall**

This event takes place every five years and is due next in 2001, 2006, etc. At 10:30am a procession from the Guildhall of ten daughters (whose function today is to dance) of local fishermen and tin workers, led by a fiddler, commemorates the provision of doles by former smuggler John Knill. After singing the Hundredth Psalm, the doles are given by the Mayor to participants and those demonstrating skills in local sea-crafts.

TAKE THE A3074 NORTH FROM LELANT OR THE B3311 NORTH FROM PENZANCE.

26th July St Anne and St Joachim's Day

Anne and Joachim are said to be Mary's parents. Anne seems to be synonymous with the ancient Earth Mother Anu, and this saint may be a Christian invention to help eliminate the memory of the pagan worship of Anu. St Anne's Well, a spa alleged to have curative powers, is at Buxton, Derbyshire.

The last Thursday in July

✞ **Pilgrimage from Grindleford Station to the Roman Catholic Chapel at Padley**   **Derbyshire**

This pilgrimage is in honour of the Catholic priests Nicholas Garlick and Robert Ludlam and the landowner John Fitzherbert found hiding at Padley on 24th July 1588 during an anti-Catholic

The Ebernoe Horn Fair, West Sussex

persecution. They were hanged, drawn and quartered at Derby 12 days later. The chapel was one at which the Fitz herberts of Padley Hall worshipped but it ceased to be used after the Reformation. It was purchased and restored in 1932 by the Roman Catholic Diocese of Nottingham to remedy damage done during the building of Totley Tunnel in the 19th Century when it was used by the labourers.

TAKE THE A625 SOUTH WEST FROM SHEFFIELD, THEN LEFT ON THE B6001.

The last Saturday in July

✛ Well-dressing, Stoney Middleton, near Bakewell   **Derbyshire**
TAKE THE A619 WEST FROM CHESTERFIELD, THEN THE A623 AT BASLOW, THROUGH CALVER.

✛ Well-dressing, Bonsall, near Matlock   **Derbyshire**
TAKE THE A6 SOUTH OUT OF MATLOCK, RIGHT ON THE A5012, THEN RIGHT AGAIN TO BONSALL.

Last week in July

✛ Congleton Wakes, Congleton   **Cheshire**
This event took place in either the last week of July or the first week in August. The old custom of monks running through the streets with leather belts with bells on, to encourage citizens to come to worship (in imitation of St Peter in chains) is no more, but the Bell-Belts have been preserved.
TAKE THE A536 SOUTH FROM MACCLESFIELD.

28th July St Botvid's Day
St Botvid was a Swede who was converted to Christianity in England and became a missionary in Europe.

29th July St Olaf's Day
St Olaf was a Christian King of Norway, who lived from AD 995-1030.

31st July St Neot's Day
Little is known for certain about the life of St Neot, who gave his name to villages in Cornwall and Cambridgeshire. He was invoked by fishermen, anxious for good catches, but the reasons for this connection with fish are unknown.

August customs

In many ways August was a continuation of July, with even more rush-bearing/hay-strewing – more frequent at this time because of the progressing harvest, church-clipping, pilgrimages and the holding of fairs, particularly sheep fairs. August was a month when many wakes or feast days were held in the Midlands and the North.

The month began with Lammas, a harvest festival of mixed pagan/Christian origins, and a time when land-use contracts were reviewed. There are no surviving customs associated with the mid-August commemoration of Marymas. Sports contests were often held in August after harvesting when workers could freely enjoy themselves before the weather changes of autumn. The latter followed soon after Bartlemas, with its fairs and holiday for indoor workers, who knew that from now on daylight would be precious.

As well as the outdoor games already mentioned, August, being a month with many fairs, saw plenty of typical fairground games, such as climbing the pole (greased or not), jumping in sacks, rolling wheelbarrows blindfolded, donkey races, muzzling in a flour tub, and the more robust cudgel-play and back-sword play.

Back-sword play *Players stood on a 4 ft (1.2m) high platform holding ash-sticks with basket handles. The object was to draw first blood. The players defended themselves by looping a strap round their non-striking hand and tying the other end to the leg. In this way they were able to fend off blows on that side.*

Variable Dates

The Champion Town Crier of England Competition, Hastings East Sussex
As This event takes place on Hastings Pier.
Hastings is on the south coast of England at the end of the A21 from London.

Late August

The Water Game, Bourton-on-the-Water Gloucestershire
Take the A429 south west from Stow-on-the-Wold.

⚘ The Aunt Sally Championships

This event is held either at the end of August or early September. It centres around teams from Oxford and Abingdon. Two public houses in Oxford where it is particularly popular are The Folly Bridge Inn in Abingdon Road and The Tandem in Kennington Road.

OXFORD IS AT THE JUNCTION OF THE A40 AND A34.

Aunt Sally *The game started as throwing sticks at tethered chickens, but is now a form of skittles. An Aunt Sally is a doll on a swivelling plinth, and teams of eight each throw six wooden batons to try and knock the Aunt Sally off the plinth. A maximum score of 48 points is thus possible. In other versions, the doll is suspended on a pole, and the batons are thrown to hit its nose or break a clay pipe wedged in its mouth.*

Fixed Dates

1st August Lammas

Lammas is thought by some to mean Loaf Mass, the thanksgiving for the wheat harvest. The first ripe corn was given to the Church to make the Communion bread for a special Mass of Thanksgiving. There was once a Lamb Mass involving feudal tenants, held at the Cathedral of St Peter in Vinculis, York, and some believe this gave rise to the name Lammas. The pagan festival of Lughnasad (Lugh was the grandson of Baal, the summer sun, and he slew him that the autumn sun would rise and oversee the harvest) was held at this time and Lammas may well have been a Christian substitute.

Lammas was a term or rent day and a Quarter Day in the Celtic Year. Land tenure and rights of pasture were often settled on this day. Some grazing lands were given over to common use from Lammas to Candlemas.

At Lammas Fairs, which were principally sheep fairs, couples used to agree to have a trial marriage for the duration of the fair, usually 11 days, and then to part if they proved incompatible.

If couples suspected that fairies had snatched their child on May Day and replaced it with a changeling then the process could be reversed at Lammas.

Freshly baked bread and lamb are traditionally eaten at Lammas.

Football is played as part of the Water Games at Bourton-on-the-Water, Gloucestershire

The Waterman's Derby or Doggett's Coat and Badge Race, River Thames   London

This event is held on 1st August or when the tides are right. It is the oldest rowing event in the world, by the Worshipful Company of Fishmongers, between Old Swan Pier, London Bridge, and the site of the White Swan Inn, Chelsea Bridge. The Bargemaster starts the race at 11am. The event was founded by Thomas Doggett in 1715, in gratitude to the young oarsman who rowed him home to Chelsea one stormy night, and as a tribute to George I to whom he had been presented.

LONDON BRIDGE IS WHERE THE A3 CROSSES THE RIVER THAMES. CHELSEA BRIDGE IS WHERE THE A3216 CROSSES THE RIVER.

2nd August St Sidwell's Day

St Sidwell of Exeter may have been a Christian invention to explain a harvest sacrifice custom.

The Sunday nearest 2nd August

Church-clipping, Burbage, near Buxton   Derbyshire

The central theme is parishioners linking hands around the church. This is a Christian modification of a pagan ritual in which adherents held hands and danced around a sacred site or object.

BURBAGE IS ON THE WESTERN EDGE OF BUXTON ON THE A53.

The Saturday before the 1st Monday in August

St Wilfrid's Feast Procession, Ripon   North Yorkshire

St Wilfrid arrived in Ripon from Rome in AD 686, and a man dressed as he, in white, heads the procession through the town to the church. The Dean meets him at the west door, after which a service of thanksgiving is held. The annual fair follows, as it has done since 1108. In the past an effigy of St Wilfrid was borne round the streets before the opening. A dish called Wilfrid Pie is served; it contains apples, sugar and cheese.

RIPON IS ON THE A61 NORTH OF HARROGATE.

1st Sunday in August

St Benet's Abbey Blessing, St Benet's, near Horning   Norfolk

The Abbot of St Benet's, a title held by the Bishop of Norwich, was the only such position to survive the Reformation. Each year the Bishop sails on a Norfolk wherry from Horning to St Benet's to deliver a blessing on the Westlands of the Norfolk Broads. A service is held in the ruins of St Benet's Hulme Abbey.

TAKE THE A1151 NORTH EAST FROM NORWICH, THEN RIGHT AT HOVETON ON THE A1062.

1st Monday in August

✠ **Well-dressing, Bradwell, near Castleton** **Derbyshire**
TAKE THE A625 SOUTH WEST OUT OF SHEFFIELD, THEN LEFT ON THE B6049.

1st Wednesday in August

✠ **Pilgrimage to the Shrine of Our Lady, Hastings Castle** **East Sussex**
Dating from the beginning of this century, the pilgrimage is to a chapel which was a Catholic shrine before the Reformation.
HASTINGS IS ON THE SOUTH COAST OF ENGLAND AT THE END OF THE A21 FROM LONDON

⊛ **Knights of the Old Green Competition, Southampton Old Green, Lower Canal Walk, Southampton** **Hampshire**
This 13th-century Bowling Green is thought to be the oldest of its kind, and this tournament similarly. The officials wear top hat and tails, are addressed as 'Sir' if they are former winners, and enforce the original rules throughout the competition. The winner is the first Gentleman Commoner to score seven ends when he becomes a Knight of the Green.
SOUTHAMPTON IS AT THE JUNCTION OF THE M3 AND M27.

1st week in August

⊛ **Grand Wardmote (Archery Competition) of the Woodmen of Arden, Meriden, near Coventry** **West Midlands**
This competition lasts from Wednesday to the first Saturday in August and also takes place in June and July. The 6 ft (2m) longbows are of yew and the targets are of original form, including clouts. Distances are measured in roods, and the prize for winning the final event is an old bugle. This association is limited to 80 men and dates from 1785. They wear green hats and coats, buff waistcoats and white trousers. The society's silver buttons adorn the coat and waistcoat.
TAKE THE B4102 EAST OUT OF SOLIHULL, THEN RIGHT TO MERIDEN AFTER HAMPTON-IN-ARDEN.

Grand Wardmote (Archery Competition), West Midlands, 1925

5th August Old St James' Day, St Oswald's Day

St Oswald was a 7th-century king of Northumbria, known for his charity to beggars and other needy people.

Oysters (for Old St James' Day) are eaten on this day as it marks the opening of the oyster season.

✠ **Church-clipping, St Oswald's Church, Guiseley, near Otley**　　　West Yorkshire

The parishioners link hands and walk round the church.

TAKE THE A6038 NORTH FROM BRADFORD.

6th August Old St Anne's Day

Tan Hill Fair, near Devizes, Wiltshire was a huge sheep and livestock fair held on this day. Salt-beef and beans were traditionally served.

The Saturday nearest St Oswald's Day

✠ **Rushbearing, St Oswald's Church, Grasmere**　　　Cumbria

At 3pm children and choristers carry bearings (decorations on biblical themes made from rushes and flowers) in procession from the church through the village and back to the church. Also in the parade are six chosen girls called rush-maidens who carry a hand-woven linen sheet full of rushes. After the 4:15pm service, **Grasmere Gingerbread** (*see p.186 for recipe*), with the figure of St Oswald on each piece, is given to the children.

GRASMERE IS ON THE A591 NORTH WEST OUT OF WINDERMERE, PAST AMBLESIDE.

8th August St Lide's day

St Lide was an 11th-century hermit on the Isles of Scilly.

✠ **Thanksgiving Service, St Lawrence's Church, Whitwell**　　　Derbyshire

This open-air service is founded on the traditional belief that the church was built from stone quarried from High Hill, although geologically the stone from the hill does not match that from which the church is made. Although it is no longer held on the crag, it is still a popular local event, starting at 2:30pm. The old hymn 'The Ballad of St Lawrence' is a distinctive feature of the service.

TAKE THE A619 EAST FROM CHESTERFIELD AND EXIT RIGHT ON AN UNCLASSIFIED ROAD AFTER BARLBOROUGH.

The Rush Bearing Festival at Grasmere, Cumbria

The three days before the second Monday in August

Cranham Feast, Cranham, near Painswick Gloucestershire

This marks the start of this three-day event at which roast deer is eaten by way of reinforcing the ancient right claimed by locals to take and eat deer.

TAKE THE A417 EAST FROM GLOUCESTER, RIGHT ON THE A46, THEN LEFT ON AN UNCLASSIFIED ROAD.

The second Monday in August

This was the day of the Horncastle Fair, Lincolnshire, immortalised in the folk song of that name.

10th August St Lawrence's Day, St Bertram's Day

St Lawrence lived in the 3rd century. St Bertram, from Ilam, Staffordshire, was an 8th-century Mercian prince.

11th August Old Lammas Eve

Many sheep fairs were held on or near this day, particularly in the south of England.

12th August

The game season opens on this day, the so-called Glorious Twelfth.

Mitcham Fair Surrey

This fair lasts for three days.

MITCHAM IS AT THE JUNCTION OF THE A236 AND A237.

The Sunday nearest 12th August

Rush-bearing, Forest Chapel, near Macclesfield Cheshire

MACCLESFIELD IS AT THE JUNCTION OF THE A523 AND A537.

The Monday after 12th August

Revel, Marhamchurch, near Bude Cornwall

The revel started as a celebration of the founding of the village by St Morwenna, whose feast day is on 5th July and is said to have brought Christianity to the village in the 6th century. The Queen of the Revel is elected and crowned by Old Father Time. Cornish wrestling is featured and Cornish teas are served.

Cornish Wrestling *The object of this sport of Celtic origin is to throw an opponent so that he falls to the ground with two hips and one shoulder, or two shoulders and one hip, squarely on the floor. The wrestlers fight bare-footed, wearing canvas jackets. They shake hands at the start and finish of a contest, are not allowed to kick – although they can strike with the sides of the foot – or take hold below the belt.*

MARHAMCHURCH IS ON AN UNCLASSIFIED ROAD SOUTH EAST OF BUDE.

13th August St Hippolytus' Day

This 3rd-century inhabitant of St Ippollitts, Hertfordshire was said to be able to cure horses.

15th August The Feast of the Assumption

Christians commemorate the Virgin Mary's Assumption into Heaven. No Marymas events survive in England.

16th August St Roch's Day

St Roch was a 14th-century saint said to be able to cure sufferers of the plague, as well as sufferers of other afflictions. This day was also used in the past for harvest feasting after the crops were safely gathered in.

The Thursday nearest 20th August

The Grasmere Sports, Grasmere   **Cumbria**

At these sports are seen Cumbrian wrestling, fell races (the Guides' Race, up, across and down the 1000ft (305m) high Butter Crags) and two hound trails.

GRASMERE IS ON THE A591 NORTH WEST OUT OF WINDERMERE, PAST AMBLESIDE.

Cumbrian Wrestling *This is an amateur sport of Celtic origin. Contestants wear white or pale pink singlets, with dark drawers over long underpants. To start, they clasp hands behind each other's back, one arm over the other's shoulder and the other arm below. The chin rests on one side of the opponent's shoulders. Then they wrestle to try and throw the other on to the ground. A contest is decided on one fall only.*

The Wednesday after the Sunday following St Lawrence's Day

Well-dressing at Barlow   **Derbyshire**

TAKE THE B6051 NORTH WEST FROM CHESTERFIELD.

18th August St Helen's Day

St Helen was the mother of Constantine, the 3rd-century first Christian Emperor of Rome.

20th August St Philibert's Day

St Philibert lived in the 7th century. The filbert nut harvest traditionally started today. Filberts are the nuts of the cultivated hazel.

The second weekend after 12th August

Saddleworth Rush-bearing Festival, villages of Saddleworth Moor (St Chad, Uppermill, Greenfield, Dobcross and Delph)   **Greater Manchester**

Rushes are piled on a cart, and this, its rider and a large copper kettle, are dragged through the villages. Barren women used to touch the cart in the hope of increasing their fertility. Morris dancers follow the cart. The cart starts in Uppermill at 9:30am on Saturday, going via Greenfield, Dobcross and Delph. On Sunday it is hauled to St Chad's for the 10:30am service, after which there is wrestling, gurning (an ugly face competition), clog dancing and various other events and entertainments.

TAKE THE A669 EAST OUT OF OLDHAM, LEFT ON THE A670 TO UPPERMILL AND THE OTHER VILLAGES.

24th August St Bartholomew's Day

St Bartholomew lived and died in 1st-century Palestine, and was martyred by being flayed alive. This fate led to his being made the patron saint of butchers and tanners. He was also the patron saint of bee-keepers and honey-makers.

From 1133 to 1855 Bartholomew Fair at Smithfield, London was held on this day, and raised revenue for St Bartholomew's Hospital. It was at this fair that apples coated in honey were first sold – the forerunner of our toffee apples. Another huge fair on this day was Stourbridge Fair at Chesterton, near Cambridge.

Currant buns are traditionally eaten by the children of Sandwich, Kent who run to St Bartholomew's Chapel to receive them. Another traditional dish is **Bartlemas Beef** *(see p.186 for recipe)*.

At Gulval in Cornwall the church is the venue for the Blessing of the Mead Ceremony.

Printers had a holiday today, to mark the closing in of the evenings and the need to light candles for the first time. They received a compensatory payment which they spent on a goose to roast.

St Bartholomew's Bun Race, St Bartholomew's Hospital, Sandwich   Kent

Sandwich is a Cinque port. In 1217 the ships of Cinque ports defeated Eustace the Monk's invading French fleet; the spoils were said to have been used to set up the Hospital. On this day the Mayor of Sandwich visits the Hospital for a memorial service for the founders and to oversee the selection of the new Master, by picking a name from the list of eligible towns people. The original children's dole of bread, cheese and beer was replaced by a race around the chapel for a currant bun, then every adult in attendance is given a souvenir of a St Barts biscuit which bears the design of the hospital seal.

TAKE THE A257 EAST OUT OF CANTERBURY.

The Blessing the Mead (wine made from fermented honey) Ceremony is held on St. Bartholomew's Day at Gulval, Cornwall

The Saturday nearest 24th August

Burning Bartle, West Witton, near Leyburn, Wensleydale **North Yorkshire**

This custom has some of the elements of a harvest sacrifice. 'Bartle' is a straw man with flashing eyes. At 9pm he is carried through the village to a traditional chant, before being thrown on to a bonfire at Grassgill End. Bartle may have originally been an effigy of St Bartholomew which the villagers were trying to save from looters, and thus the custom may be of mixed origin.

TAKE THE A684 WEST FROM LEYBURN, PAST WENSLEY.

The Sunday on or after St Bartholomew's Day

Keaw Yed (Cow's Head) Wakes Festival, Westhoughton, near Wigan **Greater Manchester**

Originally, a communal pie was made in the shape of a cow's head. A game was once played in which a cow's head was used like a rugby ball, the two features giving rise to speculation that the event may be a vestige of bull sacrificial rites. Pork pasties with clay dolls inside, furmety porridge and **Brandy snaps** *(see p.186 for recipe)* are traditionally eaten.

TAKE THE A58 SOUTH WEST FROM BOLTON, THROUGH HINDLEY.

26th August St Ninian's Day

The 4th-century St Ninian was one of the first Christian missionaries to the Picts in Scotland.

27th August St Maelrubba's Day, St Hugh's Day

St Maelrubba, a 7th-century Irish saint, may actually have been (or been confused with, it is not clear) the pagan God Mourie, to whom bulls were sacrificed.

St Hugh, or 'Little Sir Hugh of Lincoln', as the folk song says, was allegedly murdered by Jews.

29th August Feast of the Decollation (Beheading) of St John the Baptist

This was the day of Whittingham Fair, Northumberland, the song about which became famous when its title was changed to 'Scarborough Fair'.

Kirby Hill Races, Kirby Hill, near Richmond **North Yorkshire**

This event takes place every even-numbered year on or about 29th August. The 'races' are a way of electing the two wardens of the John Dakyn Trust which administers an almshouse according to his will of 1556. Residents of the six flats in the almshouse must have lived in the parish for ten

Burning 'Owd Bartle' at West Witton, Wensleydale, North Yorkshire

years and be prepared to pray for John Dakyn's deliverance each day. The names of six candidates are sealed in wax and floated in a tub of water. Two are picked, whilst the four unlucky names are left sealed and floating lest they be needed for another draw in the event of an untimely death of a warden. This is a private ceremony.

KIRBY HILL IS ON AN UNCLASSIFIED ROAD NORTH OUT OF RICHMOND, THEN EXIT LEFT.

The Preston Merchant Guild, Preston — Lancashire

This event takes place every 20 years, with the next due in 2012. The right of local traders to have a Merchant Guild was granted in 1179. This right was temporarily lost in 1974 when local government was reorganised, but restored by royal charter later in 1974.

PRESTON IS ON THE M6 SOUTH OF LANCASTER.

The last Friday in August

Crying the Neck, Helston — Cornwall

See 'Harvest Customs' for details of this ceremony, which starts at 7:30pm.

HELSTON IS ON THE A394 BETWEEN FALMOUTH AND PENZANCE.

Last Sunday in August

Plague Service, Cucklet Dell, Eyam, near Bakewell — Derbyshire

The service is held here in memory of the plague victims of 1665 who died after handling infected cloth from London. The rector 'William Mompesson' sealed off the village to protect the surrounding population, who responded by leaving food on the boundary. Coins as payment were left in a well into which vinegar had been poured to disinfect them. The procession from the church passes some surviving plague cottages.

TAKE THE A619 WEST OUT OF CHESTERFIELD, THEN TURN RIGHT ON THE A623.

The last week in August

Well-dressing at Eyam, near Bakewell — Derbyshire

TAKE THE A619 WEST OUT OF CHESTERFIELD, THEN TURN RIGHT ON THE A623.

31st August St Aidan's day

St Aidan was an Irish missionary who became the first Bishop of Lindisfarne, Northumberland, dying in AD 641.

Harvest customs

Most harvest customs in England are held in August and September. The start and finish of harvesting were always accompanied by celebrations and ritual, but it was also common for each day of the harvest to be greeted by a peal of bells. The celebrations held on the finish were called 'Harvest Home'. The organisation of the harvest was placed in the hands of an experienced worker, who was given the title of Lord of the Harvest. In earlier times the Church demanded a tithe of one tenth of the crop, but the Church's common role has now been diminished to that of blessing both the crops and workers.

The first sheaf of corn cut was often made into bread for an offering, whereas the last sheaf was thought to be the refuge of the corn spirit, and its cutting was a ceremonial affair with the corn being used to make a corn dolly or being ceremonially burned. The corn dolly had the place of honour on the feast table, would afterwards be kept (in a house or church) until the spring sowing started, and then would be taken out into the fields for the spirit to return. The actions accompanying this ritual of cutting the last sheaf are collectively referred to as Crying the Neck. A 'Neck' was a column of plaited strands of straw, representing the pole to which sacrificial victims in Phrygian times were bound before their heads were cut off with sickles so that their life blood ran into the soil. The Neck is now a columnar shaped corn dolly, like a drop dolly with a core of straws.

The last cartload of corn was brought back with much ceremony and horseplay. The cart (known as a Horkey Cart for the occasion) and horse were decorated with garlands and ribbons, and at the end of the procession to the farmer's house the Harvest-Home feast awaited. Afterwards games were played.

The next job was to clear all the corn stalks and heads left in the fields, so the gleaners moved in. The gleanings were usually women and they elected a Gleaning Queen to organise and supervise. Gleanings could be kept, and this enabled the families of poor women to survive the winter.

Corn was taken to the mill for grinding, including gleanings, and the miller would keep a portion as his fee or make a charge. At the produce markets middle-men used to try and buy up produce and sell it at a profit. These were called 'badgers'.

In an effort to 'civilise and sanctify' the often rowdy Harvest Home celebrations the Church instigated Harvest Thanksgiving services in the mid-19th century, in which produce was donated to the church, who in turn gave it to the needy after the service.

There were many supernatural tales involving fairies which emanate from harvest time, this is a recurring feature of this and other critical periods in the constant battle between ordinary people and the mysterious forces and spirits of nature. This battle is also the theme of the harvest folk-song 'John Barleycorn'. The great relief at getting in the harvest was evident on every face at the feast which followed.

The hop harvest had customs all its own. The principal hop-growing areas were Kent, the pickers coming from London, and Hereford and Worcester, the pickers coming from the Black Country towns. Tying the vines to the tops of the poles was the job of the Stilt Man. 'Cribbing', in Hereford and Worcester, was the symbolic burial and resurrection after the harvest of the Busheller (foreman) and his wife, or of an unmarried virgin. The Hop Feast would follow.

The first full moon after 21st September is called the Harvest Moon. Couples desiring a child would sleep outside under its fertile light.

Making Corn Dollies *Straw for dollies can be any corn but wheat is best. Weaving Straw is cut just above the first leaf node (and just below the head if this is not wanted), and Thick Straw, for designs like the Bridget Cross, from the base of the corn stalk. In addition to the straws you need buff-coloured thread, ribbons, elastic bands and a knife or scissors. Weaving straws, should be used within a few days. Designs such as for the Bridget Cross, Drop Dolly and Nek Dolly can be obtained from the many specialist books on making corn dollies.*

Variable Dates

After the harvest

🎧 Hanging the Corn Dolly, St Faith's Church,
Overbury, near Evesham   **Hereford and Worcester**

TAKE THE A435 SOUTH FROM EVESHAM, THEN RIGHT ON AN UNCLASSIFIED ROAD AT BECKFORD.

On Harvest Sunday

🎧 Hanging the Corn Dolly, Whalton, near Morpeth   **Northumberland**

TAKE THE A1 SOUTH FROM MORPETH, THEN RIGHT ON THE B6524.

The Cornish custom of displaying the last sheaf to signify the end of the harvest

September customs

With the Harvest drawing to a close for corn, hops and other produce, this sale was now conducted in September. Hop Processions were common in Kent and Hereford and Worcester. The hazelnut harvest began early in the month, and soon the countryside would be full of blackberry pickers. Later crab-apples would be ready for roasting or turning into jelly. Gorse was cut for fuel for ovens, bracken was cut to make bedding, the whitebait season started for fishermen.

Harvest thanksgiving services for land and sea produce were widespread, and soon after the Hiring Fairs began for labourers to seek new jobs. Goose Fairs were also a feature of this month which closed with Michaelmas, marking the effective end of summer agricultural work, celebrated with roast goose stuffed with freshly picked apples.

This was a favourite month for Hawking, as Falconry was once called. Animals also featured in several other so-called sports, such as bull-baiting, bear-baiting, dog-fighting and cock-fighting.

Variable Dates

Early September

Crying the Neck, St Ives   Cornwall
See 'Harvest Customs' section for details.
TAKE THE A3074 NORTH FROM LELANT OR THE B3311 NORTH FROM PENZANCE.

The Opening of the Whitebait Season, Southend-on-Sea   Essex
At a private function the Archdeacon and Mayor are invited to taste the first catch of the day.
TAKE THE A127 EAST FROM JUNCTION 29 OF THE M25.

Ancient Gorsedds (Bardic festivals), various sites   Cornwall
CORNWALL IS IN THE SOUTH WEST TIP OF ENGLAND.

Grand Pony Fair, Princetown   Devon
TAKE THE B3213 NORTH EAST FROM YELVERTON.

After the harvest

🌼 **Festival of First Fruits, Richmond**   **North Yorkshire**

There was something of a competition in the past to be the first farmer to have his corn inspected and ready for sale. Food and drink was the prize. This festival commemorates those days by holding a mock corn inspection after a prayer of thanksgiving; then the local farmers are toasted.

RICHMOND IS WEST OF THE A1. TAKE THE A6108 FROM SCOTCH CORNER.

Late September

🐑 **Masham Sheep Fair**   **North Yorkshire**

The fair takes place on a Saturday and Sunday afternoon.

TAKE THE A6108 NORTH WEST FROM RIPON.

⚫ **Eton College Field Game, Eton**   **Berkshire**

The game is played throughout the Michaelmas Term.

TAKE THE B3022 NORTH FROM WINDSOR.

♣ **Pipe Walk, from St Mary Redcliffe Church to Knowle, Bristol**   **Avon**

The walk takes place on a Saturday afternoon. It follows and beats the course of an underground spring, marked by 14 stones. A walker is lifted and bumped on each stone. The spring was given to the church by Robert de Berkeley in 1190.

REDCLIFFE AND KNOWLE ARE CENTRAL DISTRICTS OF BRISTOL, AND CAN BE REACHED ON THE M4 AND M5.

🔔 **Crying the Neck, St Keverne**   **Cornwall**

See 'Harvest Customs' section for details.

TAKE THE A3083 SOUTH FROM HELSTON, THEN LEFT ON THE B3293, THEN LEFT AGAIN.

Fixed Dates

1st September St Giles' Day

St Giles lived in the 8th century. He was crippled by a wound and eventually became the patron saint of cripples and beggars. Many feasts and fairs were held on this day.

👑 **Colchester Oyster Ceremony, Colchester**   **Essex**

Gathering oysters in the River Colne is an ancient right going back to the Proclamation of 1256 declaring that the right belongs to the city. The Mayor and party sail up Pyfleet Creek from Brightlingsea, where the Proclamation is read and a toast of gin and gingerbread taken. When the Mayor lowers the first trawl the season is officially open. The banquet is by invitation only.

COLCHESTER IS BETWEEN CHELMSFORD AND IPSWICH ON THE A12

Captain and officers of ship celebrate the opening of the Oyster Season, 1924

St. Giles Fair, Oxford, 1912

3rd September Nutting Day

On the old calendar this was the day when hazelnuts were collected, but today they are not likely to be ready. Lacemakers were allowed to light candles on this day to work by, and could so do until Shrove Tuesday.

✳ Tribute to Oliver Cromwell, Houses of Parliament   **London**

This takes place at his statue outside the Houses of Parliament.

THE HOUSES OF PARLIAMENT ARE BY WESTMINSTER BRIDGE.

The Monday & Tuesday after the Sunday following 1st September

✳ St Giles' Fair, St Giles' Street   **Oxford**

Originally, this was the parish wake of Walton, which in Medieval times was outside the city limits, and it grew into one of the largest trading markets in England.

OXFORD IS AT THE JUNCTION OF THE A40 AND A34.

The first Friday in September

🔔 Crying the Neck, Madron, near Penzance   **Cornwall**

See 'Harvest Customs' section for details of this ceremony, which starts at 6:30 pm.

MADRON IS ON AN UNCLASSIFIED ROAD NORTH WEST FROM PENZANCE THROUGH HEAMOOR.

The first Saturday in September

✳ Hop Hoodening, Canterbury Cathedral   **Kent**

The hop procession to the cathedral is led by Hooden Horses (like Hobby Horses, with their snapping jaws) and Invicta, the White Horse of Kent, and includes a hop bower with the Hop Queen inside and Morris dancers. At the cathedral, whose altar is draped with hops, all but the pagan Hooden Horses are admitted for the service.

TAKE THE A2 EAST OUT OF LONDON, THEN LEFT ON THE A28 INTO CANTERBURY.

The first weekend in September

This was the time of the Eccles Wake, Lancashire, at which the famous **Eccles Cakes** (*see p.187 for recipe*) were sold. This event was once notorious for-bull-baiting, cock-fighting and donkey-racing that took place, and drew huge crowds for these and more agreeable events. A variety of prizes were on offer, and cakes and ale were consumed in equal measure.

Hop Hoodening, Canterbury, Kent

The Barnet Fair, Hertfordshire

✻ The English Hop Festival, Faversham **Kent**

This event is a celebration of Kent's hop-picking past with demonstrations – including a stilt man, hop memorabilia and folklore, and traditional folk activities such as Morris dancing. There is a procession through the town on Sunday at 3pm.

FAVERSHAM IS ON THE A2 EAST OUT OF LONDON, PAST SITTINGBOURNE.

✿ Rushbearing, villages around Sowerby Bridge, near Halifax **West Yorkshire**

At 11am on Saturday at Warley church the rush-cart is blessed and is then taken by clog-wearing villagers around Sowerby, Ripponden, Triangle and Cotton Stones, in company with the Bradshaw Mummers, Morris dancers and other entertainers.

SOWERBY BRIDGE IS ON THE A58 SOUTH FROM HALIFAX.

✿ Barnet Fair, Greengate Farm, Mays Lane, Barnet **Hertfordshire**

This was an old horse, cattle and sheep trading fair, with seafood delicacies a speciality. Formerly it was held on the 4th, 5th and 6th September. Horses are still sold here, but mostly this is now a funfair.

BARNET IS AT THE JUNCTION OF THE A1000 AND THE A411.

8th September Our Lady's Birthday, Feast of the Nativity of the Blessed Virgin Mary

Christians commemorate the birthday of the Virgin Mary.

The Saturday nearest 8th September

✿ The Sheriff's Ride, Lichfield **Staffordshire**

After the election of the Sheriff by the Brethren of Lichfield, he and followers start from the Market Square at 10:30 am to ride the boundaries. This is a separate ceremony to Beating the Bounds and is done in accordance with Queen Mary's charter of 1553 establishing Lichfield as a city. One of six charters, it also stipulates an annual election of a Sheriff, who must perambulate the city boundaries and ensure that all boundary stones are in place.

LICHFIELD IS BETWEEN BIRMINGHAM AND BURTON-ON-TRENT ON THE A38.

The Sunday after 8th September

✿ Church Clipping at Wirksworth **Derbyshire**

Parishoners surround the church, hold hands and walk around it. A service follows.

FROM ASHBOURNE TAKE THE B5035 NORTH EAST AND EXIT RIGHT AFTER CARSINGTON.

The first Monday after the first Sunday after 4th September

Abbots Bromley Horn Dance   Staffordshire

This ancient dance involves the wearing of the only surviving English reindeer antlers, from animals brought by the Norsemen. They are kept in St Nicholas' Church. Six Deermen in quasi-medieval costume carry reindeer horns on poles above their heads and dance through the town, accompanied by a musician, a boy with a triangle, a boy with a crossbow, a Fool, a Hobby Horse (tourney type) and a Maid Marian (a man dressed as a woman). The dance starts from the vicarage at 8am, and has elements of a mock hunt, as perhaps a survivor from ancient times when sympathetic magic was thought to guarantee a successful hunt. **Abbots Bromley Wakes Cakes** and **Abbots Bromley Brandy Snaps** *(see p.187 for recipes)* are made and sold.

TAKE THE A518 SOUTH WEST OUT OF UTTOXETER, THEN LEFT ON THE B5013.

The second Tuesday in September

Widecombe Fair, Widecombe-in-the-Moor, Dartmoor   Devon

This was a pony and sheep fair.

TAKE THE A382 NORTH FROM NEWTON ABBOT, THEN LEFT ON THE B3387.

14th September Holy-Cross Day, Finding of the Cross, Holy-Rood Day

This is the day in AD 312 when Constantine saw a vision of the cross as he was about to go into battle against Maxentius. The cross was said to have appeared in the heavens with the words *'In hoc signo vinces'* meaning 'By this sign you will conquer'.

In 1752 when the Gregorian calendar was introduced this day followed 2nd September, and there were riots by people demanding their eleven days back.

It is said that 'The Devil goes a-nutting' on this day; young people gather nuts.

The second weekend in September

The Merrills Championships, Ryedale Folk Museum, Hutton-le-Hole   North Yorkshire

Merrills is a dialect name for the board game Nine Men's Morris.

TAKE THE A170 WEST FROM SCARBOROUGH, THEN RIGHT AT KELDHOLME ON AN UNCLASSIFIED ROAD.

Nine Men's Morris *The game is played on a board with three squares drawn one inside the other. A line is drawn through the centres of each set of parallel sides. Each player has nine counters of a certain colour. In a turn, a player places a counter on a corner or intersection. The object is to get three in a row, when one of the opponents' counters can be removed. When all 18 counters are played, a turn consists of moving one of one's counters along a line to a neighbouring free spot. If this makes three in a row then another opposing counter is removed. A player loses if left with only two counters.*

16th September St Edith's Day

St Edith lived in the 10th century and was the sister of Edward the Martyr. Water from wells dedicated to her was said to have curative powers. Wells are: Kemsing, Kent; Church Eaton, Staffordshire; and at Stoke Edith, Hereford and Worcester.

Procession to St Edith's Well, Kemsing   Kent

TAKE THE A225 SOUTH FROM DARTFORD, THEN LEFT AT OTFORD ALONG AN UNCLASSIFIED ROAD.

The Saturday nearest 18th September

The Johnson Supper, Lichfield   Staffordshire

After the laying of a wreath on the statue of Dr Johnson, and a service, there is a feast, by invitation only, consisting of his favourite dishes. Dr Johnson was born in Lichfield.

LICHFIELD IS BETWEEN BIRMINGHAM AND BURTON-ON-TRENT ON THE A38.

The Monday nearest 18th September

The Johnson Sermon, Uttoxeter Market Place   Staffordshire

This is held in memory of Dr Samuel Johnson, writer and lexicographer born on 18th September, and is read to a congregation of children. Afterwards a wreath is laid on his statue.

TAKE THE A50 SOUTH EAST FROM STOKE-ON-TRENT.

19th September Nativity of the Virgin

Worcester Great Fair   Hereford and Worcester

LEAVE THE M5 AT JUNCTION 7 AND TAKE THE A44 INTO WORCESTER.

Decorating the Rood Screen with a garland, Charlton-on-Otmoor   Oxfordshire

Today this event consists of no more than redressing the cross of box foliage which represents the statue of the Virgin Mary destroyed, along with a statue of St John, in the Reformation. Formerly a full-scale garland event was held.

TAKE THE A34 NORTH EAST FROM OXFORD, RIGHT ON THE B4027, LEFT AT ISLIP.

Pillow fight, Widecombe Fair, Devon

The first Sunday after Nativity of the Virgin

⊕ **Clipping the Church, St Mary's Church, Painswick**   **Gloucestershire**

'Clip' means 'embrace'. After a procession to the church, a traditional Clipping hymn is sung as the villagers dance round the church hand-in-hand, and Hare Pie (with a china puppy baked inside) is traditionally eaten – 'puppy dog pies', although nowadays it is a cake with almond paste on top and a small china dog inside. Whether this is a relic of a dog sacrifice, as at certain Roman customs, is not certain.

TAKE THE A46 NORTH OUT OF STROUD.

⊕ **Harvest Feast Sunday, Charlton-on-Otmoor**   **Oxfordshire**

TAKE THE A34 NORTH EAST FROM OXFORD, RIGHT ON THE B4027, LEFT AT ISLIP.

The Wednesday, Thursday and Friday preceding 20th September

⊛ **St Giles' Fair (glove), Barnstaple**   **Devon**

A white glove is hoisted to indicate freedom to trade. Cheese and toast, spiced ale and gingerbread are traditionally served.

TAKE THE A377 NORTH WEST FROM EXETER.

The Saturday nearest 20th September

⊛ **Ashby Statute Fair, Ashby-de-la-Zouch**   **Leicestershire**

This is a four-day fair, and was once an important hiring fair.

TAKE THE A512 WEST FROM LOUGHBOROUGH, OR THE A50 SOUTH EAST FROM BURTON-UPON-TRENT.

21st September The Autumnal Equinox, St Matthew's Day

St Matthew was a 1st-century tax collector for the Romans, who was traditionally the author of the first gospel. Do not pick nuts on this day as it is the Devil's principal Nutting Day, and you may be gathered in yourself. Nuts were thought to improve fertility, and girls tended to avoid collecting them lest they fall pregnant.

Druids celebrate this day on Primrose Hill, London.

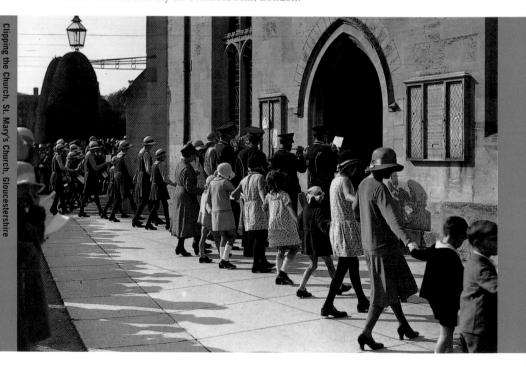

Clipping the Church, St. Mary's Church, Gloucestershire

Procession of pupils of Christ's Hospital to St Sepulchre's Church,
Newgate, and then to Mansion House **London**

This is to commemorate the founding of the school by Edward VI in 1553 in Newgate Street. The Lord Mayor is ex-officio Governor and Almoner of the school.

THE SITE OF ST SEPULCHRE'S CHURCH IS IN GILTSPUR STREET OPPOSITE THE OLD BAILEY.

The third Saturday in September

Egremont Crab Fair and World Gurning (Face-pulling) Championships,
Egremont **Cumbria**

Since its charter in 1267, roasted crab-apples have been a traditional delicacy at this fair, where the activities include racing, hound trailing and climbing the greasy pole for a leg of lamb. Each gurner puts his or her head through a horse collar and pulls as ugly a face as possible.

EGREMONT IS ON THE A595 SOUTH FROM WHITEHAVEN.

The third Sunday in September

Horseman's Sunday, St John's Church, Hyde Park Crescent **London**

At 11:30am mounted priest blesses horses.

GO NORTH FROM HYDE PARK ALONG HYDE PARK STREET.

23rd September St Tegla's Day

St Tegla lived in the 1st century; she was a hermit.

24th September Harvest Home, Feast of In-Gathering, Old Holy-Cross Eve, St Robert's Day

St Robert of Knaresborough, North Yorkshire, was a 12th-century hermit.

This was a day similar to Michaelmas Day in some rural communities. Long ago, getting a good harvest meant paying due homage to the Corn Mother or Earth Goddess. When the corn was ready, everybody helped bring it in. An experienced man would be appointed Lord of the Harvest and it was his job to organise the labourers into teams. Scythers, mainly men, would move ahead in a line, followed by women, children and the elderly who would gather and bind the cut corn into sheaves ready to be carted to the barns when dry.

In ancient times the reaper who cut the last sheaf of corn was sacrificed and his blood used to enrich the soil for next year. This sheaf was always in the centre of the field and was thought to be the refuge of the Corn Spirit or Corn Mother. The sacrifice gave rise to the symbol of death known as 'the Grim Reaper' who signified the end of the agricultural year, now, with his scythe, known as Old Father Time who symbolises the turning of the year on 31st December. Later, the last wagon of grain (the Hock or Horkey Cart) was decorated with flowers and ribbons, and the last sheaf given human form and decorated as the Corn Mother. This last sheaf was later used to make corn dollies, which were displayed during harvest festivities and kept safely, with the spirit inside, until spring sowing. They were hung up in the kitchen and taken out into the fields next Spring for the spirit to return. The Harvest Home supper was followed by much celebration, music and dancing. Two types of Harvest Cake were made, which were characteristically scored on top with a cross to make four portions. The plain bread dough cakes were called fourses and served to the labourers, but if sugar, raisins and extra shortening were added they were called **Harvest Cake** *(see p.187 for recipe)* and were made by the farmer's wife for her family.

In the middle of the 19th century churches began to hold Harvest Thanksgiving services to bless the produce, which became known as Harvest Festivals. Fishermen went to Harvest of the Sea services, for which the churches were decorated with nets, lobster pots and other fishing paraphernalia.

Sturbridge Fair, Sturbridge Common — Cambridgeshire
Once the largest fair in the land, it is held on 25th September if the 24th is a Sunday.
TAKE THE M11 NORTH FROM LONDON, AND AT JUNCTION 11 TAKE THE A10 NORTH INTO CAMBRIDGE.

25th September Old Holy Rood Day

The third week in September

Wakes Week, Sandbach — Cheshire
Brandy snaps and **Lancashire Wakes Cakes** *(see p.186 and p.187 for recipes)* are traditionally eaten.
SANDBACH IS OFF JUNCTION 17 OF THE M6.

Last Sunday in September

Penny Loaf Sunday, Newark — Nottinghamshire
In honour of his deliverance from a house fire in March 1643, Hercules Clay provided for the annual giving of a loaf of bread to the town's poor.
NEWARK IS AT THE JUNCTION OF THE A1 AND A46.

The last Monday in September

Statute Fair, Queensway Hall, Dunstable — Bedfordshire
This was once a hiring fair.
DUNSTABLE IS TO THE WEST OF JUNCTION 11 OF THE M1.

Last Wednesday in September

Bridgwater Fair — Somerset
BRIDGWATER IS OFF THE M5 AT JUNCTIONS 23 OR 24.

27th September St Barry's Day
St Barry lived on Glamorgan Island, South Glamorgan, now renamed Barry Island.

28th September Michaelmas Eve
Bonfires were lit on Michaelmas Eve in some locations and a traditional evening meal was roast lamb. In Surrey this was Nut Crack Night, nuts were even cracked and eaten during the evening service.

Blowing the Curfew Horn, Bainbridge, Upper Wensleydale — North Yorkshire
The horn blowing began as a warning of danger by Roman soldiers at the fort of Virosidum. In medieval times it became a Curfew Horn. The family maintain the tradition, at 9pm from today until Shrove Tuesday ('from Hawes back-end fair to Pancake Tuesday'). An African buffalo horn is used; two old cow horns survive, one dated 1611, the other is in the Rose and Crown.
BAINBRIDGE IS ON THE A684 EAST FROM SEDBERGH, PAST GAYLE.

29th September Michaelmas Day, St Michael's Day (St Michael and All Angels)

St Michael was chief of the archangels. He is said to have removed Lucifer from heaven, who fell to Earth, landing on a bramble bush. Ever since the devil has blighted brambles on this saint day. This gave rise to the tradition that blackberries are no good to eat after Michaelmas, although this tradition really applies to Old Michaelmas Day on 10th October.

This day also marked the end of the harvest in some rural communities. The amount of fodder available to feed livestock during the winter months would be calculated, telling the farmer how many animals could be kept and how many would have to be slaughtered. It was thus a popular time for animal sales, and also for hiring fairs, to engage farm labourers, maids and servants on a 12-month service agreement. Michaelmas was a Quarter Day and rent day. Curfew bells were often rung from Michaelmas to Lady Day. Several Derbyshire villages observe this custom.

Roast Goose Stuffed with Apple *(see p.187 for recipe)* is eaten with fresh produce and freshly baked bread. Goose is less fatty than at Christmas. Many Goose Fairs were held on this day, to which geese were often walked many miles. Tenants included a goose in their Michaelmas rent.

Payment of Quit Rent, Royal Courts of Justice, Strand   London

This event sometimes takes place in October instead. The City of London pays a Quit Rent to the Queen's Remembrancer for holdings at the Moors, Shropshire and the forge at St Clement Danes, Strand. For the Moors the Comptroller and City Solicitor pays a billhook and a hatchet, and for the Forge six horseshoes and 61 nails.

THE ROYAL COURTS OF JUSTICE ARE BETWEEN ALDWYCH AND TEMPLE.

**Election of the Lord Mayor of London, Guildhall,
followed by the procession to Mansion House**   London

THE GUILDHALL IS JUST OFF GRESHAM STREET (B128).

30th September

Tolzey Court, Stag and Hounds Inn, Old Market Street, Bristol   Avon

This event begins at 10am. The ancient court, which has attached to it the Court of Pie Poudre ('dusty feet'), is the only surviving fairground court.

BRISTOL CAN BE REACHED ON THE M4 AND M5.

Blowing the Curfew Horn, Bainbridge, North Yorkshire

Annual Quit Rent Ceremony at the Royal Courts of Justice, London

October customs

There were many fairs in October for the selling of livestock born and reared earlier in the year and for the hiring of labourers and domestic workers. The blackberry, nut and oyster seasons were closing and the last of the harvest thanksgivings and blessings were held. Shepherds traditionally held their meets in this month.

October was the favoured month for jousting and tournaments. At smaller events a popular alternative was Tilting on Horseback.

Tilting on Horseback *A ring was fixed at about shoulder height. A rider with a lance galloped up and attempted to put the lance point through the ring and carry it away.*

As the cycle of the old celtic year drew to a close, with its climax at what is now known as Hallowe'en, people's thoughts inevitably turned to ways of preparing for the hardships of the winter months and stocking up with enough fuel, dried and preserved produce, and warm clothing to last until spring. The month ends with punkies and pumpkins, witches and spirits, fire and divination, disguise and mischief.

Variable Dates

Court Leet of Laxton   **Nottinghamshire**

Laxton is the only place in the whole of England today where the medieval pattern of fields survives, and farming is still done on the open-field system. The Court determines all aspects of agricultural policy and settles demarcation and any other dispute that may occur. A jury of freeholders inspects the work of the farmers and imposes fines for poor husbandry, sowing and so on.

TAKE THE A1 NORTH FROM NEWARK TO TUXFORD, AND TURN LEFT THROUGH EGMANTON.

St Ives Charter Fair   **Cambridgeshire**

ST IVES IS ON THE A1123 EAST OF HUNTINGDON.

The Great Barmote Court, Moot Hall, Wirksworth   **Derbyshire**

See 'April Customs' section for details.

✺ Cob-Coaling, Stalybridge and Dunkinfield

Near Manchester

Children start to prepare for Bonfire Night, and in Stalybridge and Dukinfield, near Manchester, by asking residents for materials to burn (cob-coaling). They sing a cob-coaling song.

THESE TOWNS ARE ON THE EASTERN EDGE OF MANCHESTER, ON THE A635.

✺ Mop Fair, Warwick

Warwickshire

WARWICK IS BETWEEN STRATFORD-UPON-AVON AND LEAMINGTON SPA.

Fixed Dates

1st October St Mylor's day

St Mylor is the patron saint of Amesbury Abbey, Wiltshire, but little is known about his life.

The first Monday in October

A unique custom recently abandoned was the Opening of the Pudding Season at 'The Cheshire Cheese', 145 Fleet Street, London. Meat pudding (containing beef, larks, spices, mushrooms, gravy) was traditionally served.

✺ Wibsey Horse Fair, Fair Road, Wibsey, Bradford

West Yorkshire

WIBSEY IS A SOUTHERN SUBURB OF BRADFORD, ON THE A641.

✺ Mop Fair, King's Norton

West Midlands

KING'S NORTON IS ON THE A441 BETWEEN BIRMINGHAM AND REDDITCH.

The first Tuesday in October

✺ Beating the Bounds and Court Leet of Southampton

Hampshire

After the Beating the Bounds procession, the Court Leet meets in the Civic Centre. The Freemen who formed the first Court Leet, to settle disputes and deal with petty crime, before the 16th century, started what has become the oldest continuous such tradition in England. Courts Leet no longer have independent legal powers, but this one still acts as a forum for complaints, which are known as Presentments.

SOUTHAMPTON IS AT THE JUNCTION OF THE M3 AND M27.

Inspecting the fields in Laxton, Nottinghamshire

The first Thursday, Friday and Saturday in October

🪿 Goose Fair　　　　　　　　　　　　　　　　　　　　　　　　　**Nottingham**

Goose, brandy snaps *(see p.188 for recipe)* and nougat are traditionally served at this fair, once the main market for farmers from the East Midlands and the Fens to sell their geese. The fair had a Pie Powder Court.

TAKE THE A52 EAST FROM JUNCTION 25 OF THE M1, OR THE A610 EAST FROM JUNCTION 26.

The first Sunday in the October Harvest Festival

🕴 Harvest Festival of Costermongers, St Martin-in-the-Fields Church, St Martin's Place　　　　**London**

The parade and service of the costermongers (fruit and vegetable sellers) features the Pearly Kings and Queens (or 'Donahs'). The origin of the Kings was as protectors of sales pitches from rivals, but they were retained when licensing began. Now they have a ceremonial role, in their costumes decorated with patterns of pearl buttons.

THE CHURCH OVERLOOKS TRAFALGAR SQUARE.

✠ Harvest of the Sea Thanksgiving, St Mary at Hill, Lovat Lane, Billingsgate　　**London**

The church is decorated with fish, nets and other fishing paraphernalia.

LOVAT LANE IS OFF EASTCHEAP, BETWEEN THE MONUMENT AND THE TOWER OF LONDON.

✠ Harvest Festival, St Giles' Church, Stoke Poges　　　　　**Buckinghamshire**

TAKE THE B416 NORTH FROM SLOUGH.

✠ Blessing the Fishing Smacks, Brixham　　　　　　　　　　　**Devon**

BRIXHAM IS ON THE A3022 SOUTH FROM PAIGNTON.

✠ Blessing the Nets, Church of St Nicholas, Great Yarmouth　　**Norfolk**

GREAT YARMOUTH IS ON THE A47 EAST FROM NORWICH.

2nd October

💀 Old Man's Day, Braughing, near Bishop's Stortford　　　　**Hertfordshire**

In the 16th century Matthew Wall left £1 to keep alive the memory of his first(!) funeral procession along Fleece Lane to the churchyard. His coffin was dropped, and the impact revived him!

Now, at 4pm (10am if a weekend), children sweep the lane with brooms, and then a service is held round his grave. The funereal tolling of the church bells is then changed to a joyful peal, in celebration of his return to life.

BRAUGHING IS ON THE B1368.

4th October St Francis' Day

St Francis was a 13th-century hermit, said to have been charitable to animals.

The first Monday after the 4th October

Corby Glen Sheep Fair, near Grantham   Lincolnshire

CORBY GLEN IS ON THE A151.

5th October St Faith's Eve

This was another evening when an unmarried woman would engage in divination to learn the name of her future husband. Sometimes baking Faith Cakes was involved.

6th October Feast of St Faith

St Faith and her sisters Hope and Charity were martyred in the 3rd century when Emperor Hadrian ordered them put to death by being slowly grilled over a fire.

Funeral processions of unmarried girls included garlands of white flowers. After the service these would be hung in the church, with a pair of coffin-bearer's white gloves to symbolise purity. Hung for three Sundays, some became permanent, as at Abbots Ann, Hampshire.

Sloe Fair (originally Bishop's Fair 1108), Chichester   West Sussex

CHICHESTER IS BETWEEN WORTHING AND PORTSMOUTH ON THE A27.

7th October St Osyth's Day

St Osyth was the wife of the 7th-century Essex King Sighere.

Ringing the Lost in the Dark Bells, Twyford Church   Hampshire

William Davis left £1 to provide for a peal of bells and a meal for the ringers on this day to commemorate his escape from certain death in 1754. He was lost in the dark and about to ride over a quarry cliff when the sound of Twyford's bells made him realise he was riding in the wrong direction. He reined in his horse just in time. The bells are rung to this day.

TAKE THE B3354 SOUTH OF WINCHESTER TO TWYFORD.

8th October St Keyne's Day

The son of the 6th-century Welsh King Brychan, St Keyne became a missionary in South Wales and West Wales (now called Cornwall).

The second Tuesday in October

✿ **Celebration of the Wine Harvest, St Olave's Church, Hart Street**　　　　London

Masters and Wardens of the Worshipful Companies of Vintners and Distillers mark the harvest.
HART STREET IS NEXT TO FENCHURCH STREET STATION.

The second Wednesday in October

✿ **Tavistock Goosey Fair**　　　　Devon

This fair lasts all week, but the geese which gave it its name are now sold only on this day.
TAKE THE A386 NORTH FROM PLYMOUTH.

The second Saturday in October

✿ **Shepherds' Meet, Wasdale Head**　　　　Cumbria

TAKE THE A595 SOUTH FROM WHITEHAVEN, THEN LEFT AT GOSFORTH ON AN UNCLASSIFIED ROAD.

10th October Old Michaelmas Day

The Devil was said to spit on all blackberries not picked by this day. When, as the legend goes, St Michael threw the Devil out of heaven he landed in a blackberry bush, and takes an annual revenge.

Weyhill Stock Fair, Hampshire was a huge fair at which sheep and other livestock, and a variety of farm produce, were sold until recently. Shepherds used the occasion of the fair to gather at the Star Inn for a supper and to hold an initiation ceremony called Horning the Colt. New shepherds (Colts) had to put on a special headpiece with horns and an ale-cup. The cup was filled and an initiation song was sung. Then the Colt drank the ale and bought some for the other shepherds.

Preserves such as **Blackberry and Apple Jelly** *(see p.188 for recipe)* are traditionally made during this season.

✿ **Barton Fair, Tewkesbury**　　　　Gloucestershire

This is one of England's oldest surviving charter fairs, dating from the end of the 11th century.
TEWKESBURY IS BETWEEN WORCESTER AND GLOUCESTER ON THE A38.

The Monday following Old Michaelmas Day

✿ **Pack Monday Fair, Sherborne**　　　　Dorset

This fair is traditionally opened during the night by the young villagers locking arms and surging through the streets, accompanied by horns, bugles, whistles and beating on pans and tin trays (Teddy Roe's Band). This commemorates the celebrations of the masons, under their foreman Teddy Rowe, after completing the restoration of Sherborne Abbey after the fire in 1490. Then the masons packed their tools. The prelude to the band's performance is the striking of 13 by the Abbey bells.
TAKE THE A30 EAST FROM YEOVIL.

11th October St Canice's Day

St Canice was a 6th-century Irish abbot who worked on Mull.

12th October St Wilfrid's Day

In 7th-century Hexham, Northumberland, St Wilfrid persuaded the Catholic Church to grant sanctuary and immunity from persecution and prosecution to anyone within a mile 1.6 radius of the Frid (or Frith, meaning 'peace') Stool in the Abbey. It is still in existence, although the right was removed by James I in the 17th century.

Mop Fair, Stratford-on-Avon   Warwickshire

This fair is held on the previous day if the 12th is a Sunday. Roast ox is traditionally served at the fair. This, like others in the West Midlands, was originally a hiring fair for agricultural labourers and domestic servants. Domestic servants carried a mop, shepherds wore a lock of wool in their hat, and milkmaids wore a tuft of cowhair. When the 'hiring penny' or 'God's penny' was pressed in hand the year's unwritten contract started. Those whose placement did not work out had a follow-up option, for they could go to a Runaway Mop Fair, about a fortnight later. Today a smaller fair is held in the Market Place on the Friday of the following week, and a few survive elsewhere in the West Midlands.

TAKE THE A422 WEST FROM BANBURY.

The World Conker Championships, Ashton   Northamptonshire

About 1500 top-quality conkers (horse chestnuts) are required for this event, the effectiveness of which is much affected by drought and late frosts!

TAKE THE A427 EAST FROM CORBY, THEN LEFT ON AN UNCLASSIFIED ROAD TO ASHTON.

13th October St Edward the Confessor's Day

Edward (1003-1066) was King of England, and became patron saint of England after his death, until supplanted by St George in the 15th century.

Pilgrimage to Edward the Confessor's Tomb, Westminster Abbey   London

WESTMINSTER ABBEY IS OFF VICTORIA STREET (A302).

14th October St Selevan's Day

St Selevan was a Cornish saint.

A Sunday in mid-October

Blessing the Fish Harvest, St Oswald's Church, Flamborough Head   Humberside

TAKE THE B1255 NORTH EAST OUT OF BRIDLINGTON, THEN THE B1259.

Mop Fair, Stratford-on-Avon, Warwickshire

16th October

⊙The Lion Sermon, Church of St Katherine Cree, Leadenhall Street   **London**

The sermon is held on the following Monday if the 16th falls on a Saturday or Sunday. In his will of 1649 Mayor Sir John Gayer left £200 for the poor on condition that a sermon be given describing his escape from a lion whilst in Syria.

LEADENHALL STREET IS BETWEEN THE BANK OF ENGLAND AND ALDGATE.

17th October St Audrey's Day

At St Audrey's Fair in Ely, cheap bobbin lace was sold, and was known as 'tawdry lace'. Hence the use of the word 'tawdry' to refer to anything of poor quality.

18th October St Luke's Day

St Luke was a Greek doctor who became a disciple of St Paul on his missionary journeys. He was born in the 1st century in Antiock, and may have died in Greece. This day is a lucky day on which to choose a husband.

The Monday of the October school half-term

◉ Titchfield Carnival   **Hampshire**

When the Earl of Southampton imposed a toll on Titchfield boatmen in 1610, for the use of the canal linking the village to the sea, he damaged both the local economy and his reputation. As a reprisal the villagers burnt an effigy of him at the end of the local Carnival. Today, at 7pm, there is a torchlight procession and firework display.

TITCHFIELD IS ON AN UNCLASSIFIED ROAD JUST TO THE WEST OF FAREHAM.

19th October St Frideswide's Day

St Frideswide lived in the 8th century, and is said to have miraculously restored the sight of the Mercian King Ælfgar.

The London procession to Nelson's Column to mark Lord Nelson's victory at Trafalgar, London

Hoisting boots on St Crispin's Day

The Wednesday after the 18th October

⚙ **Yarm Cheese Fair**   Cleveland

Once an important livestock fair for horses, cattle and sheep as well as being a cheese market, it is now mainly a fun-fair. On the final Saturday, there is the Riding of the Fair parade and the blowing of an 18th-century horn.

TAKE THE A135 SOUTH FROM STOCKTON-ON-TEES.

The third Saturday in October

✿ **Shepherds' Meet, Buttermere**   Cumbria

TAKE THE B5289 SOUTH FROM KESWICK.

21st October St John of Bridlington's Day, St Ursula's Day

St John of Bridlington lived in the 14th century. St Ursula was a 4th-century Princess.

As this is the day in 1805 when Lord Nelson won the Battle of Trafalgar there are a number of commemorations, mainly in London and Portsmouth.

✿ **Laying the Wreath at Nelson's Column, Trafalgar Square**   London

A parade down the Mall to Trafalgar Square is organised to mark Lord Nelson's victory at Trafalgar. At the foot of Nelson's Column a service is held and a wreath laid.

TRAFALGAR SQUARE IS OPPOSITE CHARING CROSS (A4).

✪ **The Victory Service, HMS Victory, Portsmouth**   Hampshire

This starts at 8 am. Nelson's signal 'England expects that every man will do his duty' is hoisted.

PORTSMOUTH IS ON THE SOUTH COAST ON THE M275.

24th October

⚙ **Stow Fair, Stow-on-the-Wold**   Gloucestershire

The charter was granted in 1476 by Edward IV. This is the second date on which the fair is held. Originally a horse fair it is frequented by gypsies and travellers. Originally it was a sheep fair.

STOW-ON-THE-WOLD IS AT THE JUNCTION OF THE A424 AND A429.

🏛 **The Ale-Tasting, Dalton-in-Furness**   Cumbria

Originally the town held a Mop Fair, which was opened by the Steward, and his two halberd-bearers, with a Proclamation. Ale-tasters were elected to ensure local ales came up to standard during the fair. Today the ale-tasting alone has survived as a purely local event.

TAKE THE A590 NORTH EAST OUT OF BARROW-IN-FURNESS.

25th October St Crispin's Day, St Crispinian's Day

St Crispin and his brother St Crispinian were French, martyred in the 3rd century. St Crispin was the patron saint of shoemakers. Many in the trade took a holiday, some every Monday. People gave away their old shoes to the poor and bought new ones.

27th October St Odran's day

St Odran was a contemporary of St Columba c. 580 on the island of Iona.

28th October St Simon & St Jude's Day

St Simon and St Jude were 1st-century apostles. St Jude is the patron saint of hopeless cases, because he was the last saint anyone would appeal to – as his name resembled Judas!. It is said that it always rains on this day, indeed, the day had a reputation in medieval times similar to that of St Swithin's Day because the autumn weather would be breaking, giving way to gales and rain.

On this day Bedford boys sold baked **Warden Pears** *(see p.188 for recipe)* in the streets.

The last Thursday in October

ⓟ Punkie Night, Hinton St George, near Ilminster   Somerset

Children parade the streets with punkies, lanterns made from hollowed-out mangel-wurzels with a candle inside. The parade is led by the Punkie King and Punkie Queen, chosen for the best lantern pattern. They chant: 'It's Punkie Night tonight, It's Punkie Night tonight. Give us a candle, give us a light, If you don't you'll get a fright.' When making the lanterns a thin layer of flesh is left inside, and the skin peeled off rather than pierced. This is in contrast to pumpkin lanterns where all the flesh is removed and the pattern cut out of the skin. The children beg for candles to put in them.

A similar event is held in parts of Norfolk, both having their origins in the Celtic festival of Samhain and its Hallowe'en descendent.

TAKE THE A30 SOUTH WEST FROM YEOVIL, THEN TURN RIGHT AFTER CREWKERNE.

The last Friday in October

✿ The Oyster Feast, Colchester   Essex

This event, by invitation only, marks the climax of the oyster season. The sole rights to the fisheries on the River Colne were granted to the people of Colchester by King Richard I.

COLCHESTER IS BETWEEN CHELMSFORD AND IPSWICH ON THE A12

31st October Hallowe'en, All Hallows' Eve

On Hallowe'en, spirits were believed to walk abroad and the dead return to earth, to eat and drink. People believed that the souls of their departed relatives would visit them, so they left food on the table and left the door unlocked before retiring to bed. Church bells were rung, and bonfires lit, to guide returning souls to Earth. Animals were brought in for the winter. Witches were abroad, and some people were credited with being able to perform magic, see into the future and summon ghosts and spirits to appear. Ghost stories were told. Fires were lit in the open so that souls condemned to purgatory would find relief, (e.g. at Purgatory Field, Poulton, Lancashire, and at Purgatory Farm at Weston, Lancashire), and to scare witches and evil spirits away. For similar reasons torches were carried (cabbage stalks, or bundles of dried heather or brushwood, dipped in grease) and these accompanied the chanting of spells in barns and other stores to protect the contents. The image of a witch in black cloak, black pointed hat, ugly, warty face, broomstick, black cat and book of spells dates from medieval times. Rowan wood was thought to give protection from witches.

This was a Celtic Quarter Day, the Celtic festival of Samhain, summer's end or the feast to the dying sun, and the last day of the Celtic Year. It was also the Celtic Harvest Festival and the Festival of the Dead, when the verdure of summer decayed and the nights drew in. Fires were extinguished, to be rekindled later to welcome the returning spirits. At Beltane in the spring the cycle of life began again.

Many folk songs are about Hallowe'en beliefs and rituals, such as 'Tam Lin' and 'Alison Gross'.

Hallowe'en is a time for divination. Nuts are roasted by girls, or apple pips placed on hot coals, and the behaviour of the nuts or pips in the fire indicate the temperament of their future husbands. All hope for a quiet, steady burning, not a nut or pip that crackles and jumps! Nut shells are burned, and prophecies made from the ashes. Fortunes were also read from apples and cabbages. Girls bob for apples in a tub of water, although nowadays boys do this too (Apple Bobbing). Also they try to catch a suspended apple. Girls peel the apple so that the peel remains in one piece, then throw the peel in the air: it will make the shape of the initial of their future betrothed when it lands (Apple Pairing). If a girl eats an apple whilst seated in front of a looking glass she will see her future husband peeping over her shoulder. Similarly if she stands before a mirror at midnight and combs her hair three times she will see a reflection of her future husband over her shoulder. If this fails then going to bed with a sprig of rosemary or yew under the pillow will reveal the future husband in her dreams.

If each girl suspends an apple over the fire, the order in which they fall gives the order of marriage. If a girl's apple does not fall she will remain unmarried. Each boy is sat blindfolded in front of 3 bowls (luggies), one with clean water, one with foul water and one empty, and must dip a finger into one luggie. If it's the clean water he will marry a maiden, if it's the foul water he will marry a widow, and if it's the empty luggie he will remain unmarried.

Mash o' Nine Sorts *(see p.188 for recipe)* is a traditional Hallowe'en supper served to unmarried guests, in which a ring is hidden. Whoever finds it will next be married.

People used to go from house to house begging for Soul Cakes, particularly in rural Cheshire. These were rich, round fruity buns, not unlike rock cakes today. A traditional game is to try and eat buns dangling on a string.

A pumpkin lantern (made from a turnip or swede) is traditionally made before dusk and kept alight until dawn. Slice out the stalk, cut triangular eyes and nose and a zig-zag or grinning mouth. Scoop out the flesh and seeds and keep. Light a short fat candle inside.

Hallowe'en has a reputation as a Mischief Night, sometimes youngsters knocked on doors demanding a treat or they would play a trick (Trick or Treat). In the North, people dressed up (guisers) as witches, ghosts, spirits, kelpies, spunkies, with blackened faces and turnip lanterns, going from house to house getting food and money. **Hallowe'en Cakes** *(see p.188 for recipe)* were made in the North of England (Cake Day), with a variety of fillings or flavours. **Toffee Apples** *(see p.188 for recipe)* were also popular. **Pumpkin pie** and **Pumpkin Seeds** *(see p.188 for recipes)* are also eaten during Hallowe'en celebrations.

Mischief Night, Exmoor   Somerset
TAKE THE A358 NORTH WEST FROM TAUNTON, THEN LEFT ON THE B3224.

Mischief Night, in various parts of the area   Yorkshire
In the past youths played pranks such as unhinging doors, hiding implements left outside, white-washing walls, ringing bells, tying door latches, and overturning water butts.

MELTING THE LEAD

BURNING THE NUTS

November customs

As if to counter the darkness and foreboding of Hallowe'en, November begins with All Saints' Day and the Christian remembrance of the dead on All Souls' Day. Mummers' Plays mark the beginning of winter, but soon the pyrotechnics of Bonfire Night change the mood, albeit with residual anti-Catholic undertones in some formerly fiercely Protestant areas.

Many hiring agreements terminated at Martinmas and labourers with their payoff money to spend would be buying food, some to feast on then and there and some to preserve for the winter. Real and Mock Mayors were elected in November, the latter a Saxon jibe at the imposition of this Norman office. Towards the end of the month Clementing and Catterning festivities, associated with traditional holidays taken by rural craftworkers at a time when the shortening days meant a loss of good working light, were widely held, and these were scarcely over when Advent begun.

As winter had either arrived or was fast approaching, pastimes turned from the outdoor to the indoor kind, to those already mentioned under January.

Variable Dates

Court Leet of the Island and Royal Manor of Portland   **Dorset**
This Court has a jury of 24, and is concerned particularly with the use of common land. Every seven years it perambulates its bounds, and those of some other ancient Wessex towns with their own commons.

Fixed Dates

1st November All Saints' Day, All Hallows' Day, All Souls' Eve, St Cadfan's Day
Christians commemorate All Saints. Today and tomorrow originally represented an attempt to Christianise the pagan Feast-of-the-dead the remnants of which are now part of the Hallowe'en festivities. 'Hallow' is an old word for 'saint'. On this day people remembered their departed relatives and prayed for them. Food is left out tonight in case the souls of the departed visit.

St Cadfan lived in 5th-century Rhyl, Clwyd.

Up to the late 19th century this was Bonfire Day. It was a joyful day, although some aspects were the same as those on All Souls' Day, which was a solemn day. In some areas this was a Mischief Day.

All Saints' Day was a Quarter Day.

On this day, or the preceding one, or on the winter solstice, Mummers' Plays were performed to mark the beginning of winter, as a rite to revive the life-bearing sun. In Cheshire the players are called Soulers or Soul Cakers, as 'Souling' is the visiting of each house in the village begging for soul-cakes in return for a song or blessing. This practice arose in the Middle Ages when the cakes were offered as payment for prayers said for souls suffering in purgatory, or were just an offering to the departed. The Protestant Reformation saw an end to this custom and souling became no more than a traditional giving of gifts of the cakes on this day. In some places, only children maintain the custom.

Soul Cakes *(see p.188 for recipe)* – flat, oval or round buns made from eggs, milk, spices and saffron – Parkin, Treacle Toffee, apples and pears were eaten. **Lancashire Harcake** *(see p.189 for recipe)* is traditionally offered to visitors on this day.

 Antrobus Souling Play, Antrobus   Cheshire

This 400-year-old play centres around Dick Tatton, the Wild Horse of Antrobus (with snapping jaws like the Hoodening Horse), and also includes Beelzebub and Dairy Doubt, the village idiot. It is performed tonight, and from Thursday to Saturday of the next two weeks, in public houses in the vicinity, ending with the Antrobus Arms.

TAKE THE A559 SOUTH FROM JUNCTION 10 OF THE M56, THEN LEFT ON AN UNCLASSIFIED ROAD.

2nd November All Souls' Day

This was a solemn day in commemoration of, and prayer for, the faithful who remain in purgatory, in the hope they will progress to heaven. Special oval or round buns were distributed at church doors as a 'charity' for departed souls. People ('Soulers') would go from house to house singing soul verses and begging for cakes, in remembrance of the dead. The poor would offer this service to the rich in exchange for alms, supposedly to pay for prayers for the dead. Before eating a soul cake it is customary to say: A soul cake, a soul cake, Have mercy, Lord, on all Christian souls.

The observance is strongest in Cheshire and Shropshire, and also quite widely in Staffordshire, Derbyshire and Lancashire. Soul cakes were also given as a bread dole to the community poor. Bonfires, 'to light souls out of purgatory' were lit and church bells tolled.

Antrobus Souling Play, Antrobus, Cheshire, 1972

Soulcakers' Play, Comberbach   **Cheshire**
TAKE THE A559 SOUTH FROM JUNCTION 10 OF THE M56, THEN RIGHT ON AN UNCLASSIFIED ROAD.

Soulcakers' Play, Warburton   **Cheshire**
TAKE THE A6144 EAST OUT OF SALE.

Soulcakers' Play, Frodsham and vicinity   **Cheshire**
FRODSHAM IS ON THE A56 NORTH EAST OUT OF CHESTER, OR FROM JUNCTION 12 OF THE M56.

3rd November St Winefride's Day, St Clydog's Day

St Winefride was martyred in the 7th century, defending her virtue. St Clydog was a 6th-century king of the southern border lands between England and Wales.

The Sunday nearest All Souls' Day

Fish Harvest Festival, St Dunstan's-in-the-East, Lower Thames Street   **London**
LOWER THAMES STREET IS THE B132, ALONG THE RIVER THAMES WEST OF THE TOWER OF LONDON.

The first Saturday in November

Harvest Home, Putley, near Ledbury   **Hereford and Worcester**
TAKE THE A438 EAST OUT OF HEREFORD, RIGHT ON THE A4172, THEN RIGHT AT AYLTON.

Shepherds' Meet, Walna Scar, near Seathwaite   **Cumbria**
FROM BROUGHTON-IN-FURNESS TAKE THE A593 NORTH, THEN LEFT ON AN UNCLASSIFIED ROAD.

4th November St Cleer's day

St Cleer was a 6th-century Cornish hermit.

Mischief Night, various parts of region   **Yorkshire**
This event formerly took place on Hallowe'en or, in some areas, May Eve. Common pranks are ringing door bells; knocking on doors; tying door handles together; pushing objects, including fireworks, through letter boxes; smearing treacle or whitewash on walls, handles, and so on.

5th November Guy Fawkes' Day, Bonfire Night

This night commemorates deliverance from Robert Catesby's unsuccessful plot to blow up with gunpowder the king, House of Lords and House of Commons this day in 1605, but has inherited some features of Hallowe'en, particularly the use of fires or burning tar barrels to drive out evil.

Guy Fawkes was born into a York Protestant family, but he made many Catholic friends, and after he inherited his father's estate he became a Catholic. James I, under pressure from his ministers, instituted a number of anti-Catholic laws, generating much resentment in the Catholic community. Robert Catesby, another Protestant turned Catholic, devised the plot. Guy Fawkes was invited to join the conspirators as he was used to handling gunpowder – a skill he learned whilst fighting for the Spanish army against the Dutch in Belgium. The plotters gained access to the coal store (at street level) under the State Chamber of Parliament and planted the barrels of gunpowder ready for the State Opening on 31 October.

The king postponed the opening until 5th November in order to go hunting. The plotters began to worry about killing Catholic peers, and a letter was sent to Lord Mounteagle on 26th October warning him not to attend the State Opening. But the Lord stayed loyal to the king and he and the Lord Chamberlain searched the rooms below the Chamber. Guy Fawkes was discovered but not alerted to the danger he was now in. A party of soldiers was sent down on the morning of 5th November to arrest him and discovered 36 barrels of gunpowder ready to be ignited. He and some of his fellow conspirators were executed on 31st January 1606 opposite the Parliament building having been found guilty of plotting to kill the king and members of Parliament.

To this day an officer and ten men of the Yeomen of the Guard, in traditional uniforms, still search the Houses of Parliament vaults with lanterns, and notify the monarch that they are clear, before the Houses commence session. Guy Fawkes' original lantern is believed to be that on display in the Ashmolean Museum, Oxford (The Dark Lantern).

James I declared 5th November a public holiday, the first recorded bonfire celebrations being in 1607. The Hallowe'en tradition of bonfires was carried over, and it may be that the effigy of Guy Fawkes burned on this night comes from the custom of burning effigies of witches on Hallowe'en. Professional bonfire builders who made hilltop beacons plied their trade on 5th November. Bonfires on this night have now replaced the original Hallowe'en fires, banned during the Reformation, and elements of both Hallowe'en and All Soul's Day celebrations can be found. In the past, wood was often stolen to make bonfires and blazing, rolling tar barrels caused fires and mayhem.

Bonfire Societies, which celebrate this night with gusto, are mostly to be found in Kent and Sussex, where anti-Catholic resentment was particularly strong. Pope Pius IV is regarded as being the instigator of the plot, and anti-papist banners are still to be seen, and traditional verses recited.

A 'Guy', a Bonfire, fireworks and torchlight processions are traditional on this night. Children collect money for fireworks by making a guy, in Guy Fawkes' image, pushing it round in a pram or leaning it up against a wall, and asking passers-by for 'A penny for the guy?' The guy is burned on the bonfire, and then fireworks are lit. Potatoes and chestnuts were roasted in the bonfire. Many rhymes are connected with the Gunpowder Plot, as well as rhymes used by children when begging for fuel for the bonfire or money for fireworks, and rhymes chanted at the bonfire itself. Children used to blacken their faces, and they played a game called lucky stones. Each found an individual stone and put it in the bonfire. The next day it was sought in the ashes. If it was whole that child would have a year of good fortune, otherwise ill fortune.

In the West Yorkshire Pennines this day is known as Plot Night. The bonfires are called plots and there is much rivalry between plotters.

Potatoes baked in their jackets, roast chestnuts, **Lancashire Parkin** *(see p.189 for recipe)* – a Yorkshire and Lancashire cake made from oatmeal, treacle and butter, originally made to be left for the spirits of the dead returning to their family – and **Bonfire Toffee** *(see p.189 for recipe)* are eaten. **Thor Cakes** *(see p.189 for recipe)*, which are like Parkin but with added peel, are eaten in Derbyshire and Lancashire.

✳ **Guy Fawkes's Day, Lewes**   **East Sussex**

The most spectacular celebration of this night is in Lewes, where the four local Bonfire Societies (Cliffe, Waterloo, Lewes Borough, Commercial Square) engage in tar-barrel rolling, torchlit processions in ethnic costumes with anti-papist banners, commemorations at the War Memorial, and the burning of the papal effigy followed by fireworks. Marching Bonfire Boys originally adopted disguises to avoid being recognised by the police on account of past riotous behaviour on this night. Their first procession was in 1853. The original uniform of the first Lewes Bonfire Boys of a Guernsey shirt of horizontal blue-and-white stripes was replaced, as more societies sprang up, by fancy dress characteristic of each society.

   The tradition also commemorates the 17 protestant martyrs burnt, by order of Mary I, at the stake outside the Star in Lewes High Street in 1555.

TAKE THE A27 NORTH EAST FROM BRIGHTON.

✳ **Bonfire Night, Ottery St Mary**   **Devon**

This celebration starts with the firing of home-made rock cannons at 5:45am and at pm blazing tar barrels are rolled or carried through the town. The carriers protect their arms with sacking soaked in water, and pass the barrels on when they can't stand the heat any longer. It is said that the custom started to celebrate the landing of William III on 5th November 1688.

TAKE THE A30 EAST OUT OF EXETER, THEN RIGHT ON THE B3174.

✳ **Rye Fawkes and Burning the Boat, Rye**   **East Sussex**

RYE IS NEAR THE COAST AT THE JUNCTION OF THE A259 AND A268.

✳ **Guy Fawkes Night, Edenbridge**   **Kent**

There is a torchlight procession of decorated floats and a wicker guy.

TAKE THE B2026 SOUTH FROM WESTERHAM.

✳ **Guy Fawkes Night Battle**   **East Sussex**

There is a torchlight procession in front of the Battle Abbey.

Right: The 'Guy' of Lewes Borough Bonfire Society
Far right: The Cliffe Bonfire Society in Lewes

Turning the Devil's Stone, Shebbear, near Holsworthy

Devon

The Devil's Stone is a huge boulder outside the church, said to pin down Satan. He is kept trapped if the stone is turned each year, which is done at 8pm after a tuneless peal of bells. This custom exhibits shades of the battle between good and evil, as though turning this huge natural object gives the villagers power over malign forces.

TAKE THE A388 SOUTH FROM BIDEFORD, THEN LEFT ON AN UNCLASSIFIED ROAD THROUGH NEWTON ST PETROCK.

Gunpowder Plot Celebrations, Highbridge

Somerset

TAKE THE A38 NORTH FROM BRIDGWATER.

Gunpowder Plot Celebrations, Wells

Somerset

TAKE THE A39 NORTH FROM GLASTONBURY.

The Sunday nearest 5th November

Gunpowder Plot Sermon, St Mary-le-Bow, Cheapside

London

CHEAPSIDE LINKS THE NORTH SIDE OF ST PAUL'S CATHEDRAL TO MANSION HOUSE.

The Thursday nearest 5th November

Guy Fawkes Carnival, Bridgwater

Somerset

One of the interesting aspects of this big event is the use of the Bridgwater Squibs, or fireworks, made to their own formula. Rolling tar barrels used to feature here, but no longer although shop-keepers still continue the practice of closing early and boarding up their windows as if the danger of fire and riotous behaviour were still present.

BRIDGWATER IS OFF THE M5 AT JUNCTIONS 23 OR 24.

The Friday nearest 5th November

Rolling the Blazing Tar Barrels, Hatherleigh, near Okehampton

Devon

Formerly held on the Wednesday after 5th November, the tar barrels are not actually rolled now but dragged through the town on sledges and used to ignite the bonfire.

HATHERLEIGH IS NORTH OF OKEHAMPTON, ON THE A386.

6th November St Leonard's Day

St Leonard lived near Horsham, Sussex in the 6th century, St Leonard's Forest is named after him.

7th November St Willibrord's Day

St Wiilibrord was born in Yorkshire in the 7th century, and became a missionary in Europe.

8th November St Cybi's Day, St Tysilio's Day

St Cybi lived in the 6th century and St Tysilio in the 7th century, both on Anglesey, Wales.

9th November

This is a traditional day for electing both real and mock Mayors. The office of Mayor was instituted by the Normans, replacing the Saxon Portreeve, and it has been said that the election of Mock Mayors was a deliberate act of defiance towards the Norman imposition, done with much satire.

⚜ Swearing in the Lord Mayor-Elect and Lord Mayor of London's Procession   London

The Lord Mayor is chosen on Michaelmas Day (29th September) and on this day goes in state from the Mansion House to the Guildhall to be sworn in by the Chief Justice. This right of choice was enshrined in Magna Carta.

MANSION HOUSE IS AT THE JUNCTION OF VICTORIA STREET AND CANNON STREET.

The second Saturday in November (formerly 10th November)

⚜ The Lord Mayor's Show   London

This marks the day when the Lord Mayor elect takes office. A procession takes place from 10.30am at the Guildhall to the Mansion House, via St Paul's Cathedral for the blessing and the Royal Courts of Justice in the Strand for the swearing in by the Lord Chief Justice and the Master of the Rolls, then via the Embankment. The Show's climax is a firework display.

THE GUILDHALL IS JUST OFF GRESHAM STREET (B128).

10th November Martinmas Eve

There are no longer any specific customs on Martinmas Eve in England, the traditional divinations being confined to Scotland.

154 November customs

11th November Martinmas, St Martin's Day

St Martin of Tours was a 4th-century cavalry soldier. He became a monk, and gained a reputation for humility and charity to the underprivileged.

This was a day of feasting, when beasts were slaughtered, preserved and stored for winter. A whole oxen would be roasted. This may have been a survival of the Roman Feast of the Wine God Bacchus, which was held on this day. Roast Goose, hot rum and milk are also traditionally eaten.

Amongst farm labourers this day was called Pack-rag Day because it was often the last day of hiring agreements, so the labourers bundled up their belongings, slung them over their shoulders, and went to seek new employment. Perhaps this was a feast day because many people had just received payments. The day was also a Quarter Day for rent settlements and land payments.

Meeting of the Hundred of Knightlow, Knightslow Hill, and the Wroth Silver Ceremony, Knightlow Cross, Ryton-on-Dunsmore Warwickshire

Since Saxon times commoners have had the right to drive cattle over the land of the Duke of Buccleuch, provided they pay a tribute (Wroth Silver) at first light, and no later. The commoners who represent the 25 parishes of the Hundred meet before sunrise. (A Hundred is an ancient legal subdivision of a shire.) The name of each parish is read out at dawn and the representative steps forward and pays its due. When the tribute is paid to the Duke, he provides a drink of hot rum and milk for all at the Dun Cow Inn. Failure to pay incurs a fine of 100 pence for every penny owed or of a white bull with red nose and ears (similar to those of the ancient Chillingham herd in Northumberland).

TAKE THE A45 SOUTH EAST FROM COVENTRY TO RYTON-ON-DUNSMORE.

Firing the 'Penny Poppers', Fenny Stratford, near Bletchley Buckinghamshire

This ceremony dates from 1730 and commemorates the founding of St Martin's Church by Dr Browne Willis. The six small cannons, presented by Dr Browne and kept padlocked on a shelf in the church tower, are fired at 8am, noon, 4pm and 8pm. As part of Dr Browne's bequest, after the firing, a special sermon is preached and an endowed supper enjoyed.

FENNY STRATFORD IS SOUTH OF MILTON KEYNES, JUST OFF THE A5.

Firing off the 'Penny Poppers' Stratford, Buckinghamshire, 1952

14th November St Dyfrig's day

St Dyfrig lived in the 6th century, and was said to have been the bishop who crowned Arthur.

16th November St Margaret's Day

St Margaret of Scotland was the wife of the 11th-century king, Malcolm III.

17th November St Hilda's day

St Hilda lived in the 7th century, founded Whitby Abbey and presided over its Synod. It was this body which fixed the way in which Easter's date is calculated.

This day was granted as a public holiday by Elizabeth I in 1570 to mark the 12th anniversary of her coronation. Even today the Bank of England and the Exchequer take this day as a holiday, although no one else does.

The third Wednesday of November

✺ **The Court Leet and Court Baron of Sidbury Manor, near Sidmouth**　　　**Devon**

The courts elect officers whose function was originally to ensure that all provisions purchased for the Manor were of good quality. Appointments such as Bread-weigher, Ale-taster, and Meat-taster are made. When the courts' business is done there follows the Leet-ale, a feast which seems to now be the main reason for convening at all.

SIDBURY IS ON THE A375 BETWEEN SIDMOUTH AND HONITON

The third Saturday of November

✺ **The Mardale Shepherds' Meet, St Patrick's Well Inn, Bampton, near Penrith**　　　**Cumbria**

This is the oldest continuously held shepherds' meet, at which shepherds hold a Foot Hunt (a fox hunt with hounds, but with the shepherds on foot), tell stories and exchange experiences, and which ends with a rendering of 'While shepherds watched their flocks by night'.

TAKE THE A6 SOUTH FROM PENRITH TO SHAP, THEN TURN RIGHT ON AN UNCLASSIFIED ROAD THROUGH ROSGILL.

19th November St Ermenburga's Day

St Ermenburga was a Kentish princess who founded a nunnery at Minster on the Isle of Thanet.

20th November St Edmund's Day

St Edmund was a 9th-century king of East Anglia, who was murdered by Vikings when he refused to champion their pagan cause. He was buried at Bury St Edmunds, Suffolk.

✠ **Giving St Edmund's Buns, Southwold**　　　**Suffolk**

At 2:45pm a church service dedicated to St Edmund is held, and afterwards in the church porch the Mayor gives each school child a bun. This is followed by the planting of a tree, another long-standing tradition, in the town.

TAKE THE A12 NORTH OUT OF SAXMUNDHAM, THEN RIGHT ON THE A1095.

21st November Old Martinmas Eve

Casual seasonal workers on farms and in fishing ports would work their last day today, and would feast to celebrate, sometimes at the expense of a satisfied employer and sometimes at their own.

22nd November St Cecilia's Day, St Clement's Eve

St Cecilia was a 3rd-century Roman Christian, who took a vow of chastity – after marrying – and was martyred when she refused to recognise pagan gods. She is the patron saint of musicians.

St Clement's Eve was a day when hatters had a holiday in honour of their patron saint St Clement. Hatters claim he invented felt by stuffing wool between his sweaty feet and sandals on a long pilgrimage.

The Wednesday nearest St Cecilia's day

✛ **St Cecilia's Day Service**   London
Formerly at St Sepulchre (Church of the Holy Sepulchre without Newgate), Giltspur Street, this commemorative service is now held at three venues in rotation: Westminster Abbey, Westminster Cathedral and St Paul's Cathedral.

23rd November St Clement's day
St Clement was a 4th-century Christian martyr, drowned by being bound to an anchor, who became the patron saint of blacksmiths, lighthousemen and hatters. Influence from the Church brought about the replacement of the Saxon smith-god Wayland, who forged mail for the gods, by Clement. Blacksmiths would fire gunpowder on their anvils in honour of the saint they called Old Clem, and hold a feast. To collect money for the feast they would parade an effigy of Old Clem around their village and ask for alms (Clementing). One of the biggest Clementing celebrations, including Firing the Anvil, was at Twyford, Hampshire until 1880. The feast was held at the Bugle Inn. Fishing villages also had Clementing festivities. Later, children took up Clementing and sang songs in return for apples or spiced Clements cakes or **St Clement's Tarts** *(see p.189 for recipe)*. They would play the games with apples that are also associated with Hallowe'en, i.e. Apple Bobbing and Apple Pairing. Clement's Cakes were also traditionally sold at the Berkshire Clementide Sheep Fair.

24th November St Catherine's Eve
After work, lace-makers used to prepare a Cathern Bowl. Cider in a bowl is spiced with cinnamon and a little sugar, and placed in the hearth. Above it are suspended some apples which the heat of the fire turns to pulp. The pulp falls into the cider, which is then strained and given to fellow lace-makers and guests. Afterwards a kind of purification ceremony was undergone by each lace-maker, as they jumped over a lighted candle placed on the floor. If the flame was blown out then bad luck would follow for the rest of the year. This was one of many examples of the belief that jumping through fire could change one's fortunes.

25th November St Catherine's Day
St Catherine of Alexandria was reputed to be an early Christian martyr who was tortured on a wheel in AD 310, hence the Catherine Wheel firework and the Catherine or Rose Window. She is patroness of spinners, lace-makers, rope-makers and spinsters. It may be that there is a connection with the story of Catherine being tortured on a wheel and the Church's attempt to rid people of their ancient sun-worshipping tradition of wrapping a wheel in straw, setting light to it, and rolling it round the fields as a fertility rite. Furthermore, a confusion may exist between St Catherine and Catherine of Aragon, the first wife of Henry VIII, who she married in 1509. It was she who introduced Spanish lace-making techniques into England. There is no certainty at all that Catherine ever existed.

Lace is worn in commemoration of the traditional lace-makers' holiday, taken because the nights were drawing in and it was too dark to see properly to make lace. Festivities included holding a procession (Catterning), collecting money and electing a Cattern Queen. A game played during St Catherine festivities was Jumping the Cattern Candle, which was about two ft (6m) high. If the flame was extinguished bad luck would follow. This would also appear to be part of pagan sun worship, with its connection of fire and fertility.

At the beginning of the 20th century machinery for lace-making superseded much of the handicraft, and observance of this day lapsed. However, children persisted with the custom of Catterning by going to houses and farms signing songs about St Catherine and asking for pennies, apples or other little gifts.

Cattern Pie *(see p.189 for recipe)*, Cattern's Cakes (bread dough with butter, caraway seeds, sugar and eggs kneaded in), and Wigs (batter of flour, butter, sour milk, ginger and spices, cooked in muffin pans) are eaten in Bedfordshire. Apples and beer are also traditionally consumed, as is Hot Pot, a hot mixture of rum, beer and eggs.

The Sunday before Advent Sunday Stir-up Sunday

The name 'Stir-up Sunday' comes from the start of the Collect of the day 'Stir up we beseech thee, O Lord, the wills of thy faithful people.' It is the traditional day to start the Christmas pudding. Everyone should take a turn at stirring the pudding and make a wish as they do so, but not reveal it to anyone. Money is put into the pudding, traditionally silver threepenny pieces. Puddings should be made from 13 ingredients, one for Jesus and one for each apostle, and a total of 13 should be made. The last, or Judas Pudding, should be thrown away.

After a cordial visit by Elizabeth I to the lawyers at Middle Temple she ordered a Christmas pudding made for them as a token of her appreciation. Each year the lawyers decided to create a tradition and saved a bit to be added to next year's pudding that they would make themselves. This continued until the 1960s when the custom lapsed. In 1971 Queen Elizabeth, the Queen Mother revived it by presenting a new pudding.

The four evenings before the last Friday in November

🏛 The Court Leet, Wareham   Dorset

This is a surviving Norman Court which now has only the function of checking on weights, measures and other standards in local shops and public houses. The Ale-tasters, with pewter ale-measure, Bread-weighers, with scales, Leather Sealer, Scavengers, to check rubbish, Hayward, and Surveyors and Searchers of Mantles and Chimneys comprise the team of inspectors.
TAKE THE A35 WEST OUT OF POOLE, THEN LEFT ON THE A351 TO WAREHAM.

28th November St Juthwara's Day

St Juthwara lived in South West England, but little is known about her.

Advent

'Advent' means 'coming', of the Messiah. Christians celebrate the coming of Christ during Advent – the four weeks before Christmas. Advent Sunday is the nearest Sunday to 30th November, before or after. The Advent wreath, with four candles, one to light on each Sunday, is made on the day before Advent Sunday. This tradition may have started in Germany. The third Sunday is Gaudete, a day of rejoicing. Cribs are erected during Advent, and on 1st December children can start an Advent calendar, opening a window each day until Christmas. These were first produced in Germany about 1890.

In the North of England before the Reformation poor women made two dolls, called the Advent Images (representing the Virgin and Christ-Child) and went round the neighbourhood singing the ancient carol 'The first joy that Mary had, it was the joy of one', and people contributed a coin. The 24 little images behind doors in the Advent calendar have their origins in these Advent images, although Advent only starts on the 1st December if this day is a Sunday.

30th November St Andrew's Day, Andermass

St Andrew was a fisherman and is the patron saint of Scotland and of lace-makers in the English Midlands. He was crucified on a cross shaped like an 'X' at his own request, as he felt too humble to be accorded the same shape cross as Jesus had had. This gave rise to the saltire on the Scottish flag. On this day young girls would take off their clothes and ask of St Andrew whom they would marry.

This was Mischief Night in Northamptonshire. Squirrel-hunting was an annual event on this day, particularly in South and South East England.

Elderberry wine and Tandra cake or **St Andrew's Cake** *(see p. 189 for recipe)* – a bread dough base to which is added lard, sugar, currants or raisins, lemon peel and eggs – are eaten in England in areas of lace-making such as Bedfordshire, Buckinghamshire, Hertfordshire and Northamptonshire. The holiday was known as 'Tander'.

The Saturday nearest St Andrew's Day

Eton College Wall Game, Eton   Berkshire

At 11am two teams, the Collegers (scholars) and Oppidans (boarders), play this idiosyncratic game on a long, narrow pitch including a wall and a tree. Scrimmages, called 'bullies', are held to try to score, or 'boss', a goal by getting the ball into the other side's 'calx' (chalk marks on the wall and tree). The last goal to be scored was in 1911.

TAKE THE B3022 NORTH FROM WINDSOR TO ETON.

At the end of November, during National Tree Week

Arbor Day, Southwold   Suffolk

This is part of the St Edmund's celebrations, moved to coincide with National Tree Week.

TAKE THE A12 NORTH OUT OF SAXMUNDHAM, THEN RIGHT ON THE A1095.

The Eton College Wall Game, Berkshire

December customs

After the first few days of Advent, St Nicholas' Day and the election of Boy Bishops are held, after which there was little to interrupt the preparations for the winter solstice and Christmas, a period of extraordinary mixing of pagan and Christian customs and symbolism. Slaughtering of beasts for the Christmas table began on 17th December.

Once the climax of Yule, Midwinter Day became, as St Thomas' Day, the time when Christmas activities such as carolling, putting up decorations and wrapping up gifts began – a far cry from the hijacking of the seasonal distinctiveness of Christmas by commercial interest as early as October. Wassailing, carolling, Mumming and sword dancing, the latter two particularly on Boxing Day, are all much in evidence throughout the Yuletide season. Like November this was a month for mainly indoor games, including those associated with the festive occasions in the month.

As if children were not spoiled enough on Christmas Day they had unbounded license on Holy Innocents' Day, barely drawing breath before preparations for New Year's Eve began. The calendar year was ending and divination was again a common theme.

Variable Dates

Candle Auction, Grimston Leicestershire
TAKE THE A6006 WEST FROM MELTON MOWBRAY, THEN RIGHT ON AN UNCLASSIFIED ROAD.

The Venison Warrant Gift, Mansion House London
This is the second of the two gifts under the warrant, four does presented to the Lord Mayor of London. Four bucks were received in July.
MANSION HOUSE IS AT THE JUNCTION OF VICTORIA STREET AND CANNON STREET.

Fixed Dates

1st December
Although this is not necessarily the start of Advent, it is the customary day when children open the first window of their Advent calendars.

The first Monday in December

Election of the Deputy of the Cinque Port Liberty, Brightlingsea   Essex

The Cinque Ports of Kent and Sussex achieved special status in medieval times because they were the home of the Navy. The original five were: Dover, Hastings, Hythe, Romney and Sandwich: later they were joined by Rye and Winchelsea. Special associate status was granted to Brightlingsea in 1360, and the town still commemorates this event by electing a new Deputy each year in the belfry of All Saints Church. The new Deputy pays the Mayor Ship Money, and is given a silver chain of office.

TAKE THE A133 EAST FROM COLCHESTER, THEN RIGHT AT FRATING GREEN ON THE B1029.

3rd December St Birinus' Day

St Birinus became the first Bishop of Dorchester, Oxfordshire in the 7th century, and was to die in AD 650 of an adder bite.

4th December St Barbara's Day, St Osmund's Day, Old St Clement's Day

St Barbara was invoked by miners and soldiers for protection against injury by explosions, but the reasons for this are as obscure as the details of her life.

St Osmund was Bishop of Salisbury, Wiltshire in the 11th century.

The big Sheep Fair at Lambourn, Berkshire took place today, at which was sold a delicacy called Clementy Cake – spiced fruit buns.

5th December St Justinian's Day

St Justinian travelled from his native Brittany to Ramsey Island off the coast of Dyfed, Wales, where he lived as a hermit.

6th December St Nicholas' Day

St Nicholas was the Bishop of Myra in Asia Minor (southern Turkey) in the 4th century. He was known for his kindness and generosity to children. He died on 6th December AD 326. According to one legend, St Nicholas gave away three bags of gold for the dowries of three poor sisters. This is remembered in the pawnbroker's sign of three gold balls.

By tradition he visits homes to see if children have been good, and if so leaves small gifts. He is

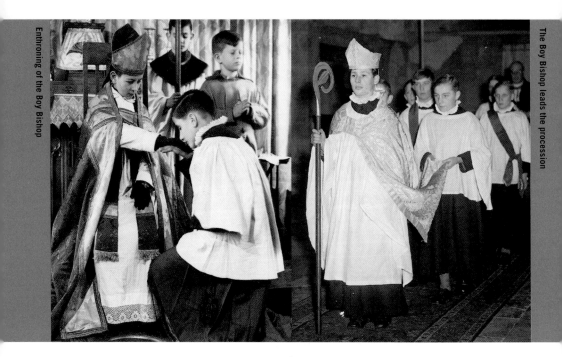

accompanied by Black Peter, a mischievous imp who carries a bundle of canes for use on naughty children. This association is maintained today in Holland. Sailors used to invoke St Nicholas when in distress, and referred to him as 'Old Nick', a term that became attached to the Devil, presumably responsible for the distress.

After the Reformation – the Feast of St Nicholas – a Catholic saint day – was amalgamated with Christmas Day, but the emphasis on presents and entertainment for children remains. 'Santa Claus' is a corruption of the Dutch name for St Nicholas. The origin of 'Father Christmas' is quite different from the origin of 'Santa Claus' but the two characters are thought of today as one.

Cathedral towns used to elect a Boy Bishop on this day, who served until Holy Innocents' Day (28th December), in commemoration of St Nicholas' compassion towards children. The Boy Bishop undertook all duties except taking Mass. The Eton College Captain elected on Montem Day may have originally been a Boy Bishop. Schoolboys in many places 'barred-out' their teachers on this day, as on Shrove Tuesday, in another display of boys taking an adult role.

✚ Enthroning of Boy Bishop (who holds office until Holy Innocents' Day, 28th December), Berden, near Bishop's Stortford   **Hertfordshire**
TAKE THE B1383 NORTH FROM BISHOP'S STORTFORD, THEN LEFT AT QUENDON.

✚ Enthroning of Boy Bishop (who holds office until Holy Innocents' Day, 28th December), Boston   **Lincolnshire**
BOSTON IS ON THE A16 NORTH OF SPALDING.

✚ Enthroning of Boy Bishop (who holds office until Holy Innocents' Day, 28th December), Bristol   **Avon**
BRISTOL CAN BE REACHED ON THE M4 AND M5.

✚ Enthroning of Boy Bishop (who holds office until Holy Innocents' Day, 28th December), Par   **Cornwall**
PAR IS ON THE A3082 WEST OF FOWEY, BETWEEN FOWEY AND ST AUSTELL.

✚ Enthroning of Boy Bishop (who holds office until Holy Innocents' Day, 28th December), Edwinstowe   **Nottinghamshire**
TAKE THE A60 NORTH OUT OF MANSFIELD, THEN RIGHT ON THE A6075.

162   December customs

7th December St Diuma's Day

St Diuma was a 7th-century bishop, about whom little can be certain.

8th December Feast of the Conception, St Budoc's Day

Christians celebrate St Anne's conception of the Virgin Mary. St Budoc was a 6th-century saint, possibly from the South West of England.

10th December

Boston Beast Mart   Lincolnshire

Dating from 1576, this is not a market anymore, but the Proclamation is still read on the old site (now part of Boston Grammar School) by the Mayor with local dignitaries in attendance.
BOSTON IS ON THE A16 NORTH OF SPALDING.

11th December Old St Andrew's Day

Northamptonshire lace-makers took a holiday today, the festivities being characterised by their dressing in men's clothes and drinking hot elderberry wine.

The weather is supposed to be fine today for a while, the first of the halcyon days when the kingfisher was said to start nesting; this unlikely legend was probably imported from Greece.

12th December St Finnian's Day, St Lucy's (Lucia's) Eve

Formerly in Scandinavia, St Lucy's Eve was similar to our Hallowe'en, with belief in witches and fairies strong, but although this tradition survived longest in the areas of Britain settled by Vikings, there are few remnants of it. Those that still exist seem to have found their way into stories about St Finnian, a 6th-century Welsh saint.

13th December St Lucy's Day

St Lucy was a 4th-century virgin of great charity and virtue, the stuff of which saints are made. Before the calendar change, festivities in Lucy's honour were held in Norse areas of Britain as part of the Yule celebrations around the winter solstice.

Candle Auction every 3rd year, Aldermaston   Berkshire

Bidding for a1 acre (1 ha) of land is done, the last bid before a pin, inserted into the candle 1 in (2.5cm) below the wick, falls gets the use of the acre.
ALDERMASTON IS ON THE A4 EAST OF NEWBURY.

The first Sunday after 12th December

Broughton Tin Can Band, St Andrew's Church, Broughton, near Kettering   Northamptonshire

This is a surviving charivari of unknown origin, but it may be connected with Old St Andrew's Day. It has elements of Beating the Bounds and of scaring away evil spirits, and starts just after midnight. The Canners meet outside the Rectory and parade while beating their tin cans lustily.
TAKE THE A43 SOUTH WEST FROM KETTERING.

16th December

The making and eating of mince pies traditionally starts on this day.

17th December Sow Day

Sows were slaughtered in readiness for preparation for Yule. Boar's Head was a favourite dish at festive times among the Celts and Norsemen, who admiring the strength, stamina and ferocity of the boar hoped to acquire these characteristics. A few customs involving boar's heads remain.

In Roman times this was the start of Saturnalia, a week-long feast and orgy, from which many of the Christmas characteristics come, such as over-indulgence and giving presents.

At the End of Michaelmas Term

✿ Boar's Head Dinner, Queen's College   **Oxford**

This famous event, accompanied by the rendering of the Boar's Head Carol' by choristers, was formerly held on Christmas Day. The Boar's Head, with orange in mouth (perhaps representing the sun), is carried in on a silver platter. After the carol, the orange is given to the principal chorister and the garnishes of rosemary, bay (as mentioned in the carol) and holly are given to the guests.

OXFORD IS AT THE JUNCTION OF THE A40 AND A34.

20th December St Thomas' Eve

Traditionally, this was a holy day on which no work was done. Unmarried girls would put a sprig of evergreen under their pillow before retiring and hope to dream of their future husbands.

21st December St Thomas' Day, Midwinter Day (Winter Solstice)

St Thomas the apostle, whose saint day was formerly 3rd July, refused to believe in the risen Christ until he had touched his wounds. This alleged incident gave rise to the term 'doubting thomas'. It may not be coincidence that much of our Christmas custom and imagery (for example, resurrection, child effigies, burning logs, fire and light) could be found throughout Europe, the Middle East and East Asia, and can be traced back with reasonable surety through Norse Yule customs, further to the cult of Mithras, the Persian Sun God, and even further back to the Phrygian Sun God Attis.

The old Norse festival of Yule fell on this day, where evergreens (holly, ivy, conifers) were used to symbolise the eternity of life and fires were lit in honour of Thor and kept alight until the shortest day was passed and the new-year dawn had started. The Yule Log was kept burning throughout, symbolising warmth, and is remembered by the chocolate Swiss roll cake, the **Chocolate Yule Log** *(see p.190 for recipe)*. Candles were lit, Yule cakes eaten and cider drunk. A remnant of the Yule Log was preserved and used to light the next one, symbolising the continuance of life. Our present Christmas celebrations are a mixture of Christian and pagan. Saturnalia was the Roman celebration of the winter solstice, when the sun was welcomed back after the shortest day. Elements of this have fused with the Yule customs to give us our modern Christmas on 25th December in western Europe, but which was celebrated on 6th January in eastern Europe. The adoption of Christianity by the Roman Emperor Constantine in the 4th century began the changes in Christmas customs.

This evening is a good time for carol singing with lanterns, as carol-singing traditionally was done from today until Christmas morning. Most common Christmas carols today were written in either the 19th century or 20th century, but Christmas folk carols can still be heard in North

Derbyshire and South Yorkshire. The earliest collection of English Christmas carols was published in 1521. Bands of professional musicians, called 'Waits', used to hire themselves out on festive occasions like Christmas. Local carollers sometimes carried and showed boxes with wax effigies of Mary and Jesus in, to encourage contributions. This was called 'vesselling', a corruption of wassailing. The latter, as practised in the Christmas season, was similar to the later carolling but revellers carried a 'wassail bowl' full of Lambswool (see 5th January) from house to house to offer to the occupants, along with songs and good wishes. Wassailers were often accompanied by a man dressed as a bull, who would show his face when money was given. This animal-god association may point to the pagan origin of vesselling.

It is also a traditional time to put up the Christmas tree – decorated with lights and a fairy at the top – and Christmas decorations, to keep active all evening and night until dawn heralds in the new year. Prince Albert is often credited with introducing the Christmas fir tree into England in 1841, shortly after marrying Queen Victoria, but German immigrants in Manchester were erecting them in the 1820s. In any case, evergreen decorations were a feature of Yule long before, as putting lighted candles on a pine tree furnished light for the woodland spirits sheltering there after the deciduous trees had lost their leaves and cover. A floral wreath is hung on the front door. Other traditional decorations adorn the house. Green decorations include holly, ivy, bay, rosemary and laurel. Presents are put under the tree, to be opened after Christmas lunch. Christmas Cards received are put on display.

Mistletoe is hung up, and any woman who passes underneath may be kissed, provided a berry is plucked, giving both good-luck. No kisses may be offered when the berries are gone, and to refuse a kiss means certain spinsterhood. Mistletoe was venerated by the Druids, especially when it grew on oak, as a good luck emblem with magical properties for it appeared to be able to grow without soil. It was originally hung over dwellings to protect the occupants, and must never touch the floor.

When mistletoe was not available a Kissing Bush (or Bough) was used. This was a small holly or yew bush uprooted and hung upside down from the kitchen ceiling. It was decorated with ribbons, tinsel, gifts, sweets and fruit. Dipping it in a flour and water paste and leaving it to dry gave the appearance of snow, whilst dipping it in Epsom Salts and water caused the leaves to sparkle. Sometimes two boughs made into loops and hung together at right angles were used. The Kissing Bough declined in popularity in the mid-19th century when the Christmas Tree was introduced from Germany. In remote parts of Northumbria, Derbyshire, Cheshire and Staffordshire people

The Wassail Bowl

still hang the Kissing Bush, a framework of evergreens, decorated with candles and ornaments, with a spray of mistletoe suspended in the centre. Years ago, poor people went from house to house begging gifts for Christmas, including flour and other ingredients for bread and cakes, some offering sprigs of mistletoe or holly in return. This was called 'Thomassing', 'gooding', 'mumping', 'corning' or 'doleing'. Some towns used to give out doles to the needy on this day.

Animal disguises were once a feature of winter customs. One survivor in North-east. Derbyshire, north-west. Nottinghamshire and south Yorkshire is the Old Tup Play. It is performed at Christmas time by teenagers, the central character being a man dressed as a tup (a castrated ram). An old man has the ram and he sends his wife for a butcher to kill it. The play ends with a doctor resurrecting it, and with the song 'The Derby Ram' about a monster ram. These plays appear to have elements of animal sacrifice and sympathetic magic. Another play in this area involves an old horse and a blacksmith who mimes his shoeing. A collection is taken afterwards.

On St Thomas' Day children barred out their teachers as on Shrove Tuesday and asked for a holiday. This is the traditional day to plant broad beans, which have pagan links with doom. If a bean comes up white there will be a death in the family.

Pork is traditionally eaten on this day, plus something baked and something brewed.

The Sunday nearest 21st December

William Underhill's Charity (money), Eldersfield Hereford and Worcester
In his will of 1647 William Underhill left money to the 'honest poor, not Bastards nor any known dishonest poor', who receive alms placed on his tomb on the floor of the aisle by kneeling to pick it up. Nowadays the vicar calls the names of the chosen, who receive the money from the churchwarden whilst the latter is sitting on a chair at the head of William Underhill's tomb.
TAKE THE A438 WEST FROM TEWKESBURY, LEFT ON THE B4211, THEN RIGHT ON AN UNCLASSIFIED ROAD.

23rd December

Tom Bowcock's Eve, The Ship, Mousehole Cornwall
According to locals, 200 years ago the villagers were near starvation because fishing boats were coming back empty when Tom Bowcock managed to bring in a catch, containing seven different sorts of fish. This event is celebrated with Stary Gazy Pies, containing seven different sorts of fish, and the singing of a folk song written about it.
MOUSEHOLE IS SOUTH OF PENZANCE ON AN UNCLASSIFIED ROAD.

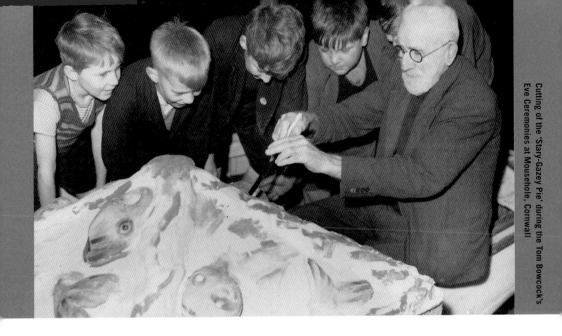

24th December Christmas Eve

Bring in a burning log or faggot (bundle of ash sticks bound with bramble binds) on Christmas Eve, light it with a piece of last year's log, and keep it alight throughout Christmas Day for good fortune throughout the coming year. The smoke from burning green ash was held to protect the house from evil. Bringing in the ashen faggot was a Saxon tradition similar to those involving the Norse Yule Log, and survived well in the West Country until recently. Only Dunster in Somerset maintains the custom now. In some places, holly, ivy and other greenery were never brought into the house before sunset on Christmas Eve. Holly has male associations in folklore and ivy female, so the entwining of them in wreaths and other decorations symbolises harmony in the home at Christmas.

Also kept alight during Christmas was the Yule Candle, made by pouring fat and colouring into a mould. It was placed in the centre of the table and decorated with holly and ivy. In Derbyshire miners used to drink **Posset** *(see p.190 for recipe)* as they sat round the candle. Posset is ale with milk and nutmeg added, drunk from a communal bowl with a large spoon. After eating a simple evening meal, often of fish, the family sits round the tree singing carols and listening to readings.

The twelve-day period of the Christmas season, which traditionally starts on Christmas Eve, is the 'image of the year' according to folk belief. Whatever is done during these days reflects on the good or bad luck of the coming year. Christmas Eve was a traditional time for divination, as though it was effectively the end of the year. Most customs involved with looking into the future persisted longest amongst unmarried women, the unlucky and impecunious.

Stockings are hung up on the ends of beds or by the chimney, a custom dating from the 19th century. Father Christmas is left a glass of sherry and mince pie, plus carrots for his reindeer. Traditional gifts in stockings include sweets, bags of chocolate coins, fruit, new coins, nuts and small toys.

A traditional Christmas Eve game is snapdragon. Raisins are put in a broad, shallow bowl, brandy poured over and lit. All try to pluck out and eat a raisin without burning themselves. Another game is flapdragon, where contestants drink from a cider jug which has a lighted candle floating in the cider.

Christmas Eve is a traditional time for Nativity plays and for Mummers' Plays, the latter often including the legend of St George and the Dragon, including also the characters of the Grand Turk, the gallant knight, the doctor, the Fool or Jester, and Old Father Christmas (or Sir Christmas) as Narrator and Master of Ceremonies. Father Christmas may have been modelled on the Scandinavian Odin (Saxon Woden), as Odin had a long beard and cloak trimmed with fur, and rode on his horse Sleipnir to deliver gifts to his followers at Yule. Generally, Father Christmas had a green coat. Underlying all Mumming Plays is the seasonal theme of the conflict between good and evil, darkness and light.

In medieval times, in large manor houses and the Royal Court the Master of Ceremonies appointed for Christmas entertainments also acted as Fool or Jester, in a similar role to the Lord of Misrule. In the 19th century, Father Christmas took on this role, quite a different origin to

St Nicholas/Santa Claus the bringer of presents to children on Christmas Eve. Gradually these two characters became one and the same, and when in the 1860s Christmas cards showed Father Christmas leaving presents for children on Christmas Eve the merger was complete. The image of a gift-laden sleigh pulled by reindeer also comes from Victorian Christmas cards. The earliest Christmas card known is that designed by J C Horsley back in the year1843 for his friend Sir Henry Cole.

American authors, referring only to Santa Claus/St Nicholas, claim that the image of a jolly, rotund, bearded man in a bright red, fur-lined coat was invented by the Swedish-American artist Haddon Sundblom for a series of advertisements for Coca-Cola in 1931. Whilst the red colour may have become standard as a result of these, the rest of the image, that of Father Christmas, is very much older than Coca-Cola, or, indeed, the Pilgrim Fathers. The earliest American image of Santa Claus in a red jacket, (and wide black belt, boots and clay pipe) was in fact an illustration by Thomas Nast in 1863.

In Kent the Hooden Horse was taken round houses and songs sung to be admitted. If admitted, there was general foolery and the Mollie swept the floor and asked for money. This has echoes of New Year's Eve practice. A 'Hoodening Play' is a type of Mumming Play featuring the Hooden Horse, with its snapping jaws, and also a Jockey who tries with varying degrees of success to ride him. Unlike the Cheshire souling Horse, the Hooden Horse has a mane adorned with ribbons and a tail made from horse hair.

In North Lincolnshire, around the mouth of the River Trent, a horse resembling a Hobby Horse accompanied the Wooing Play, which may be staged from now until Plough Monday. Such Horses also accompanied other celebrations and events such as civic pageants, guild processions and Morris dancers.

First-footing was done on Christmas Eve long ago, but is now generally associated with New Year's Eve.

The last window of Advent Calendars is opened today.

Yuletide Frumity *(see p.190 for recipe)* – also known as frumetty or frumenty – is traditionally eaten on this day, as is Pestle Pie made from beef, tongue, fowl, eggs, sugar, raisins, lemon and orange peel and spices in a pastry case. Pastry dolls were made for the children from the left over pastry, using currants for eyes, a glace cherry for a nose and candied peel for a mouth. They were put in a box made up as a crib with linen, lace and ribbons.

Burning the Ashen Fagots, Devonshire, 1854

Hanging the Wheatsheaf, Ackworth Moor Top — West Yorkshire

This old Norse tradition is a Christmas gift to wild birds.

TAKE THE A628 SOUTH FROM PONTEFRACT.

Giving the Christmas Sheaf, Walmer — Kent

It was an ancient custom to give cocks an extra good feed on Christmas Eve so that they would warn of any evil spirits about that night. The special cake of fat and grain, called the Christmas Sheaf, was made. The ducks on the village pond in Walmer are now the only recipients.

WALMER IS ON THE SOUTHERN EDGE OF DEAL, ON THE COAST.

Singing of the Coventry Carol, Coventry Cathedral — Warwickshire

COVENTRY CAN BE REACHED BY DRIVING SOUTH FROM JUNCTIONS 2 OR 3 OF THE M6.

Tolling the Devil's Knell, Dewsbury — West Yorkshire

This 700-year-old custom keeps the Devil from the parish for the coming year. The bell called 'Black Tom of Southill' is struck once for every year since Christ's birth, finishing exactly at midnight. Then an extra ring ensures that the Devil is vanquished.

DEWSBURY IS BETWEEN HUDDERSFIELD AND WAKEFIELD ON THE A638.

Wassailing, Wakefield — West Yorkshire

Bands of wassailers visit houses, receiving spiced Yule Cake and cheese, and cider or wine.

TAKE THE A61 NORTH FROM BARNSLEY.

Sword Dancing, Grenoside — South Yorkshire

This team does clog-and step-dancing.

GRENOSIDE IS A NORTHERN SUBURB OF SHEFFIELD, ON THE A61.

Festival of 9 lessons and carols, King's College — Cambridge

LEAVE THE M11 AT JUNCTIONS 11, 12, 13 AND 14 FOR ROADS INTO CAMBRIDGE.

Burning the Ashen Faggot, The Luttrell Arms, Dunster — Somerset

The Ashen Faggot, a bundle of 12 ash sticks bound with green ash withies, is brought in and burned while 'The Dunster Carol' is sung. A withy can be nominated by a couple and a wish made, which will come true if the wish has been said before the withy burns through. Unmarried couples nominating withies will marry in the order that they burn through.

DUNSTER IS ON THE A39 EAST OF MINEHEAD.

Hoodening Play, Whitstable — Kent

TAKE THE A290 NORTH FROM CANTERBURY.

Hoodening Play, Sandgate, near Folkestone — Kent

SANDGATE IS ON THE A259 ON THE WESTERN EDGE OF FOLKESTONE.

Hoodening Play, Charing, near Ashford — Kent

CHARING IS ON THE A20 NORTH WEST OF ASHFORD.

Hoodening Play, Margate — Kent

MARGATE CAN BE REACHED BY TAKING THE A28 EASTWARDS FROM CANTERBURY.

Hoodening Play, Ramsgate — Kent

RAMSGATE IS ON THE A254 SOUTH OF MARGATE.

Christmas Eve Mummers Play, Andover — Hampshire

TAKE THE A343 SOUTH FROM NEWBURY.

Christmas Mummers, Overton   Hampshire
TAKE THE B3400 EAST FROM ANDOVER.

The Vessel Cup, Carlton-in-Cleveland   Cleveland
The Vessel Cup, although a variant of Wassail Cup (*see* 6th January), here refers to the song sung
when children take round the doll-in-the-box. This was originally Mother and Child, but came to
be just one doll in a decorated box, for which the children asked Christmas contributions.
TAKE THE A19 NORTH FROM THIRSK, RIGHT ON THE A172, THEN RIGHT ON AN UNCLASSIFIED ROAD.

Calling the Waits, Pickering   North Yorkshire
PICKERING IS ON THE A170 WEST FROM SCARBOROUGH.

Christmastide Wassailing, Little Wittenham   Berkshire
TAKE THE A415 EAST FROM ABINGDON.

The Keynsham Dole   Somerset
The Holbin Charity set up in 1619 is for the distribution of bread to the poor and aged of the parish.
KEYNSHAM IS ON THE A4 WEST OF BATH.

Presenting the Mock-Boar's Head to the Lord Mayor of London   London
This is a 12th-century tradition by the butchers of Smithfield, the 'boar' in fact being a boar-
shaped meat-loaf.

Poor Horse Plays, Richmond   North Yorkshire
These Mumming Plays, with the song 'Poor Old Horse', portray the life, death and resurrection of
a man disguised as a horse. Whether this hearkens back to sacrificial rites or totemism is not certain.
The plays are performed in public houses and other venues during the week before Christmas.
RICHMOND IS WEST OF THE A1. TAKE THE A6108 FROM SCOTCH CORNER.

Singing Folk Carols, Castleton   Derbyshire
TAKE THE A625 WEST FROM SHEFFIELD.

Singing Folk Carols, Oughtibridge   South Yorkshire
TAKE THE A6102 NORTH WEST FROM SHEFFIELD.

Singing Folk Carols, Bradfield   South Yorkshire
BRADFIELD IS ON AN UNCLASSIFIED ROAD WEST OF OUGHTIBRIDGE.

Singing Folk Carols, Ecclesfield   South Yorkshire
TAKE THE A6135 NORTH FROM SHEFFIELD.

Singing Folk Carols, Worrall   South Yorkshire
WORRALL IS ON AN UNCLASSIFIED ROAD SOUTH OF OUGHTIBRIDGE.

The Mayor's Audit Money, Richmond   North Yorkshire
This may well be the only surviving St Thomas' Day dole, now given out by the Mayor to local pen-
sioners on or near the 22nd December. Specially minted coins called 'Richmond Shillings' are given.
RICHMOND IS WEST OF THE A1. TAKE THE A6108 FROM SCOTCH CORNER.

25th December Christmas Day
Christians celebrate the birth of Christ. Christmas Day was a Quarter Day. In the 5th century all
churches except the Armenian Church commemorated the birth of Christ on 25th December,

extending the festivities until 6th January to encompass the visit of the Magi twelve days after Christ's birth. This day is called Epiphany. As Christmas Mass was originally held at midnight on the 24th December, the end of the twelve days of Christmas is, on this basis, midnight on the 5th January. Hence 5th January is known as Twelfth Night. The Puritans banned Christmas celebrations by Act of Parliament in 1644, making 25th December a fast day. This came into force in 1652. With the restoration of the monarchy in Charles II Christmas celebrations were once again permitted in 1660.

On this day in medieval times a servant would be crowned Lord of Misrule in a reversal of roles. This tradition has survived in the armed forces where officers serve the ranks at Christmas dinner.

Christmas cards and gifts are sent. Children open their stockings in the morning; other presents, put under the tree beforehand, are opened by the family together after lunch. A Christmas spread was originally Boar's head served first, then **Plum Porridge** *(see p.190 for recipe)* – meat broth thickened with bread crumbs, raisins, currants, prunes and spices – then meat dishes (fowl, game, beef, venison), then sweetmeats such as mince pies. When boar became rare beef, turkey, capon or goose replaced it. Turkey was first introduced into England in 1542 from America. Nowadays cranberry sauce is served with the turkey.

Christmas Pudding *(see p.190 for recipe)*, a plum pudding cooked in a cloth, replaced Plum Porridge in the 17th century. Brandy was poured over it and lit, and nowadays a sprig of berried holly and **Brandy Sauce** or **Hard Sauce** *(see p.190 and p.191 for recipes)* are added. Silver coins (usually threepenny pieces) and charms were added to the Plum Pudding in Victorian times. A ring meant you would have a sweetheart and a thimble meant a year unmarried. Other traditional foods are **Christmas Cake** *(see p.191 for recipe)* – descended from Twelfth Cake *(see 5th January)* – Yule Log *(see 21st December)*, and **Mince Pies** *(see p.191 for recipe)*. Yule-dough or Yule cakes are images of a baby in pastry or gingerbread given by bakers to their customers at Christmas. The hands are crossed in front and features and buttons are of raisins. In northern England they are called 'Doos'.

The idea for Christmas crackers probably arose from the French custom of wrapping sweets in paper and twisting each end *(bon-bons)*. Thomas Smith, a Baker, adopted the idea, adding a love motto and then a novelty to the wrapping. He invented the banger later, and the modern Christmas cracker was born in the late 1870s.

Popular Christmas games were charades, buff (trying to make people smile, for which they pay a forfeit), hunt the slipper, spinning the trencher, musical chairs and postman's knock.

The custom of hunting and killing a wren on Christmas Day and carrying it round the village on St Stephen's Day appears to have been confined to South West England.

In the Midlands it is traditional to eat pikelets baked on a griddle at 5 o'clock in the afternoon. In Shrewsbury 'Wigs' (caraway-filled cakes made from fine white flour and moulded into various shapes) are eaten.

26th December Boxing Day, St Stephen's Day

St Stephen was stoned to death in AD 35 and became the first Christian martyr. As he was the apostles' keeper of alms for the poor the giving of alms has always been associated with this day. Collecting alms used to be called 'Stephening'.

Collection boxes for the poor were put in churches before Christmas and opened on this day for distribution of their contents. This practice largely ceased after the Reformation, so poor tradesmen used to collect a 'Christmas Box' from their satisfied customers. This was also the day when the remains of the Christmas feast were put in boxes and given to the servants or those who had given service during the previous year – another possible origin of the term 'Christmas Box'. It is a day to visit relatives, friends and neighbours during the day, and a pantomime in the evening. Pantomimes are traditional shows based on folk tales, in which the leading male parts are played by women and the leading female roles are played by men – another example of role reversal.

In Norfolk handbell ringing was traditional on this day.

Hunting foxes and squirrels was traditional on this day, as was shooting birds - particularly the wren. The biological name for the wren is *Troglodytes troglodytes*, literally cave dweller, after its tendency to nest in dark places including tombs and caves. Thus it acquired the reputation of being a go-between with the underworld and the forces of darkness. Killing it was a way of ensuring that the sun's light would win through and return. Furthermore, there is an ancient legend that the wren was regarded by birds as their king. This is told in the folktale about a contest between an eagle and a wren to see who could fly highest. The wren flew on to the eagle's back, and when the latter had exhausted himself, so high did he fly, the wren simply took off and flew a little higher. From this it may follow that killing the wren was making a royal sacrifice for the return of the sun. Wren Boys, having caught a wren, paraded it, singing a wrenning carol. The bird's carcass was hung on a pole, or carried in a garland of holly or gorse, and paraded around the town. Donations were given in exchange for a wren's feather, which was considered lucky. This custom was prevalent in South West England.

Another explanation for this custom is that it represents a seasonal role reversal, when servants and masters changed places, and the smallest bird became king of the birds. If the wren could be killed, then perhaps the temporary role reversal would become permanent. Amongst sailors a wren killed on St Stephen's Day was thought to protect the killer from shipwreck or other disaster.

The traditional lunch on Boxing Day is cold turkey, **Bubble-and-Squeak** *(see p.191 for recipe)* and cranberry sauce or pickle.

The Paper Boys Mummers, Marshfield, near Bath — Avon
The players have elaborate headwear – high crowns with long paper ribbons – the chief mummer having his own special design. The players are: St George, Father Christmas, Beelzebub, a Turkish Knight, the Doctor, Saucy Jack, Tenpenny Nit and Mince Pie.
MARSHFIELD IS ON THE A420 WEST OF CHIPPENHAM.

Crookham Village Mummers' Play, near Fleet — Hampshire
This features King George, Bold Roamer, Bold Slasher, Father Christmas and Little Johnny Jack who kills Father Christmas at the climax to the play.
FLEET IS ON THE A323 NORTH WEST FROM ALDERSHOT. CROOKHAM VILLAGE IS JUST TO THE SOUTH OF FLEET.

Mummers' Plays at Headington, near Oxford — Oxfordshire
The Headington Quarry Mummers' Play from 10am until 3pm in public houses.
HEADINGTON IS A NORTH-EASTERN SUBURB OF OXFORD, ON THE A40.

St Albans Mummers' — Hertfordshire
The players gather outside the Town Hall at midday.
ST ALBAN'S IS BETWEEN HEMEL HEMPSTEAD AND HATFIELD ON THE A1057.

Traditional Christmas Mummers' Play, Chailey — East Sussex
TAKE THE A275 NORTH FROM LEWES.

Traditional Christmas Mummers' Play, Moulton, near Northampton — Northamptonshire
MOULTON IS ON THE NORTHERN EDGE OF NORTHAMPTON, JUST OFF THE A43.

Traditional Christmas Mummers' Play, Coventry — West Midlands
COVENTRY CAN BE REACHED BY DRIVING SOUTH FROM JUNCTIONS 2 OR 3 OF THE M6.

Traditional Christmas Mummers' Play, Andover — Hampshire
TAKE THE A343 SOUTH FROM NEWBURY.

Traditional Christmas Mummers' Play, Uttoxeter — Staffordshire
TAKE THE A50 SOUTH EAST FROM STOKE-ON-TRENT.

Traditional Christmas Mummers' Play, Evershot — Dorset
TAKE THE A37 SOUTH FROM YEOVIL, THEN RIGHT ON AN UNCLASSIFIED ROAD.

Broomstick fighting, Bridgnorth
Shropshire

A unique custom, small boys from Low Town go in the morning up to High Town, with blackened faces, jackets inside out, decorated with coloured cloth, carrying a broomstick. In pairs they engage in mock stave fights, and singing ten verses of 'This old man, he played one', and collect money.
BRIDGNORTH IS ON THE A454 WEST FROM WOLVERHAMPTON.

St Stephen's Day Walk, Runwell
Essex

This is a walk along local footpaths from the village to Running Well.
TAKE THE A132 NORTH FROM WICKFORD

Grenoside Longsword Dancers, near Sheffield
South Yorkshire

Dancing starts at the Old Harrow Inn at 11am.
GRENOSIDE IS A NORTHERN SUBURB OF SHEFFIELD, ON THE A61.

Handsworth Longsword Dancers, near Sheffield
South Yorkshire

Dancing starts at Handsworth Church, then in Woodhouse.
HANDSWORTH IS ON THE A57 IN THE SOUTH-EASTERN SUBURBS OF SHEFFIELD.

Flamborough Sword Dancers
Humberside

Dancing starts at midday.
TAKE THE B1255 NORTH EAST FROM BRIDLINGTON, THEN THE B1259.

27th December St John the Evangelist's Day

St John wrote his Gospel and other parts of the biblical manuscript.

The Boar's Head Supper, St John's College
Cambridge

LEAVE THE M11 AT JUNCTIONS 11, 12, 13 AND 14 FOR ROADS INTO CAMBRIDGE.

28th December Holy Innocents' Day, Childermas

Christians think of the babies slaughtered in Bethlehem by Herod in his attempt to kill the Christ Child. Children, paradoxically, were often beaten as a reminder of the suffering of the slain children. Church bells would sound in their memory. Church altars were draped in black or violet. Fasting by adults, indulgence by children, is also a tradition.

A sword battle between King William and Little Man John during the Mansfield Mummers Play

The last Monday in December

This is traditionally Judas' birthday, and was considered an unlucky day.

29th December **Martyrdom of St Thomas a Becket**

St Thomas was Archbishop of Canterbury under Henry II, and was slain on this day in 1170 for resisting royal attempts to limit church power.

30th December **St Egwin's Day**

St Egwin founded Evesham Abbey, Hereford and Worcester, in the 7th century.

31st December **New Year's Eve, St Sylvester's Day**

St Sylvester was born in Rome and was known for the way he defended the Church during the Diocletian disturbances. He was made the next pope in AD 314, and died on this day in AD 335. It is tradition to stay up until midnight to see in and toast the New Year. Scots sing 'Auld Lang Syne', although this is now widely sung in England. Put out a piece of coal, a piece of bread and a silver sixpence, and bring them in on New Year's morning to ensure the family has warmth, food and prosperity during the year. In some areas the back door is opened on New Year's Eve and then closed as the front door is opened to let the New Year in. Gifts were often given on this day, often a capon for a New Year's Day meal. Children gave oranges or lemons stuck with cloves to their god-parents, asking for their blessing. Women often cleaned their houses from top to bottom, and polished their silver, to make a clean start to the New Year.

Watchnight services at midnight were started by the Methodist Church in the 18th century, and similar are held in many churches and cathedrals today. It was also a favourite time for bell-ringing.

In the Pennines, Sweepers (or Mummers) – men dressed as women and vice versa, with clothes inside out, blackened faces, and carrying a broom – visit each house and sweep around the room, especially the hearth. They ask for money for sweeping the old year out. Dressing up as animals, for example, bulls, goats, deer, on this day was a custom descended from pagan animal-god worship, one fiercely attacked by the church. Divination games and fortune-telling are traditional on this day, some resembling those done on Hallowe'en. Girls may learn the name or profession of their future husbands by dropping egg white, candle wax or melted lead into water and studying the shapes produced. An initial seen would be that of the one they would marry. In similar fashion fruit peel was thrown over the shoulder. New Year's Resolutions were often made on this day.

Baking the cake, New Years Eve

Wassailing, Minchinhampton — Gloucestershire
MINCHINHAMPTON IS JUST SOUTH OF STROUD ON AN UNCLASSIFIED ROAD.

Wassailing, Randwick — Gloucestershire
RANDWICK IS ON AN UNCLASSIFIED ROAD NORTH WEST OF STROUD.

Wassailing, Avening — Gloucestershire
TAKE THE A46 SOUTH FROM STROUD, THEN LEFT ON THE B4014.

Wassailing, Stow-on-the-Wold — Gloucestershire
STOW-ON-THE-WOLD IS AT THE JUNCTION OF THE A424 AND A429.

Wassailing, Stroud — Gloucestershire
STROUD IS ON THE A419, WEST OF CIRENCESTER.

Wassailing, Westbury-on-Severn — Gloucestershire
TAKE THE A40 WEST FROM GLOUCESTER, THEN LEFT ON THE A48.

Tar-Barrels Parade and Welcoming the New Year, Allendale, near Haltwhistle — Northumberland

This parade and celebration starts just before midnight. This is basically a fire ceremony which probably has its origin in the celebration of the winter solstice and the first signs of life in the new year.

Male, behatted guisers in fancy dress, some in women's costume, carry blazing tar barrels on their heads from the churchyard to the square in a spectacular parade. Their faces are blackened. They are preceded by the Braes of Allen Band, a silver band, and once at the square they circle the bonfire from right to left then cast their barrels on to it. The ceremony is followed by singing, dancing, and much jollity and exchange of good wishes. As the embers die the villagers and guisers go first-footing.

Even under the blackout regulations of the World War II, this ceremony continued, under an iron canopy.

ALLENDALE IS ON THE B6295, NORTH OF COWSHILL.

Tar Barrels Parade, Allendale, Northumberland

Additional customs

Annual Customs of Variable Date

Applications by Freemen to the Manorial Court, Malmesbury   **Wiltshire**

The people of Malmesbury were granted land by King Athelstan in AD 930, and freemen are allowed to claim a plot for an allotment, a capital burgess a plot of 8 to 15 acres (3 to 6 ha), by applying in person to the Court. To formally apply for an allotment, turf from the Common is placed in front of the Steward, and the commoner-elect places one shilling under the turf. The Steward then strikes him on the shoulder with a twig, also taken from the Common, and says: 'Turf and twig I give to thee, the same as King Athelstan gave to me. I trust that you a true subject will be.'

MALMESBURY IS ON THE A429 NORTH OF CHIPPENHAM.

Candle Auction, Diseworth   **Leicestershire**

TAKE THE A6 NORTH FROM LOUGHBOROUGH, THEN LEFT ON THE B5401.

Candle Auction, Congresbury   **Somerset**

This auction follows the letting of two pieces of land by the drawing of marked apples.

TAKE THE A370 SOUTH WEST OUT OF BRISTOL.

Ale-Tasting and Bread-Weighing, Ashburton   **Devon**

Each inn within the town is visited once a year for the ale to be tasted and bread to be weighed. If they are found to be satisfactory an evergreen sprig is given to the landlord, which he then hangs over the door.

TAKE THE A38 SOUTH OF EXETER.

Court Baron of Painswick   **Gloucestershire**

This has three jurymen from the commoners of the four parishes that make up the manor, Sheepscombe, Edge, Slad and Painswick.

TAKE THE A46 NORTH OUT OF STROUD.

The Great Barmote Court, Ashford-in-the-Water (formerly Monyash)   Derbyshire
This court, regulating the lead mining industry in the High Peak, and the Low Peak Court (twice annually) are England's oldest surviving industrial courts, established by Edward I in 1288.
TAKE THE A6 EAST FROM BUXTON.

A Saturday in May or June, Flower Parade, Spalding   Lincolnshire
TAKE THE A16 NORTH EAST FROM STAMFORD.

Summercourt Fair, Cornwall
TAKE THE A3058 SOUTH EAST FROM NEWQUAY.

Burrator Reservoir Company Commemoration, Burrator Reservoir, near Yelverton   Devon
An annual pilgrimage to drink the health of Sir Francis Drake (great-great-nephew of the famous Admiral, and Recorder of Plymouth from 1696 to 1717), who founded Plymouth's water supply.
TAKE THE A386 NORTH FROM PLYMOUTH.

Conker Championships, Walton-on-Trent   Derbyshire
TAKE THE A38 SOUTH WEST FROM BURTON-UPON-TRENT, THEN LEFT ON AN UNCLASSIFIED ROAD.

Broughton-in-Furness Fair   Cumbria
Hot pennies are thrown for children to scramble for.
TAKE THE A595 NORTH FROM BARROW-IN-FURNESS, THEN LEFT AT GRIZEBECK.

Brough Horse Fair   Cumbria
BROUGH IS ON THE A66, EAST FROM PENRITH , PAST APPLEBY.

Bampton Pony Fair   Devon
TAKE THE A396 NORTH FROM TIVERTON, THEN RIGHT ON THE B3227.

Ye Fyshinge Feast, Plymouth   Devon
This feast is held on a summer Saturday.
PLYMOUTH IS ON THE SOUTH COAST, ON THE A38 SOUTH FROM EXETER.

The sale of Exmour Ponies at Bampton Pony Fair

🜲 **The Yeomen of the Guard search the Houses of Parliament** London

It takes place on the morning of the State Opening of Parliament. Public not admitted.

THE HOUSES OF PARLIAMENT ARE BY WESTMINSTER BRIDGE.

🜲 **The Silent Change, Guildhall** London

The incumbent and elect Lord Mayors, Aldermen and High Officers assemble in the Guildhall for the annual surrender of the Lord Mayor's seat and office to the newly elected Lord Mayor. The whole ceremony is conducted in silence after the new Lord Mayor's Declaration. The symbols of office – the Sword and Mace, the Crystal Sceptre, the Seal and City Purse – are handed over and the City Plate signed for.

At the start of a new term, the Butchers' Company present the Lord Mayor with a boar's head, a traditional payment for land used 'for cleansing the entrails of beasts'.

In the autumn of the Lord Mayor's year, the Fruiterers' Company present fruits, a very old payment of a toll on fruit to bring it into the City.

THE GUILDHALL IS JUST OFF GRESHAM STREET (B128).

✠ **Samuel Pepys Memorial Service, Church of St Olave, Hart Street** London

This is where Samuel Pepys and his wife worshipped. The Lord Mayor lays a wreath on his memorial.

HART STREET IS NEAR FENCHURCH STREET STATION.

✠ **Sir John Cass Memorial Service, Church of St Botolph, Aldgate** London

Staff and pupils of Sir John Cass School wear a red plume, which represents the blood-stained quill in Sir John Cass' hand when he died of a haemorrhage as he was signing his will.

THE CHURCH IS BY ALDGATE UNDERGROUND STATION.

Customs Held Regularly at Intervals

🜨 **Verderer's Court of Attachment of the Forest of Dean, Speech House, Coleford, Forest of Dean** Gloucestershire

This Court takes place every 40 days. The Forestry Commission is represented by the Deputy Surveyor, and nowadays the Commission usually takes the necessary action against offenders. However, the Court still technically has legal powers to try offences against 'vert and venison', that is, against growing plants and trees and the animals of the forest. There are four verderers who look after the use and amenities of the forest. The office of verderer was established by King Canute.

TAKE THE A4136 FROM MONMOUTH, THEN RIGHT ON THE B4231.

Sailing the bounds of Poole harbour by the Admiral of the Port
Dorset

This is done by barge every third year (due 2000).

POOLE IS ON THE COAST TO THE WEST OF BOURNEMOUTH.

The Wakefield Miracle Plays
West Yorkshire

The plays are held irregularly every five to ten years (possible next in 1998).

TAKE THE A61 NORTH FROM BARNSLEY

Riding the bounds, Lancaster
Lancashire

This takes place every 7th year.

LANCASTER IS ON THE M6 NORTH OF PRESTON.

Candle Auction, Chedzoy, Sedgemoor
Somerset

The auction is held every 21st year (due 2009). A pin is not used in the candle; the bidding ceases when the flame sputters out.

TAKE THE A372 SOUTH EAST FROM BRIDGWATER, THEN LEFT ON AN UNCLASSIFIED ROAD TO CHEDZOY.

Occasional Customs

Hanging of maidens'/virgins' garlands, held at churches in various locations

On the death of a young man or woman at Abbotts Ann, Hampshire, a garland (a crown decorated with paper roses with white paper gloves hanging from it) is carried at the head of the funeral procession by two girls dressed in white. It is hung from the church gallery for three Sundays to see if anyone challenges the bestowing of this honour (the white gloves symbolise throwing down the gauntlet), and if not is then hung permanently from the church roof. The garlands, or Virgins' Crowns, were blessed every St Faith's Day (6th October).

Virgins' Crowning Ceremony, Abbotts Ann, Hampshire

In the church at Ashford-in-the-Water, near Bakewell, Derbyshire, there are four maidens' garlands, consisting of a frame made of wood and wire over which are arranged rosettes, ribbons, paper gloves and handkerchiefs. One garland was for Ann Howard, who died on 12th April 1747 aged 21 whilst betrothed and still a virgin.

Other maidens' garlands can be seen hanging in churches at: Astley Abbotts, Shropshire; Ilam, Staffordshire; Matlock, Derbyshire; and Trusley Georgian Church, Derbyshire.

ABBOTTS ANN IS ON AN UNCLASSIFIED ROAD OFF THE A343. ASHFORD-IN-THE-WATER IS ON THE A6. ASTLEY ABBOTTS IS ON THE B4373. ILAM IS ON AN UNCLASSIFIED ROAD OFF THE A515. MATLOCK IS ON THE A6. TRUSLEY IS ON AN UNCLASSIFIED ROAD OFF THE B5020.

Peace and Good Neighbourhood Dinner, Kidderminster — Hereford and Worcester

More than 500 years money was left to buy loaves for the children born or living in Church Street and to set up a meeting to resolve quarrels. Then, 300 years later more money was left to buy ale and tobacco for the men of Church Street. The charities are now administered by a committee that organises the dinner.

TAKE THE A451 SOUTH WEST FROM STOURBRIDGE.

Baking of the Denby Dale Pie, Denby Dale — West Yorkshire

Giant pies have been baked on selected national occasions since the first to commemorate George III's recovery from illness on 3rd September 1788. Other pies have been baked to mark the repeal of the Corn Laws in 1846, Queen Victoria's Golden Jubilee in 1887 and the Bicentenary Pie of 1988. An 18-ft (5.5m) long pie dish can be seen outside the Pie Hall.

TAKE THE A635 WEST FROM BARNSLEY.

Horse Shoe Tax, Oakham Castle, Oakham — Leicestershire

A tax of horse shoes is made on every peer visiting Oakham for the first time.

OAKHAM IS ON THE A606 WEST OF STAMFORD.

Walking the Bounds, Spaunton Manor estate, near Kirkbymoorside — Cumbria

The Bounds are walked every time a new member of the Darley family inherits the estate.

KIRKBYMOORSIDE IS ON THE A170 WEST FROM SCARBOROUGH.

Beating the Bounds, River Medway — Kent

The Mayor of Rochester, Kent goes by barge around his domain, between Garrison Point and Hawkwood, in his capacity as Admiral of the River Medway.

ROCHESTER IS ON THE NORTH KENT COAST ON THE A2.

Cornish Wrestling at St Columbs, St Wenn (where the championships are held), St Kew, St Merryn and Perranporth — Cornwall

ST COLUMB MAJOR AND MINOR ARE ON THE A3059. ST WENN IS ON AN UNCLASSIFIED ROAD OFF THE B3274. ST KEW IS ON AN UNCLASSIFIED ROAD OFF THE A39. ST MERRYN IS ON THE B3276. PERRANPORTH IS ON THE B3285.

Court Leet of the Manor of Balneath — East Sussex

This court sat in 1959 after a lapse of 46 years.

Verderer's Court (or Court of Swaincote and Attachment of the New Forest), Verderer's Hall, Queen's House, Lyndhurst — Hampshire

This Court is held at about six-week intervals. Ten verderers look after the animals, plants, use of and amenities in the forest. One is appointed by the Crown, four by bodies such as the Forestry Commission and the Council for the Preservation of Rural England, and five elected by the commoners of the forest, who must own at least one acre (0.4 ha) with common rights. The verderers appoint agisters to patrol the forest. The proceedings of the Court are open to the public.

LYNDHURST IS ON THE A35 SOUTH WEST OF SOUTHAMPTON.

⚜ Ceremony of the Accession, St James' Palace   London

On the accession of a monarch the Heralds meet on Friary Court Balcony, St James' Palace, where the State Trumpeters sound a fanfare. Then the Garter King of Arms proclaims the successor. This is repeated at Charing Cross, Temple Bar (where the Lord Mayor, Aldermen, other City officers, and the City Marshall, ceremonially challenge Her Majesty's Officers of Arms) then in the City at Chancery Lane, and on the steps of the Royal Exchange.

ST JAMES'S PALACE IS IN MARLBOROUGH ROAD, OFF THE MALL.

⚜ Entry of the Monarch into the City of London, Temple Bar   London

Temple Bar is the western boundary of the City of London, at the junction of Fleet Street and Strand. When the monarch enters the City in state he or she is met by the Lord Mayor at Temple Bar, who presents the City's Pearl Sword. Since Charles I returned the sword, the monarch has always done so before entering the City.

The Temple Bar is the only surviving gate of the City of London, and is now in Theobalds Park, Cheshunt, Hertfordshire. The other gates, Aldgate, Bishopsgate, Moorgate, Cripplegate, Aldersgate, Newgate and Ludgate were all demolished before the end of the 18th century.

THE NEAREST UNDERGROUND STATION IS TEMPLE.

⚜ Ceremony of the Loving Cup, City of London   London

At City banquets guests rise in threes, one to drink, another to lift the cover, and the third to protect his back. This custom is said to have arisen in AD 978 when King Edward the Martyr was assassinated while drinking from the stirrup cup offered by the treacherous Elfrida.

Dates for Moveable Feasts

	1997	1998	1999	2000
Shrove Tuesday	11th Feb	24th Feb	16th Feb	7th Mar
Ash Wednesday	12th Feb	25th Feb	17th Feb	8th Mar
Mothering Sunday	9th Mar	22nd Mar	14th Mar	2nd Apr
Easter Sunday	30th Mar	12th Apr	4th Apr	23rd Apr
Hock Sunday	6th Apr	19th Apr	11th Apr	30th Apr
Rogation Sunday	4th May	17th May	9th May	28th May
Ascension day	8th May	21st May	13th May	1st June
Whit Sunday	18th May	31st May	23rd May	11th June
Trinity Sunday	25th May	7th June	30th May	18th June
Corpus Christi	29th May	11th June	3rd June	22nd June

Recipes appendix

January

Plum Pudding
1½ lb (600 g) finely chopped suet
1 lb (400 g) raisins
the yolks and whites of 6 eggs
6 tablespoons milk
¾ lb (300 g) flour
1 teasspoon salt
a large spoonful of brandy

Mix suet, raisins, eggs and milk together, putting flour in by degrees. Add salt and brandy then boil uncovered for 5 hours. Use more fruit, less suet and fewer eggs if required.

Coventry Godcakes
8 oz (225 g) flaky pastry
mincemeat
milk
sugar

Roll out pastry and cut into 4 in (10 cm) squares. Place a spoonful of mincemeat in one corner of the pastry, fold over the opposite corner to make a triangular pastry, seal and decorate edges. Brush with milk, sprinkle with sugar and bake in a very hot oven (475-550°F/240-290°C) for 15 minutes.

Twelfth Cake
8 oz (200 g) butter
8 oz (200 g) caster sugar
4 eggs
3 tablespoons brandy
8 oz (200 g) plain flour
8 oz (200 g) currants
8 oz (200 g) raisins
8 oz (200 g) sultanas
2 oz (50 g) chopped nuts
cinnamon
a dried pea
a dried bean

Beat eggs and add brandy. Cream the butter and sugar together and stir in the egg-and-brandy mixture. Fold in the flour, cinnamon, fruit and nuts, a portion at a time, and finally the pea and bean. Grease and line a 12 in (30 cm) tin, and pour in the mixture. Bake in a slow oven (300°F/150°C) for about 3 hours, until an inserted knife comes out clean. Allow to cool and glaze with melted honey. Decorate with glacé cherries and crystallised fruits.

Lamb's Wool
4 pints (2 l) ale
2 pints (1 l) white wine
1 grated nutmeg
2 teaspoons ground cinnamon
1 tablespoon demerara sugar
roasted crab apples

Heat ale and wine together and when hot add spices and sugar. Serve in a deep bowl with roasted apples floating on top.

Epiphany Tart
8 oz (200 g) plain flour
¼ teaspoon salt
4 oz margarine
2 tablespoons water
a selection of jams

Sieve flour and salt into a bowl, add the margarine in pieces and rub with the flour between the finger-tips until the whole resembles breadcrumbs. Add the water and knead until smooth. Wrap in greaseproof paper and leave in a cool place for 30 minutes.

Roll out the pastry and use it to line a 9 in (22.5 cm) tart tin. Use the trimmings to make a lattice pattern across the base and add the jams (warmed if necessary) to each of the areas created. Bake in a fairly hot oven (400°F/200°C) for about 25 minutes. Serve with custard.

Venison with Port Wine Sauce
For the venison
a saddle of venison
oil
vinegar
1 onion
salt and pepper
bacon rashers
orange juice
For the port wine sauce
2 oz (56 g) ham
1½ oz (42.5 g) butter
1 carrot
1 onion
1 oz (28 g) mushroom stalks
bunch of mixed herbs
salt and pepper
4 tablespoons white wine
1 oz (25 g) flour
1¼ pints (625 ml) stock
5 tablespoons port wine
3 tomatoes

Marinate the venison for 2 hours in a mixture of oil, vinegar, chopped onion and seasoning, basting frequently. Put into a roasting pan and cover with rashers of bacon. Roast for 20 minutes in a moderately hot oven (325-350°F/160-180°C), then reduce to very moderate (250°F/120°C) and cook for about 1¼ hours, basting frequently. Sprinkle with orange juice and serve with port wine sauce.

To make the sauce, dice ham and fry gently in a little melted butter, adding the diced carrot, onion and mushroom stalks, herbs, salt and pepper. When golden, add white wine and simmer until reduced by half. Meanwhile melt the rest of the butter in another saucepan and add flour. Brown it without burning, and when glossy gradually add half the stock and the mixture from the first saucepan. Simmer slowly for 1½ hours. Sieve and return to pan. Add port wine, chopped tomatoes and the rest of the stock. Cook for another 30 minutes then strain again.

February

Feasten Cakes

1 lb (400 g) plain flour
½ teaspoon cinnamon
4 oz (100 g) unsalted butter
2 teaspoons dried yeast
2 oz (50 g) sugar
¼ teaspoon of saffron
¼ pint (150 ml) milk
6 fl oz (175 ml) clotted cream
2 eggs
4 oz (100 g) currants

Warm the milk and make an infusion of the saffron. Cream the yeast with a little sugar. Sieve the flour and cinnamon into a bowl and mix. Rub in the butter. Strain the saffron milk and beat in the cream. Add the yeast to this mixture and leave for the yeast to activate. Beat the eggs.

Pour the frothy yeast mixture into the flour and cinnamon and add the eggs, currants and remaining sugar. Knead well, cover and leave for dough to rise. Shape dough into small, flat cakes and leave until dough is springy to the touch.

Put on to a lightly greased baking sheet, brush milk and sprinkle sugar on each, then bake in a fairly hot oven (375°F/190°C) for 25 minutes. Serve cold with whipped or clotted cream.

Valentine Cakes (Plum Shuttles)

1½ lb (600 g) plain flour
4 oz (100 g) castor sugar
2 oz (50 g) chopped peel
½ pint (250 ml) milk
4 oz (100 g) butter
4 oz (100 g) currants
1 oz (25 g) yeast

Rub the fat into the flour and add, with mixing, the sugar, peel and currants. Add the yeast and milk and sufficient water (about 1/2 pint (250 ml) to make a soft dough. Leave for about 45 minutes then work the dough on a floured board until homogeneous. Cut pieces off and mould into the shape of weavers' shuttles (traditionally) or into heart shapes. Leave for about 15 minutes then bake in a fairly hot oven (375°F/190°C) until golden brown.

Valentine Biscuits

3 oz (75 g) flour
3 oz (75 g) butter
1 egg yolk
the rind of half a lemon
¼ teaspoon baking powder
1½ oz (37.5 g) sugar

Cream the butter and sugar together, add lemon rind, and beat in the yolk. Add the flour and baking powder and mix. Roll out and cut with a heart-shaped cutter. Bake in a hot oven (425°F/220°C) for 20 minutes.

Shrovetide

Minced Beef Collops

½ oz (12.5 g) butter
1 lb (400 g) lean minced beef
2 oz (50 g) shredded suet
1 chopped onion
1 tablespoon tomato sauce
½pint (250 ml) thick gravy or rich stock
salt and pepper

Melt butter in a saucepan and add all the other ingredients. If using stock, thicken it with a little flour. Simmer gently for 20-25 minutes.

Pancakes

4 oz (10 g) plain flour
½ teaspoon salt
1 egg
½ pint (250 ml) milk
lard or fat for frying
castor sugar and a lemon

Sieve flour and salt, make a well in the centre and add the egg, working the flour in from the sides. Add the milk gradually, beating to make a smooth batter. Melt just enough lard to coat the bottom and sides of a pan; when hot and just beginning to smoke pour in a little pancake batter. Cook until set and browned underneath, toss or turn and cook the second side. Sprinkle with castor sugar and a squeeze of lemon juice.

Baldock Doughnuts

1 cup sugar
1 cup milk
2 oz (50g) butter
2 eggs
1½ teaspoons cream of tartar
¼ teaspoon bicarbonate of soda
currants

Mix the sugar, butter, cream of tartar, bicarbonate of soda and currants thoroughly and add the milk and eggs. Mix again and sprinkle on flour, with further mixing, until a pliable paste is obtained. Mould into traditional doughnut shapes (not rings) and deep fry. Roll in sugar and serve warm.

Coquille Buns

1 lb (400 g) self-raising flour
2 oz (50 g) lard
2 oz (50 g) margarine
½ cup sugar
2 teaspoons mixed spice
2 tablespoons mixed fruit
1 egg

Rub the lard and margarine into the flour. Beat the egg with milk and add it until a pliable dough is obtained. Roll out 2 in (5 cm) thick on a floured board and cut into squares. Cook in a moderate oven (350°F/180°C) until golden-brown. Serve with butter.

Lent

Lenten Kedgeree

one tin of sardines
3 cups of brown rice
1 teaspoon mixed herbs
1 onion
salt

Slice and fry the onion. Boil the rice with a little salt. Put the deboned sardines with their oil into a bowl, chop and stir in the mixed herbs and a pinch of salt. Add the onions and rice and mix thoroughly. Heat through in the oven.

Frumenty

2 oz (50 g) wheat grains
½ pint milk
2 teaspoons sugar
whatever flavouring you wish to add to the frumenty
  e.g. raspberry or other garden soft fruit

Soak the wheat grains in water overnight. Strain the wheat grains and add to the milk in a saucepan. Bring to the boil and simmer while stirring until the milk has thickened. Add the flavouring and sugar and cook for another two minutes. Add more milk if it thickens too much.

Simnel cake

For the cake
4 oz (100 g) blanched sweet almonds
8 oz (200 g) currants
8 oz (200 g) sultanas
8 oz (200 g) raisins
4 oz (100 g) mixed peel
2 oz (50 g) glace cherries
11 oz (312 g) plain flour
2 teaspoons mixed spice
8 oz (200 g) margarine
grated rind of 1 orange
1 teaspoon almond essence
5 eggs
¼ teaspoon bicarbonate of soda
1 teaspoon milk
For the almond paste
2 lb (800 g) almond paste
3 tablespoons apricot jam and 1 egg yolk
12 oz (300 g) ground almonds
4 oz (100 g) icing sugar
½ oz (12.5 g) castor sugar
juice of 1 lemon
2 eggs
1 dessertspoon orange flower water
½ teaspoon vanilla essence

To make the cake mixture, chop almonds and mix with currants, sultanas, stoned raisins, chopped peel and quartered cherries. Sieve flour and spice. Cream together margarine and sugar until fluffy. Beat in grated orange rind and almond essence. Beat in eggs one at a time, alternately with a little flour. Fold in half flour and fruit mixture. Mix thoroughly, then fold in the rest. Finally add bicarbonate of soda, dissolved in milk.

To make the almond paste, sieve icing sugar and mix together dry ingredients. Add vanilla essence to lemon juice and stir this and beaten eggs into the mixture. Knead to a paste and roll out on a board.

Roll out half the almond paste to a circle to fit inside an 8 in (20 cm) cake tin, spread half cake mixture evenly, smooth top and place the circle of almond paste on top. Add the remaining cake mixture and spread evenly. Tie a double sheet of paper round the tin, to come 1½ in (4 cm) above the top. Bake on the middle shelf of a slow oven (250-300°F/120-150°C) for 4¼-4¾ hours. Cool in tin for about 5 minutes, then turn out, strip off paper and finish cooling on a wire tray.

While cake is cooling boil jam for 2-3 minutes and sieve. Roll out 8 oz (200 g) almond paste to a thin round to cover top of cake. Spread top of cake with jam and press round of paste on evenly. Roll out a thin strip of almond paste about 1½ in (4 cm) wide, spread with jam and press on round side to join top layer of almond paste. Roll out two thin strips and twist together, press round top outer edge of cake with jam to form a plait, and finally form remaining almond paste into little eggs, and arrange these round the cake, inside the plaited border. Eleven are traditionally used to represent the eleven loyal apostles. Brush with beaten egg yolk and put into a very hot oven (475-550°F/240-290°C) for 7 minutes to brown.

Fig Pie

2 cups cooked figs
a pastry shell
¼ cup currants
¾ cup sugar
½ teaspoon mixed spice
1 tablespoon orange rind
1 tablespoon treacle or syrup
2 egg whites

Prepare the pastry shell and figs beforehand (if using dried figs soak them in water overnight first). Cut up the figs and add currants, sugar, treacle, rind and spices. Beat egg whites until stiff and fold into mixture, stirring well. Add to pastry shell and bake in a moderate oven (350°F/180°C) until golden-brown.

Northumberland Carlings

peas
beans
butter
salt and pepper

Peas and beans are soaked in water overnight, fried in butter and seasoned with pepper and salt. Sometimes sugar and rum are added.

Pond Pudding

4 oz (100g) self-raising flour
2 oz (50 g) grated suet
⅙ pint (100 ml) milk
4 oz (100 g) butter
2 oz (50 g) demerara sugar
2 oz (50 g) currants

Mix the flour and suet and add sufficient milk to make a dough. Roll enough of the dough to line a buttered 1 pint (600 ml) pudding basin. Cream the butter and sugar together, mix in the currants and add the mixture to the basin. Roll out the remaining pastry and make a top for the pudding. Cover with greaseproof paper and steam for 2½ hours. Serve with hot custard.

Easter

Tansy Pudding

½ pint (250 ml) milk
3 oz (75 g) breadcrumbs
1 tablespoon chopped young Tansy leaves (or equivalent in ginger)
2 eggs
1 oz (25 g) sugar
½ oz (12.5 g) butter

Boil milk and pour it over breadcrumbs. Leave to soak for 30 minutes. Add chopped Tansy leaves to beaten eggs and sugar. Mix with milk and breadcrumbs, put into a buttered dish, dot with butter and bake in a very moderate oven (300°F/150°C) for 1 hour. Serve with cream.

Cheese Cake

For the filling
2 lb (800 g) cottage cheese
½ pint (250 ml) cultured (sour) cream
2 oz (50 g) fine semolina
4 oz (100 g) castor sugar
4 eggs
3 tablespoons lemon juice and the grated rind of 1 lemon

For the pastry
2 oz (50 g) flour
2 oz (50 g) fine semolina
pinch salt
2 oz (50 g) butter
water to mix
raisins for topping

For the topping
¼ pint (125 ml) cultured cream
chopped nuts

Rub the cottage cheese through a sieve. Blend smoothly and thoroughly with the cream, semolina, sugar, eggs, lemon juice and rind.

Sift flour, semolina and salt. Rub in butter and mix to a dry dough with water; roll and line the bottom of spring form cake tin 8½-9 in (20-23 cm) diameter and 3 in (7.5 cm) deep. Grease sides of tin and sprinkle with flour. Top pastry with raisins and spoon in the cake mixture.

Bake in a moderate oven (325-350°F/160-180°C) for 1½ hours. Top with cream and return to oven, cooking for about 7 minutes. Turn out oven and leave cake in oven until cold. Sprinkle chopped nuts round edge of cake.

Hot Cross Buns

1 oz (25 g) yeast
3 oz (75 g) castor sugar
½ pint (250 ml) milk
1 lb (400 g) flour
1 teaspoon salt
¼ teaspoon cinnamon
¼ teaspoon grated nutmeg
4 oz (100 g) currants
1 oz (25 g) chopped peel
2 oz (50 g) melted butter
1 egg
milk and sugar to glaze

Cream yeast and sugar and add a little milk. Sieve flour and salt, add yeast and all the milk, sprinkle with a little flour, cover and leave for 15 minutes. Add cinnamon, nutmeg, melted butter and beaten egg and mix well, adding more milk if necessary. Cover and leave to prove for 1 hour, or until the dough is twice the size. Add currants and chopped peel, knead and form dough into buns. Arrange on greased baking trays and mark a cross in the top of each. Leave for 15 minutes, then brush with a milk and sugar glaze and bake in a hot oven (425-450°F/220-230°C) for 15 to 20 minutes.

Easter Biscuits

8 oz (200 g) self-raising flour
4 oz (100 g) margarine
4 oz (100 g) granulated sugar
pinch of salt
1 level teaspoon cinnamon
2 oz (50 g) currants
1 egg

Rub fat into flour. Add sugar, cinnamon and salt, then the currants. Add egg to bind. Work the mixture until it is pliable, then roll it out thinly and cut into biscuits. Do this on a floured board. Bake at gas 350°F/180°C until golden-brown.

May

Junket

milk
cream
sugar
cinnamon

Put warm milk in a bowl; turn it into rennet; then put some scalded cream, sugar and cinnamon on the top, without breaking the curd.

Old-fashioned Gingerbread

2 oz (50 g) almonds
2 oz (50 g) candied peel
¾ oz (18 g) powdered ginger
1 teaspoon mixed spice
1 lb (400 g) flour
4 tablespoons golden syrup
6 oz (150 g) butter
4 oz (100 g) sugar
1 egg
½ teaspoon bicarbonate of soda
2 teaspoons milk

Chop almonds and peel and mix in with the sieved flour, spice and ginger. Warm the syrup, butter and sugar and beat together. Add the beaten egg. Dissolve the soda in milk and add this too. Stir well together and bake in greased and lined tin in a slow oven (250-300°F/120-150°C) for 2 hours.

Egg Custard

2 eggs
1 pint (500 ml) milk
1 oz (25 g) sugar
pinch of salt
flavouring (grated nutmeg or orange or lemon rind)

Beat the eggs and add milk and the salt. Strain into a greased pie dish and stir in the sugar. Sprinkle the flavouring on top and bake for 1 hour in a slow oven (275°F/140°C) then for 40 minutes with the heat turned up to 300°F/150°C.

May Cup
4 glasses white wine
8 glasses cider (both sweet if preferred)
1 glass brandy
orange slices and
Ladies' Bedstraw (a spring wildflower)
Mix together white wine, cider and brandy and add orange slices and washed Ladies' Bedstraw. Keep in a cold place for 2 hours, filter into a bowl and serve.

Plum Pudding
4 oz (100 g) flour
4 oz (100 g) breadcrumbs
1 cup milk
pinch of salt
4 oz (100 g) currants
3 oz (75 g) shredded suet
2 tablespoons treacle
½ teaspoon mixed spice
1 chopped apple
3 oz (75 g) sugar.
Mix flour and crumbs in a bowl and add apple, sugar, suet, currants, spices and salt. Warm the treacle and add to the milk, then pour on to the dry ingredients. Mix and turn into a well-greased basin. Cover with greaseproof paper and steam for 6 hours.

Whitsuntide

Banbury Cakes
½ lb (220 g) puff pastry
1 oz (25 g) butter
2 oz (50 g) sugar
1 small egg
1 oz (25 g) cake crumbs
2 oz (50 g) mixed peel
4 oz (100 g) currants
a pinch of mixed spice
Roll out pastry to ⅛ in (3 mm) thick and cut into 6 in (15 cm) rounds. Beat the egg. Put butter into a bowl, add sugar and beat until creamy. Add the beaten egg, cake crumbs, peel, currants and spice and mix thoroughly. Put a portion on each pastry round, wet the edges of the pastry and turn up to make parcels, sealing at the top so that none of the mixture can seep out. Turn cakes over, pat down, moisten and sprinkle with a little sugar. Bake in a fairly hot oven (400°F/200°C) until golden-brown.

Gooseberry Pie
For the shortcrust pastry
8 oz (200g) plain flour
5 oz (125g) margarine
2 tablespoons water
For the filling
1 ½ lb (600 g) gooseberries (top and tailed)
4 oz (100 g) sugar
¼ pint (125 ml) water
Put margarine, water and one third of the flour into a mixing bowl and cream with a fork. Stir in the remaining flour to form a firm dough. Knead on a floured board until smooth. Roll out sufficient pastry to line the bowl. Add layers of gooseberries (or other soft garden fruit if preferred), sprinkling each layer with sugar and water.

Roll out the remaining pastry and make a top for the pie, trimming off the surplus. Make a hole in the top for the steam to escape, brush with water and sprinkle with caster sugar. Bake in a fairly hot oven (400°F/200°C) for 30 to 40 minutes. Serve with hot custard.

July

Heg Peg Dump
For the dough
8 oz (200 g) self-raising flour
4 oz (100 g) grated suet
¼ pint (125 ml) water
1 teaspoon baking powder
½ teaspoon salt for the pastry.
For the filling
1 lb (400 g) stoned plums (or damsons)
8 oz (200 g) sliced cooking apple
6 oz (150 g) sugar
1 tablespoon cake crumbs and 1 tablespoon water for the filling.
Mix the flour, suet, salt and baking powder and add sufficient water to make a soft dough. Knead until smooth.

Roll enough of the dough to line a buttered 2 pint (1200 ml) pudding basin. Fill up with layers of fruit, sugar and crumbs, and add the water. Roll out the remaining pastry and make a top for the pudding. Cover with greaseproof paper and steam for 3 hours. Serve with custard or cream.

Oysters
Serve plain on the deep shell, in their own liquor. Accompany with brown bread and butter, lemon wedges and wine vinegar, and serve a dry white wine or stout.

August

Grasmere Gingerbread
8 oz (200 g) plain flour
¼ teaspoon bicarbonate of soda
1 teaspoon ground ginger
4 oz (100 g) butter
4 oz (100 g) brown sugar
Sieve flour, bicarbonate of soda and ginger, rub in butter and add sugar. Line shallow baking tin with greased greaseproof paper and press the mixture into it. Bake in a moderate oven (325-350°F/160-180°C) for about 30 minutes.

Bartlemas Beef
beef
¼ teaspoon each of ground nutmeg
ginger
cinnamon
cloves and mace
⅓ teaspoon salt
This is just braised beef, but the beef is rubbed with the mixture of spices and seasoning before being covered with water and braised until tender.

Brandy Snaps
4 oz (100 g) butter
4 oz (100 g) sugar
4 tablespoons golden syrup
4 oz (100 g) flour
1 teaspoon powdered ginger
pinch of salt
a few drops of vanilla essence.

Melt butter with sugar and syrup. Add flour, ginger, salt and vanilla essence. Drop mixture in teaspoons on to well greased baking trays, far apart. Bake in the middle of a very moderate oven (325-350°F/160-180°C) until brown (about 15 minutes). Leave there for a few minutes then slip a palette knife under each and roll up quickly before they harden. Serve with whipped cream.

September

Eccles Cakes
For the pastry
8 oz (200 g) of short or puff pastry.
For the filling
2 oz (50 g) margarine
4 oz (100 g) currants
2 oz (50 g) soft brown sugar
3 oz (75 g) mixed fruit
1 oz (25 g) peel
lemon juice a pinch of allspice
Roll out the pastry and cut into circles 4 in (10 cm) diameter.Melt the margarine, add the other ingredients and keep warm. Place spoonsful into the centre of the pastry circles, damp around the edges of the pastry ring and gather up to cover the filling. Turn the cake over and lightly flatten. Brush with egg white and sprinkle with caster sugar. Make two small cuts in the top and bake in a hot oven (375°F/190°C) for 20 minutes.

Abbots Bromley Wakes Cakes
For the paste mixture
4 lbs (1.6 kg) cake flour
½ oz (12.5 g) baking powder
½ oz (12.5 g) salt
1½ oz (37.5 g) ground mixed spice and 2 lbs (800 g) butter
all rubbed together to form a paste.
For the sugar and egg mixture
1 ½ lbs (600 g) sugar and 7 ½ oz (180 g) eggs mixed together
Combine the two mixtures and roll out on a lightly floured board. Cut out with a 3½ in (9 cm) scalloped cutter. Bake in a hot oven (400-425°F /200-220°C) until golden brown and dust with sugar.

Abbots Bromley Brandy Snaps
For the meal mixture
2 lbs (800 g) all-purpose flour and 1 lb (400 g) butter rubbed together until they are like meal
For the sugar mixture
2 lbs (800 g) molasses
3½ lbs (1.4 kg) sugar
1 oz (25 g) ground ginger and 5 oz (125 g) water mixed together
Combine the two mixtures and knead the dough (with wet hands) into a cylinder. Pinch off pieces of dough the size of a walnut and place 4 to 5 inches (10-12 cm) apart on heavily greased tins. Bake at 380-400°F/190-200°C until tinted brown, but not too hard. Remove from oven.

When the snaps begin to cool, loop over a wooden stick, or a cornucopia mould. When cold, store in tightly closed tins. Fill with whipped cream before serving.

Harvest Cake (Fourses Cake)
1 ½ lb (675 g) plain flour
½ tablespoon salt
2 teaspoons mixed spice
6 oz (175 g) lard
½ oz (15 g) fresh yeast
2 teaspoons sugar
¾ pint (450 ml) and 6 oz (175 g) currants
Using a little sugar and warm water make a cream of the yeast. Sieve the flour, salt, and mixed spice into a bowl and rub in the lard. Add the yeast and stir in the remaining water. Mix until a smooth, pliable dough is obtained. Knead and leave to rise. Knead in the currants, and put into a loaf tin. Leave until fully risen then bake in a fairly hot oven (400°F/200°C) for about 45 minutes.

Lancashire Wakes Cakes
8 oz (200 g) plain flour
¼ teaspoon salt
6 oz (150 g) butter
6 oz (150 g) sugar
1 oz (25 g) currants
1 egg
milk to mix
castor sugar for topping
Sieve flour and salt, rub in butter, add sugar and currants. Mix in beaten egg and enough milk to make a stiff dough. Roll out thinly on a floured board, cut into rounds round a saucer and bake on a greased and floured baking sheet in a moderate oven (325-350°F/160-180°C) for about 25 minutes. Sprinkle castor sugar on top.

Roast Goose Stuffed with Apple
a goose
some sage and onion stuffing
1 apple
some flour
seasoning
stock
Stuff a mature bird with sage and onion stuffing mixed with grated apple, but roast goslings plain. Truss and prick the skin of the breast to allow the fat to escape. Put into a roasting pan with the giblets and roast in a hot oven (425-450°F/220-230°C) for 20 minutes, then lower the heat to very moderate (250°F/120°C). Allow 15 minutes per pound. Strain off excess fat during cooking.

When almost cooked dredge the breast with a little flour, baste with hot fat and return to the oven to get a crisp brown finish. Take out bird, and keep hot. Strain off fat, add a little stock to form gravy, season and strain.

October

Nottingham Goose Fair Brandy Snaps

4 cups flour
2 cups butter
3 cups brown sugar (firmly packed)
1¼ cups corn syrup
2 tablespoons ground ginger
1 tablespoon lemon juice

Combine the butter, sugar and corn syrup in a saucepan and melt over a low heat. Add lemon juice and flour sifted together with ginger. Combine thoroughly. Place teaspoonsful of the mixture on a well-greased baking sheet, allowing ample space around each spoonful.

Bake for 15 minutes in a slow oven at 300°F/150°C. Allow to stand for 2 minutes before lifting with a knife and roll up quickly, with one fold, while still warm. When cold, fill the hollow roll with clotted cream.

Blackberry and Apple Jelly

Take 2 lb (800 g) blackberries
sugar
2 lb (800 g) apples

Wash, core and slice the apples and put into a preserving pan. Add the blackberries and cover with water. Bring to the boil and boil for about 20 minutes, stirring well to prevent burning. Strain and measure the volume of juice. Return to the pan and add 11/4 lb (500 g) sugar for every pint (500 ml) of juice. Bring again to the boil and boil for three minutes. Bottle and seal.

Warden Pears

Take fresh pears
½ pint (250 ml) red wine
1 oz (25 g) brown sugar
a pinch of cinnamon
ginger
saffron

Peel pears and place in an oven-proof dish. Prepare a mixture of the other ingredients and pour over. Bake in a moderate oven (350°F/180°C) for 20 minutes, or a little longer if not yet tender.

Mash o' Nine Sorts

1 lb (400 g) potatoes
2 carrots
1 turnip
1 parsnip
2 leeks
4 oz (100 g) peas
salt and pepper
single cream.

Prepare and boil all the vegetables. Mash together the potatoes, carrots, turnip and parsnip and season with salt and pepper. Add sliced leeks and mix in some single cream. Stir in the peas and ring, and transfer the whole to an oven-proof dish. Cook in a moderate oven (350°F/180°C) until golden-brown.

Hallowe'en Cakes

2 oz (50 g) butter
2 oz (50 g) sugar
2 oz (50 g) self-raising flour
1 egg
1 teaspoon filling (e.g. chopped glace cherries chopped nuts, raisins, sultanas, currants) and flavouring to taste (e.g. coffee
cocoa
coconut
caraway seeds).

Cream the butter and sugar together, add beaten egg, flour and a little milk if too stiff. Portion out into bun cases and cook on a baking tray in a fairly hot oven (400°F/200°C) until golden-brown.

Toffee Apples

½ lb (220 g) sugar
clean unbruised apples and pointed hardwood sticks.

Melt the sugar slowly in a shallow pan, stirring constantly, until it caramelises. Pierce each apple with a stick and roll in the molten toffee until covered all over. Allow to harden in a rack.

Pumpkin Pie

8 oz (200 g) sweet shortcrust pastry (made using butter instead of lard or margarine and adding 1 oz/25 g of brown sugar to the flour)
1 cup mixed dried fruit
1 tablespoon brown sugar
grated rind of 1 lemon
1 grated peeled apple
sweet sherry
2 eggs
3 oz (75 g) brown sugar
pinch salt
1 cup evaporated milk or double cream
1 teaspoon mixed spice
whipped cream
walnuts to decorate
2-3 cups of mashed stewed pumpkin pulp

Line a flan dish with the pastry. Spread the next 4 ingredients into the pastry case, sprinkling with the sherry. Beat the eggs, mixed spice, remaining brown sugar and salt together, add the cream and the pumpkin pulp, then warm gently, stirring all the time. Do not boil or overheat. Pour it over the fruit mixture and bake in a moderate oven (325-350°F/160-180°C) until set. Cool and decorate with whipped cream and walnuts. Keep in fridge until served.

Pumpkin Seeds

pumpkin seeds
oil
salt

Fry seeds in oil, and toss them in salt. Serve as 'nibbles' with drinks.

November

Soul Cakes

6 oz (175 g) butter
6 oz (175 g) caster sugar
3 egg yolks
1 lb (400 g) plain flour
1 teaspoon mixed spice
3 oz (75 g) currants
some milk.

Mix the flour and mixed spice together. Cream the butter and sugar together in a bowl and beat in each egg yolk. Then add the flour and spice mixture, currants, and a little milk. Mix to form a soft dough.

Make dough into flat cakes, mark a cross on each one and put on to a greased baking sheet. Bake in a moderate oven (350°F/180°C) until golden-brown - about 10 to 15 minutes.

Lancashire Harcake

1 lb (400 g) oatmeal
2 oz (50 g) butter
½ oz (12.5 g) ground ginger
12 oz (350 g) golden syrup
1 egg
some brown ale

Rub the butter into the oatmeal, add the ginger and stir in the syrup. Add a beaten egg and a little brown ale, and mix. Pour into a greased tin and cook in a moderate oven (350°F/180°C) for 1-11/2 hours, when it should be firm. When cool cut into squares.

Lancashire Parkin

8 oz (200 g) plain flour
1 teaspoon baking powder
2 teaspoons ground ginger
1 teaspoon ground caraway seed
8 oz (200 g) medium oatmeal
8 oz (200 g) black treacle
4 oz (100 g) lard
4 oz (100 g) demerara sugar
1 egg
4 tablespoons milk.

Sieve together flour, baking powder, ginger and caraway, then add the oatmeal. Put the treacle, lard and sugar into a saucepan and heat gently, stirring until the sugar and fat have dissolved. Remove from heat and add beaten egg and milk. Combine with flour and oatmeal mixture, mix well together and put into a shallow baking tin (10 x 8 in/25 x 20 cm) lined with greased greaseproof paper. Bake for 1 hour in a very moderate oven (300°F/150°C). Cut into squares when cold.

Bonfire Toffee

1 lb (400 g) of demerara sugar
¼ pt (125 ml) water
3 oz (75 g) butter
4 oz (100 g) black treacle
4 oz (100 g) golden syrup
¼ level teaspoon cream of tartar
5 drops of vinegar

Well grease a tin. Heat all ingredients gently in a heavy-bottomed pan until the sugar dissolves. Increase the heat, boil rapidly for 8 to 10 minutes, stirring all the time. Test by dropping a little into cold water. When brittle, take off the heat. Allow to cool in the pan for 5 minutes, pour into a tin and leave to set for 12 hours. Break into pieces and store in an air-tight jar.

Thor Cakes

1 lb (500 g) oatmeal
1 lb (500 g) flour
¾ lb (375 g) butter
1 lb (500 g) sugar
1 lb (500 g) treacle
2 oz (50 g) chopped candied peel
2 teaspoons baking powder
1 teaspoon salt
1 teaspoon caraway seeds
1 teaspoon ground ginger

Mix all ingredients together except the butter and treacle. Rub in the butter and then add the treacle slightly warmed. Knead and roll out on a floured board until the thickness of biscuits. Make or cut into rounds and place on a baking tray. Cook in a moderate oven (325°F/160°C) for 10 minutes.

St Clement's Tarts

For the pastry
8 oz (200 g) plain flour
5 oz (125 g) margarine
2 tablespoons water
the juice and peel of 1 orange
For the filling
the peel of 1 lemon
3 oz (75 g) butter
3 oz (75 g) sugar
2 eggs
¼ teaspoon vanilla essence

To make the pastry, put margarine, water and one third of the flour into a mixing bowl and cream with a fork. Stir in the remaining flour to form a firm dough. Knead on a floured board until smooth. Roll out the pastry and line tart tins.

To make the filling, separate the egg yolks and whites. Chop the orange and lemon peel finely. Cream the butter and sugar together and beat in the egg yolks. Add orange juice, chopped peel and vanilla essence. Whisk the egg whites until stiff and fold into the mixture. Pour into the pastry cases and bake in a fairly hot oven (400°F/200°C) for 25 minutes. Serve cold.

Cattern Pie

shortcrust pastry
sweet mincemeat
honey and breadcrumbs.

Line a flan dish with shortcrust pastry, and fill it with sweet mincemeat. Spoon melted honey over the top and sprinkle generously with breadcrumbs. Place pastry 'spokes' over the top of the pie, to resemble a wheel. Cook in a moderate oven (325-350°F/160-180°C) until the pastry is golden brown. Serve with cream. People don't get a 'piece', they get a 'spoke'.

St Andrew's Cake

1 lb (400 g) plain flour
1 teaspoon salt
½ oz (12.5 g) fresh yeast (or ½ tablespoon dried yeast)
1 teaspoon caster sugar
½ pint (250 g) water
1 egg
4 oz (100 g) lard
4 oz (100 g) currants
4 oz (100 g) sugar
1 oz (25 g) chopped crystallised lemon peel

Mix flour and salt and sift into a mixing bowl. Warm the water in another bowl and to it add a mixture of the yeast and caster sugar. Blend and leave until the frothing stops. Then mix in a beaten egg, and add the mixture to the flour and salt. Melt the lard slowly and, when cooled, add it to the mixture and stir until smooth. Knead, cover and leave to rise.

Knead in the currants, sugar and peel and transfer to a 2 lb (1 kg) loaf tin. Leave until the dough has risen to the top, then bake in a moderate oven (350°F/180°C) for about 1 hour or until golden-brown.

December

Chocolate Yule Log

For the cake
3 oz (75 g) self-raising flour
3 oz (75 g) caster sugar
2 eggs for the cake
For the filling
jam
lemon curd or buttercream
For the chocolate icing
4 oz (100 g) ground almonds
4 oz (100 g) sifted icing sugar
4 oz (100 g) caster sugar
1 large egg and lemon juice
for the almond paste.
2 ½ oz (62.5 g) margarine
4 tablespoons cocoa
8 oz (200 g) icing sugar
3 tablespoons hot scalded milk
1 teaspoon vanilla essence

To make the cake, whisk the eggs together in a bowl and add the sugar. Whisk again until a thick cream is obtained. Fold the flour in lightly, a little at a time. Spread the mixture on a well-greased 9 x 12 in (22.5 x 30 cm) Swiss Roll Tin and bake in a hot oven (400-425°F/200-220°C) for 7 to 8 minutes. Do not overcook. Turn upside-down on to a sugared greaseproof paper. Turn in the short end and roll, not too tightly. Fold the paper around it and leave for a few minutes to set. Unfold and spread the filling on, then roll up.

To make the almond paste, beat the egg. Mix the dry ingredients in a bowl and add the egg and sufficient lemon juice to give a pliable paste. Knead on a board dusted with icing sugar until smooth. Roll it out and cut two disks to fit on the ends of the cake. Paste them on with a little filling. Keep the remaining paste for decoration.

To make the icing, melt the margarine and cocoa together, and stir in the remaining ingredients. Beat until thick. Cover the cake with chocolate icing and use a fork to get a bark effect. Decorate with almond paste figures and shapes, and dust with icing sugar for a snow effect.

Posset

2 slices stale bread
salt
grated nutmeg
1 dessertspoon caster sugar
1 pint (500 ml) milk
1 tablespoon brandy or a measure of ale

Trim the crusts off the bread and cut the remainder up into small pieces. Put in a bowl and add a pinch of salt, a pinch of nutmeg and the sugar. Heat the milk, but do not boil, and pour over the bread. Cover and leave to stand for 15 minutes. Add the brandy or ale and mix thoroughly.

Yuletide Frumity

2 pints (1 l) pearled wheat (or frumity corn)
5 pints (2.5 l) water
½ teaspoon cinnamon
milk
sugar
grated nutmeg

Cover the wheat with the cold water. Put in a warm oven for 12 hours. Then bring to the boil, add cinnamon, and, stirring frequently, boil until the wheat is swollen and soft. Pour into a vessel and leave to cool, when it should be a stiff glutinous mass. This is called cree'd wheat. When required boil again with double its quantity of milk until thick and creamy. Serve with sugar, nutmeg and milk.

Plum Porridge

beef or mutton
broth
brown bread
raisins
currants
prunes
cloves
mace
ginger

Boil beef or mutton with broth, thickened with brown bread. When half-boiled, add remaining ingredients. Finish boiling, with stirring.

Christmas Pudding

4 oz (100 g) almonds
1 lb (400 g) currants
1 lb (400 g) raisins
1 lb (400 g) sultanas
4 oz (100 g) candied peel
4 oz (100 g) glace cherries
8 oz (200 g) flour
8 oz (200 g) breadcrumbs
1 lb (400 g) suet
½ teaspoon mixed spice
½ teaspoon cinnamon
¼ teaspoon salt
5 eggs
2 tablespoons marmalade
4 tablespoons brandy
rind and juice of 1 lemon
milk to mix
gravy browning or caramel

Blanch and chop almonds. Clean fruit by rubbing it in flour on a sieve. Chop peel and cherries. Mix together all the dry ingredients and fruit. Add beaten eggs and marmalade, brandy, lemon juice and enough milk to give a stiff dropping consistency. You can add gravy browning or caramel to colour the mixture – it will darken when cooked.

Grease basins and fill three-quarters of the way up. Cover with greased paper and steam for 8 hours, or boil for 5 hours. The puddings should be made at least a month before they are to be eaten, so that they have time to mature. When required for use steam for 3 hours. Serve with brandy or hard sauce.

Brandy Sauce

3 egg yolks
½ pint (250 ml) single cream or milk
1 tablespoon brown sugar
¼ pint (125 ml) brandy

Beat egg yolks and stir in cream or milk. Cook very slowly in a double boiler, stirring frequently, until it will just coat the back of a spoon. Add sugar and brandy, whisking well.

Hard Sauce

3 oz (75 g) unsalted butter
6 oz (150 g) icing sugar
1 tablespoon brandy

Cream butter until soft. Sift the icing sugar and cream into butter, then work in the brandy.

Christmas Cake

For the cake
8 oz (200 g) butter or margarine
8 oz (200 g) brown sugar
1 teaspoon vanilla essence
1 teaspoon almond essence
2 tablespoon orange marmalade
4 eggs
6 oz (150 g) plain flour
4 oz (100 g) fine semolina
4 level teaspoons mixed spice
1/4 level teaspoon salt
1 level teaspoon bicarbonate of soda
8 oz (200 g) raisins
8 oz (200 g) sultanas
8 oz (200 g) currants
8 oz (200 g) dates
4 oz (100 g) glace cherries
4 oz (100 g) dried figs
4 oz (100 g) mixed peel
4 oz (100 g) crystallised ginger
4 oz (100 g) chopped almonds
4 tablespoons brandy or sherry
apricot jam
For the marzipan
marzipan and royal icing
8 oz (200 g) fine semolina
8 oz (200 g) icing sugar
8 oz (200 g) castor sugar
2 egg yolks
½ teaspoon almond essence
½ teaspoon vanilla essence
1 tablespoon sherry or milk
For the royal icing
Take 3 egg whites
1 ½ lb (600 g) icing sugar
2 to 3 drops of glycerine

To make the cake, beat butter, sugar and essences to a smooth cream. Beat in the marmalade. Beat in the eggs one at a time. Stir in the sifted flour, semolina, spice, salt and crushed soda. Add the prepared fruit (seeded and chopped), chopped peel and ginger and almonds. Stir in brandy or sherry. Turn into a greased 8 in (20 cm) cake tin with 3 linings of paper at bottom and sides, smoothing down evenly. Place in a moderate oven (325°F/160°C) (middle or lower half) and cook slowly, covering for the first or second half of cooking time with 2 thicknesses of paper. Bake for about 4 hours in a slow oven (250-300°F/120-150°C).

The cake is cooked when it is firm and elastic to touch and has shrunken slightly from the sides of the tin, and when a bright skewer pierced into the centre comes out undimmed. Cool in tin and leave paper on until ready to cover with marzipan.

To make the marzipan, mix semolina, sieved icing sugar and castor sugar. Mix in egg yolks, essences and sherry or milk. Blend into a smooth, pliable paste, taking care in the mixing that this is not wet, and roll out. Brush top and sides of cake with apricot jam, cover with marzipan, then wrap in aluminium foil for 2 or 3 days for the paste to set firmly.

To make the royal icing, lightly whisk egg whites and then gradually add sufficient sieved icing sugar to form a fairly stiff icing. Stir in glycerine then beat thoroughly till smooth and pure white. Cover cake with royal icing and decorate.

Mince Pies

For the mincemeat
take 4 oz (100 g) chopped apples
12 oz (300 g) mixed dried fruit
juice and rind of 1 lemon
4 oz (100 g) suet
4 oz (100 g) sugar
2 teaspoons marmalade
½ teaspoon mixed spice
½ teaspoon cinnamon
½ teaspoon grated nutmeg
¼ teaspoon salt
2 tablespoons ale or brandy.
For the pie cases
8 oz (200 g) flaky or shortcrust pastry
1 egg
sugar

To make the mincemeat, chop fruit and suet very finely. Mix together all the ingredients, and put into jars. Store in a cool place.

Roll out pastry ⅛ in (0.3 cm) thick and stamp out rounds to fit tins, making those for the tops of the pies a little smaller than those for the base. Line greased tins with pastry, put a good teaspoon of mincemeat in each, damp edges and put on lids. Flute the edges and make a small hole with a skewer in the top of each. Glaze with beaten egg and a little sugar and bake in a hot oven (425-450°F/220-230°C) for about 25 minutes.

Bubble-and-Squeak

left-over potatoes
Brussels sprouts
a pinch of salt

Mash potatoes and sprouts together with a little salt, then fry until surface is brown and crisp.

games appendix

crafts appendix

acknowledgements

The Publisher wishes to thank the organizations listed below for their kind permission to reproduce the photographs in this book. Every effort has been made to acknowledge the pictures properly, however we apologize if there are any unintentional omissions which will be corrected in future editions.

Barnabys Picture Library 37 right, 58 right, 109 right, 120, 124, 133, 135, 137 left, 153
Collections */Jarrold Publishing* 161, */Brian Shuel* 22, 26 left, 71, 93, 100 right, 100 left, 105, 139, 140, 149, 152 left, 152 right, 175, 178 right
Fortean Picture Library 69 right
Hulton Getty Picture Collection 7, 9, 13 left 13 right, 14, 24, 25, 26 right, 29, 31, 35, 37 left, 39, 40 left, 40 right 41, 44, 45, 48, 53, 54, 56, 58 left, 59, 61, 63, 64, 67, 69 left, 70, 72, 75 left, 76, 83, 84, 85, 87 left, 87 right, 90, 92, 98, 99, 102 left, 102 right, 108, 109 left, 110, 111, 114, 115, 117, 118, 119, 122, 123, 125, 127, 129, 130, 131 left, 131 right, 132, 134, 137 right, 141, 143, 144 left, 144 right, 147, 154, 155, 158, 159, 162 left, 162 right, 164 left, 164 right, 165, 166, 167, 168, 173, 174, 177, 178 left, 179, 181
Reed Consumer Books Ltd. 19, 32, 73, 75 right, 78, 81, 89, 112, 151